PHILOSOPHY AND PSYCHO-ANALYSIS

Jay Atlas

By John Wisdom

OTHER MINDS

PHILOSOPHY

AND

PSYCHO-ANALYSIS

JOHN WISDOM

Professor of Philosophy in the University of Cambridge

UNIVERSITY OF CALIFORNIA PRESS

Berkeley and Los Angeles

1969

UNIVERSITY OF CALIFORNIA PRESS
BERKELEY AND LOS ANGELES
CALIFORNIA

*Originally published in Great Britain in 1953 by
Basil Blackwell, Oxford*

FIRST CALIFORNIA PAPER-BOUND PRINTING, 1969

LIBRARY OF CONGRESS CATALOG CARD NUMBER: 69-15943

Manufactured in the United States of America

CONTENTS

ACKNOWLEDGMENTS

The thanks of the author and the publisher are due to the Editors of the following Journals for permission to reprint extracts from their publications.

Psyche, The Aristotelian Society, Mind, The Library of Living Philosophers, Polemic, Politics and Letters, and to the Cornell University Press and Professor Max Black for permission to use the extract *A Note On Probability* from *Philosophical Analysis.*

OSTENTATION
(*Psyche Vol. XIII*)

THIS paper is designed to show that *ostentation* is the main means to satisfying the desires of the philosopher.

I am not imagining that in maintaining this I am maintaining anything which is new in any exciting sense. On the contrary, I believe that philosophers have always employed ostentation although they have seldom said so because, being busy philosophizing, they have had little time to philosophize about philosophizing. I believe that Jeremy Bentham meant by his word 'paraphrasis'[1] something very like what I mean by 'ostentation' and that those philosophers, such as Russell and Moore, who have spoken of 'incomplete symbols' and 'logical constructions' have had in mind the same ideas.

Ostentation is a species of substitution. I substitute one sentence, S', for another, S, if I state that anyone who utters S' is saying the same thing as anyone who utters S.[2]

I perform the operation of *ostentation* upon a sentence S, when I substitute S' for S and S' reveals more clearly than does S, the structure of the fact (or facts) they *locate*.[3] Next 'locate' must be defined.

Anybody who utters a sentence is claiming that there is a fact (or facts) having such and such an internal structure — such and such elements arranged in such and such a way. Any fact which answers to the description is said to be *located* by the sentence. The description may of course be more or less complete.

The sentences which completely locate facts are those which are made up from adjectives, verbs and prepositions and proper names (grammar-book sense) only. The sentences which incompletely

[1] Bentham, *Works*, Vol. VIII, pp. 246–8. For the relation between paraphrasis and logical constructions, see my *Interpretation and Analysis*. For the relation between logical constructions and ostentation see my articles on logical constructions in *Mind*, April, 1931, October, 1931, October, 1932, January, 1933, April, 1933.

[2] 'To substitute' may mean *to state that S' may be put for* S or it may mean *to put S' for* S. 'To translate' is subject to the same ambiguity.

[3] This definition is not the same as that which I give in articles in *Mind*. There I define ostentation as the substitution of sentences which more nearly Display Facts. Display is not defined in terms of insight but of identity of structure. That definition is superior but is long and difficult.

locate facts are those in which common nouns and an article are used. They are derived from complete sentences by substituting 'something' for one or more of the proper names in the complete sentence. Thus 'Bob is happy', 'England fought France', and 'Othello was jealous of Desdemona on account of Cassio' completely locate facts. (Words like 'of' and 'to' and auxiliary verbs are neglected.) 'Something is happy', 'Something which is wicked is happy', 'Everything which is wicked is happy' incompletely locate facts. 'Something wicked is happy' is obtained from 'Bob is wicked and Bob is happy'. 'Everything which is wicked is happy' means 'Something wicked is happy and it is not the case that something wicked is not happy'. 'The thing which is wicked is happy' means 'Something wicked is happy and it is not the case that something else is happy'. 'Bob loves Jessie' completely locates the fact that *Bob loves Jessie* and no other fact such as *Bert loves Jessie*. 'Something loves Jessie' incompletely locates *Bob loves Jessie* and *Bert loves Jessie* but not *Bob loves Elizabeth*. 'Something loves something' still more incompletely locates *Bob loves Jessie* and any other case of love.

When a sentence completely locates a fact it expresses it.[1] But we must not say of a sentence which incompletely locates a fact that it expresses that fact. It is customary, however, to say of an incomplete sentence, say 'Joan loves someone' that it expresses an incomplete (or general) fact. This is just a misleading way of saying that it incompletely locates a fact. And if we spoke only in the best style we should never use the expression 'incomplete fact'. Obviously there is a sense in which 'incomplete fact' is a nonsensical expression. 'Incomplete fact' is a nonsensical expression if 'fact' is used in the way it is when we speak of the fact (complete) that Peter loves Joan. There are not two species of fact, the one complete, the other incomplete; there are sentences which completely and incompletely locate facts. Whatever is said about the incomplete fact that F, could be said by speaking about the sentence 'F' which incompletely locates C, a fact (complete). The form (incomplete) of the fact (incomplete) *Something loves Joan* is the form of the fact which 'Something loves Joan' locates. Joan is an element in the fact *Something loves Joan* means Joan is an

---

[1] S expresses the fact that F if and only if S and the sentence 'F' locate with equal completeness the same fact, i.e. if 'F' is substitutable for S.

element in the fact which 'Something loves Joan' locates and is (unlike Peter) specified by 'Something loves Joan'. Thus do incomplete facts vanish, though their grins, of course, remain.

A fact (complete) is either of the sort *This is* Q, where Q, like 'red' names a quality; or of the sort *This* R *that*, where R like 'adjoins' names a relation; or of the sort *This* R *that to that*, where R like 'gives' names a relation; and so on to facts with n-terms. The this's and that's are the *terms* or *constituents* of the facts; the relations and qualities are the *components* of the facts; the *elements* of a fact are its constituents and components. Two facts are of the same *form* when they have the same number of terms. The fact aRb differs from the fact bRa, not in its elements, nor in its form, but in *arrangement*.

Ostentation, I have said, is substitution which results in insight into the structure of the fact a sentence locates — a clearer, though not more complete, apprehension of the elements of that fact and of how they are arranged. No doubt you will find this statement obscure but I hope to remove the obscurity later.

I. THE PHILOSOPHIC RESPONSE

If you stimulate a philosopher in a suitable way he will begin to philosophize. To philosophize is to analyse.[1] When a man analyses he makes statements of a certain kind with a certain intention. What kind of statement? One about words. What kind of intention? Insight into structure. Let us consider these two points.

1. *The philosopher's statement is verbal.* All philosophic statements are, of course, made *in* words. We may go further, however; for all philosophic statements *mention* words. [Contrary to *Analysis and Interpretation* (p. 16) 'The fact you considered yesterday has such and such an analysis' is no exception.]

Philosophic statements are of the form 'The fact located by S has the elements and arrangement revealed by S''. For example: *The fact expressed by 'The average man has an intelligence quotient of 60' has the elements and arrangement revealed by 'The sum of human intelligence quotients divided by their number equals 60'.*

---

[1] Apart from speculative philosophy, which is the deductive study of the existence of God and the immortality of the soul.

There are many who would refuse to say that philosophic statements, even when confined to statements in analytic philosophy,
are statements about words. And since to deny what they say
would be to take a paradoxical and surprising view,[1] we may
expect that what they say is in some important sense correct.
Closer investigation will confirm this; it will also, however, show
that it is very easy to make a mistake about the sense in which
philosophic statements are not about words and that in a very
important and proper sense they *are* only about words.

I used to say that philosophic statements are not about words. I
did not, of course, mean that they are not made in words, nor even
that they do not mention words. I meant that what the philosopher primarily intends to locate by his sentence is a fact which
is not about words.

I *primarily* intend to produce a situation, S, when I intend for its
own sake to produce it. I *secondarily* intend to produce a
situation, S, when I intend to produce it as a means to another
situation, S'.

Suppose now that I say 'The man on the donkey is the Sultan'.
If my primary intention is merely to tell you which man is the
Sultan, then although I mention a donkey and therefore, in some
sense, my sentence is about a donkey, nevertheless there is a sense
in which my sentence is not about a donkey — it is not *primarily*
or *essentially* about a donkey. This being so I should of course be
annoyed if you objected: 'You are wrong. That is not a donkey,
it is a mule'. I mentioned the donkey merely in order to draw
your attention to a fact which is not about a donkey at all, the fact
That is the Sultan.

Now it may be claimed that things are like this with the philosopher; that his primary intention is to draw attention to facts
which are not about words at all, that he only secondarily intends
to draw attention to facts about words. But this won't do.

For what could this non-verbal fact, to which the philosopher
primarily intends to draw our attention be? Take the case:
'The fact expressed by "England fought France" has the structure
revealed by "Englishmen fought Frenchmen".'

From 'The tallest man is older than the smallest' we can obtain

---

[1] Surprising conclusions may be a sign of one's devotion to logic but they are also a
sign of the falsity of one's premisses *or the ambiguity of one's language*.

a fact which makes no reference to size, by substituting names for descriptions thus – 'Bob is older than Bert'. Can something similar be done when we have 'The fact expressed by "England fought France" has the structure revealed by "Englishmen fought Frenchmen"', and wish to obtain a fact which has no reference to words?

We could do this if the relation involved were anything other than the pseudo-relation *identity-of-structure*. But as it is we cannot remove the descriptions without talking nonsense; just as we cannot remove descriptions when we have the pseudo-relation of *identity* between things. 'The tallest is identical with the smallest' yields falsity or nonsense when names are substituted for the descriptions. For if 'Bob is identical with Bert' is not false, we can re-write it 'Bob is identical with Bob'; and that is nonsense.[1] Similarly we cannot substitute the name 'this' for the descriptive phrase 'the fact expressed by "England fought France"', and the name 'that' for the descriptive phrase 'the fact expressed by "Englishmen fought Frenchmen"', and then write: This is identical in structure with that. For since no two facts have the same structure if 'This is identical in structure with that' is true, we can re-write it 'This is identical in structure with this' – which is nonsense.

How would it do to write, not 'The fact located by "England fought France" has the structure revealed by "Englishmen fought Frenchmen"', but 'The fact that England fought France has the structure of the fact that Englishmen fought Frenchmen' or '*England fought France* has the structure of *Englishmen fought Frenchmen*'?[2] It would not do at all.

For *Englishmen fought Frenchmen* is an incomplete fact and therefore has neither structure, nor form, nor elements, nor arrangement in the sense in which the complete fact *England fought France* has. Still less is the structure of the one identical with the structure of the other.

---

[1] Some people would say 'trivially tautologous'. I believe that 'nonsense' is right.

[2] It might be thought that the expression 'The fact that England fought France', and the expression '*England fought France*', are alternative expressions for 'The fact expressed by "England fought France"'. This of course would give me what I want – the verbalness of philosophic statements – at once. But I do not think it is true. I do not think that *It is good that he is happy* means *The fact expressed by 'He is happy' is good*. Similarly I do not think that *That England fought France has the structure, etc.* means *The fact expressed by 'England fought France' has the structure, etc.*

Shall we say that *England fought France* is identical in structure not with the incomplete fact *Englishmen fought Frenchmen*, but with the complete fact which 'Englishmen fought Frenchmen' incompletely locates, namely the fact that Tom, Dick and Harry (Englishmen) fought Henri, François and Jean (Frenchmen)?

But this is not true. *England fought France* is a two-termed fact and contains England as a term; it is not 6-termed and it does not contain Tom as a term.

We could say if we liked that *England invaded France* has six (say) *ultimate* terms and contains Tom, Dick and Harry as *ultimate* referent terms, *fought* (as applied to individuals) as *ultimate* component, and Henri, François and Jean as *ultimate* relata terms.

But when we have given 'ultimate' a meaning which is compatible with the fact that a fact has in some sense only one set of terms, we shall find that the above statement is only a clumsy and obscure substitute for the following verbal statement: 'England fought France' *finally* locates what 'Englishmen fought Frenchmen' *directly* locates.

It remains (*a*) to find the sense in which the philosophic response is not merely a statement about words, and (*b*) to see more clearly what the statement about words is, by defining 'finally locates' and 'directly locates'.

2. *The philosopher's intention is not verbal.* It is obvious that the philosopher's work is not the same as that of the translator; it is obvious, in other words, that analysis is not translation. We cannot say that the difference is that the primary intention of the translator is to convey a fact about words, while the primary intention of the philosopher is to convey a fact which is not about words. For we have just seen the attempt to say *what* non-verbal fact it is the primary intention of the philosopher to convey, break down. We can, however, say:

A translator is one who substitutes a sentence, S', for a sentence, S, (in a different language) with the primary intention of teaching us the verbal fact which his sentence expresses, namely the fact about the meaning of S. It is not the primary intention of the philosopher to convey a fact about words; this is not because it is his primary intention to convey a fact which is not about words, but because it is not his primary intention to convey a fact at all. His primary intention is not to provide information but to promote insight – insight into the structure of the fact located by the sentences which he equates.

His primary intention is clearer apprehension of the form, elements and arrangement of facts already known. Thus the philosopher does not differ from the translator in *what* he says but in the *intention* with which he says it.[1] The philosopher intends of course to say what he does about words but only as a means to insight; any other fact, whether about words or not, would do as well for his purposes, provided it would produce the same insight. An English-French dictionary could not be written in German and Spanish; but a philosophy done in English and French could as well be done in German and Spanish, that is to say, it could as well fulfil the primary intention of him who wrote it. For it could as well promote the intended insight into the structure of facts.

3. *The nature of the philosopher's intention.*

3.1. *Increased clearness in the apprehension of the structure of a fact must not be confused with knowing the fact more clearly.* If one has never clearly observed the difference between *loathing* and *despising* and consequently writes indifferently 'Bob loathes Bert' or 'Bob despises Bert' and the distinction is then pointed out to one, then there will probably result an increase in the clarity of one's knowledge of the fact that Bob despises Bert. This kind of increase in clearness of knowledge is often produced by removing ambiguity from sentences – a very different thing from ostentation. To know a fact clearly is not the same thing as to see its structure clearly.

Someone may say: 'What stuff! To know a fact is to know that its elements are arranged in the way they are. Hence one cannot know a fact without knowing its structure, nor clearly know it without clearly knowing it structure. To know the fact that England fought France is to know that England fought France. To *tell us about* the structure of the fact that England fought France by writing "There is a two-termed fact with England as referent, France as relatum and *fought* as component", instead of *exhibiting* the structure by writing "England fought France", is to gain nothing.'

(*a*). I do not imagine for a moment that anything much is

---

[1] A liar does not differ in *what* he says from one who *un*intentionally deceives.

gained by re-writing 'England fears France' as the sentence 'There is a two-termed fact with England as referent, etc.' To do so would be to confuse changing apprehension of structure with knowledge about structure, with increasing clearness of apprehension of structure.

(b). It is false that one cannot know a fact clearly without knowing clearly its structure. For this happens when sentences are compressed. Thus there is no doubt that one's apprehension of the structure of the complex fact located by[1] 'The church in Hyde Park is large' becomes clearer when it is translated (i) Something is a church in Hyde Park; (ii) Something, the same thing, is large; (iii) It is not the case that Something, another thing, is a church in Hyde Park. Again, the similarity of the structure of *A ruler of the universe exists* to the structure of *The big man is injured (by something)* is not obvious till we substitute for the former sentence the new sentence 'The universe is ruled by something'. Yet we may know quite clearly the facts *The church in Hyde Park is large* and *A ruler of the universe exists*, in the sense that we have not the slightest tendency to confuse them with other facts, without expanding the sentences and so obtaining the consequent increased clearness in the apprehension of the structure of the facts they locate.

3.2. *The philosopher's intention is not increased clearness in the apprehension of the non-ultimate structure of facts.* I do not, however, wish to assert that it is the philosopher's business to promote increased clearness in the apprehension of structure in *this* sense of 'structure'. This kind of improvement is the business of the logician and results from formal definition or expansion, an operation much easier than ostentation. It is possible to apprehend ever so clearly the structure of a fact, in this sense, without approaching the goal of the philosopher.[2] For his goal is not increased clearness in the apprehension of structure but increased clearness in the apprehension of ultimate structure or Structure. This distinction is difficult but important.

3.3. *The philosopher's intention is increased clearness in the apprehension of the ultimate structure of facts.*

---

[1] More accurately — 'the structure of a representative selection from the facts located by'.

[2] Thus the definition of *x is the brother of y* which I gave in *Interpretation and Analysis*, is not an example of philosophical analysis but of formal definition or analysis.

4. '*Ultimate structure*' means '*Structure*'. When, on p. 4, we were considering the fact *England fought France* we supposed a nation to be 'reducible' to its nationals, in the sense that to say anything about a nation is merely to say something (though not the same thing) about its nationals. If we suppose that men are similarly reducible to their mental and bodily states, then we may write out a series of sentences which more and more reveal the ultimate structure of the fact *England invaded France*.

(1) 'England invaded France'.

(2) 'Englishmen sent men who moved threateningly on to land owned by Frenchmen'.

(3) 'The E-groups of states (corresponding to, though not identical with, Englishmen) included decisions which caused a threatening movement included in the S-groups of states (soldiers) and "on" the L-group of sensa (the land of France) "owned by" the F-groups of states (Frenchmen)'.

We shall do well to write down now something like the complete forms of the above sentences. 'England invaded France' is itself complete so we write:

(a) 'England invaded France'.

(b) 'Tom, Dick and Harry sent Harry to France owned by Henri, François and Jean'.

(c) 'T_d, D_d and H_d (decisions) members respectively of $T_1 \ldots T_n$ (states of Tom), $D_1 \ldots D_n$ (states of Dick) and $H_1 \ldots H_n$ (states of Harry) caused H_m (movement of Harry) 'on' $F_1 \ldots F_n$ (sensa of France) 'owned by' $h_1 \ldots h_n$ (states of Henri), $f_1 \ldots f_n$ (states of François), and $j_1 \ldots j_n$ (states of Jean)'. Here the letters are names not variables; otherwise (c) would mean the same as (3). [For 'X (some person) killed him' would mean the same as 'Some person killed him' if 'X' were used as a variable; though it would of course mean the same as 'Bob killed him', if 'X' were a name.]

Let us say: (i) that each sentence in the second series *directly* locates the fact it expresses, i.e. 'aRb' directly locates the fact that aRb; (ii) that each sentence in the first series *directly* locates the fact which its complete form (in the second series) expresses; (iii) that each earlier sentence in each series *indirectly* locates the fact (perhaps very complex) directly located by any later sentence. Let us say that each of the sentences *finally* locates the fact located with varying degrees of directness and completeness by every one of the sentences, i.e. the fact expressed by the sentence 'T$_d$, D$_d$, H$_d$, etc.' The elements of the fact finally located by all the sentences, though directly located only by the two last in each series, are the *ultimate* elements of the facts those sentences locate. In other words: the ultimate structure of the fact that aRb is the structure of the fact which the sentence 'aRb' finally locates.

On this interpretation of 'ultimate structure' it is not that a fact has many sets of elements and many structures but that the sentence which expresses it locates with differing degrees of directness many facts, each of these facts having its own structure. Now this is as it should be. A fact *is* a set of elements arranged in a certain way: how then can it also be a different set of elements in a more complicated arrangement?

A refinement may now be introduced. It is obvious that the sense in which Tom is an element in the fact located by 'England invaded France' is different from the sense in which England is; and we have said what this difference is; England is an element of the fact which 'England fears France *directly* locates, Tom is an element of a fact which it *in*directly locates, sense data are elements of a fact which it still *more* indirectly locates. It is not equally but I hope that it is sufficiently obvious that the sense in which Tom is an element in the Tom-Dick-and-Harry-fact is different from that in which England is an element in *England invaded France*; while the sense in which the states are elements in the T$_d$-D$_d$-H$_d$-fact is different again.

If this is not sufficiently obvious the following proof may be read. If a nation is reducible to its nationals (and it *is*) then statements about nations are statements about their nationals, i.e. predicates applicable to nations are definable in terms of predicates applicable to their nationals. Therefore the predicate applicable to England, *element of the fact that England fears France*, is definable in terms of a predicate applicable to Englishmen. It is now obvious that that predicate is *element of the fact located by* 'Englishmen, etc.' Thus it appears that the sense of 'element' in which England is an element, so far from being identical with, is definable by, the sense of 'element' in which Tom is an element. Similarly it may be shown that if Tom is reducible to his states then the sense in which he is an element is definable in terms of the sense in which his states are.[1]

Let us write that sense of 'element' in terms of which all the others are to be defined, 'Element'; and the sense of 'arrangement' in terms of which all the others are to be defined, 'Arrangement'; and the sense of 'structure' in terms of which all the others are to be defined, 'Structure'.

We may now write the final definition of 'ultimate structure' as follows: The ultimate structure of the fact that aRb is the Structure of the Fact finally located by the sentence 'aRb', e.g. the ultimate structure of the fact that England invaded France is the Elements and Arrangement of the Fact which 'England invaded France' finally locates. The structure of the fact that aRb is its ultimate structure when the fact which 'aRb' directly locates is the fact it finally locates.

5. *The ultimate elements of a fact must not be confused with the simple elements of a fact of the second order, i.e. a fact about facts.* Miss Stebbing's language in her paper 'The Method of Analysis in Metaphysics'[2] suggests that she is taking this view. And the language of others has less clearly suggested the same thing. To take such a view is to confuse such a series as (1) (*That) gives me satisfaction*, (2) ([*That*]. *is good) gives me satisfaction*, (3) ([*He is happy*] *is good) gives me satisfaction*, with the England-to-states series.

Such serial translation as this results in clearer apprehension of the vertical structure of facts. But like the revelation of horizontal structure (3.1 and 3.2) it is still a revelation of structure, not Structure; and to confuse it with the serial translation in the 'England etc.' to 'T_d, D_d, H_d, etc.' series is to confuse a species of expansion with ostentation.

From the view that philosophic analysis consists in revealing the elements of a fact which are simple in the sense of not having elements, it would follow that philosophic analysis is applicable only

---

[1] In general: If x is reducible to y then facts about x are reducible to facts about y. And then the sense in which facts about x have elements will be reducible to that in which facts about y have elements. Compare incomplete facts. It will be noticed that all the complete facts above are complete only relatively to their incomplete forms and the facts above them in the series; they are incomplete relative to the facts below them. Only the T_d–D_d–H_d fact is absolutely complete. Thus England invaded France must be incomplete in some sense since the incomplete 'Englishmen sent etc.' can be substituted.

[2] *Proceedings of the Aristotelian Society*, December, 1932.

to facts of the second or third or fourth or etc., order. But *England fears France* is of the first order – it is not a fact about facts. The ultimate elements of a fact are, when they are not its elements, simpler in some sense than its elements; but they are not simpler in the sense that the non-ultimate elements are facts of which the ultimate elements are elements. England is not a fact of which Tom, Dick and Harry are elements.

6. It should now be clear why I speak of 'the philosophic response' instead of 'the philosophic proposition'. For the philosopher should be defined, not in terms of what he does but in terms of his intention. This is always useless though harmless – it is insight into the Structure of the Facts which our sentences finally locate.

7. Ostentation is defined as the translation of sentences which less reveal, and more mislead as to, this Structure into sentences which more reveal, and less mislead as to, this Structure. It should be noticed that 'England invaded France' does not merely not reveal the structure of the fact it finally locates, but by its verbal similarity to 'Tom hit Bob', it suggests that the Structures of the facts located are of equal complexity.

8. *It is clear then that if ostentation is possible it is a philosophic method. It is possible.* The case of 'England invaded France' which we have considered does not prove that ostentation is humanly possible; for the translation was not in that case carried out correctly and in detail. It was, however, carried out roughly and in outline. And ostentation has been successfully practised in 'reducing' propositions to judgments and general facts to sentences and complete facts.

9. *And there is no other method of fulfilling the philosophic intention, half so potent.*

10. *We are therefore entitled to accept the proposition that ostentation is the main philosophic instrument.*

II. THE PHILOSOPHIC STIMULUS

The same conclusion is reached from a study of the philosophic stimulus. I say 'stimulus', not 'question', because the philosophic stimulus is not a request for information, but a request for insight.

1. The philosopher asks What is the Self? What is the State? What is Time?

2. The expression 'What is . . . ?' is very ambiguous. Anyone who asks 'What is an anemometer?' is asking 'What functions does an anemometer perform?' The philosopher, of course, is not asking 'What functions does the self perform?' The psychologist does that.

3. The philosopher is not using 'What is . . .?' in the scientist's sense. When the philosopher asks 'What is a chair?' 'What is water?' he is not asking for the chemical formulae for these. This may seem too obvious to be worth mentioning. But there are people who speak as if it is the business of the philosopher to carry the work of the scientist a stage further. Mr. Joad once tried to persuade me to give up putting the philosophic stimulus in the form 'What is the analysis of *This is a table?*' and to put it in the form 'What makes up a table?' This latter formulation has a healthy, none-of-your-philosophical-hocus-pocus, look about it. But it is as ambiguous as, and perhaps even more misleading than, the orthodox formulations, 'What is the nature of X?' 'What is the ultimate nature of X?' 'What is X?'

'What is water?' asked with a profound look and in the philosophic manner, has a confusing verbal similarity with 'What is water?' asked briskly and in the scientific manner. But the two requests differ in kind, not merely in degree. When has a philosopher ever pushed a scientific inquiry a stage further? And supposing it were found that the neutron is scientifically ultimate, would that be a philosophic discovery?

No – the philosopher is asking for a certain kind of definition of the Self, of the State.

4. He is not of course using 'What is . . .?' in the foreigner's sense and asking for a verbal definition.[1]

5. He is not asking for formal definition.

---

[1] We are often told to begin by 'defining our terms'. But what does this mean? Our instructor should follow his own advice. Certainly we should begin a book on Ethics or Economics by verbally defining ambiguous expressions such as 'good', 'useful', 'interest'. And if we wish to proceed from the logically simple to the logically complex, we should next provide formal definitions or formal analyses of *good*, *rent*, etc. But if we wish to proceed from the certain to the less certain, we should set out first the laws of the science or the more obvious laws and then analyse. This analysis might then bring to light less obvious laws which in their turn would improve analysis. *Philosophical analysis should not appear at all in a scientific work.*

6. It is not that a nation is a fact and the philosopher asking for its elements.

7. Is it that there is another kind of unity, not to be identified with a fact, nor to be identified with the sort of unity of which the scientist finds the elements? If we call such a unity a philosophic unity and its elements philosophic elements, then we might ask: 'Is a nation a philosophic unity and a philosopher one who asks what are its philosophic elements?' Let us consider this view which though objectionable is not without excuse.

If we ask 'What is a nation?' 'What is England?' there appear to be two possible answers: (1) A nation is its nationals and England is Tom, Dick and Harry; (2) A nation is a unity 'over and above' its nationals and England is a unity 'over and above' Tom, Dick and Harry. These may be set out more clearly as follows: (1) To say something about England is to say it about Englishmen; (2) To say something about England is not to say it about Englishmen, but about a unity in which they are elements, (though something about the elements may follow from what is said about the unity).

(2) is objectionable. For if we have said all there is to be said about Tom, Dick and Harry, including of course statements about their interrelations, we shall have said all there is to be said about England, even if none of our statements mention England. When England makes war on France, is there besides the fact that Tom, Dick and Harry are fighting Henri, François and Jean, some other fact about a unity (philosophic) England and a unity (philosophic) France? And is there besides the fact that Englishmen each acknowledge a king, another fact, that England is a monarchy? But (2) is not without excuse; for we cannot accept (1).

For to say that England is a monarchy is not to say *that* about Englishmen. 'Every Englishman is a monarchy' is nonsense but 'England is a monarchy' is sense; therefore to say the one is not to say the other.[1]

This dilemma arises because we put the philosophic requests in the substantival manner: 'What is a nation?' If we had asked instead: 'What is the Structure of national facts?' 'What is the structure of facts about England?' then we should have

[1] 'The group of Englishmen is a monarchy' is no use. It is as redundant as England is a monarchy. See Susan Stebbing's *Logic*, p. 147.

seen that besides the alternatives (1) *To say something of England is to say it (the same thing) of Englishmen*, (2) *To say something of England is not to say it (the same thing) of Englishmen*, there is a third alternative, (3) *To say something of England is to say something but not the same thing of Englishmen*. And (3) is clearly the right alternative. 'England *is a monarchy*' means 'Englishmen *acknowledge a king*'. Again 'What is Time?' is hopeless. But 'What is the structure of the fact *Time heals all wounds?*' is not.[1]

It is, however, a mistake to put the philosophic stimulus in the form: 'What is the structure of the fact that aRb?' As we have already seen, we might in this way accidentally start the logician. This could be avoided by asking 'What is the Structure of the fact which the sentence 'aRb' finally locates?'

But even this form is open to objection. For it suggests that we do not know what the Elements of the fact finally located by 'aRb' are and how they are Arranged. Yet to know the fact that aRb *is* to know the Elements of the fact which 'aRb' finally locates and how they are Arranged.

8. We must then put the philosophic stimulus in the form, not of a question, but of a prayer — *Please give me clearer apprehension of the Arrangement of the Elements of the Fact finally located by the sentence 'aRb'*.

[1] See Moore, *Philosophical Studies*, p. 209.

IS ANALYSIS A USEFUL METHOD IN PHILOSOPHY?
(*The Arist. Soc. Supp. Vol. XIII*)

MR. BLACK does not directly concern himself with the question which forms the title of this symposium, but asks instead *What is philosophical analysis?* His example may well be followed, because when it is clear what philosophical analysis is, then it will be clear that it is an old and very useful method in a certain kind of philosophy.

In order that people may know what philosophical analysis is before they consider its ultimate nature I shall begin with examples of it. Philosophical analysis is most easily confused with *material* and *formal* analysis.[1] Hence examples will be chosen and a definition worded so as to bring out the distinction between it and these two.

As to the relations between analysis and what I have ventured to call ostentation. Whenever one analyses the fact that S is P one gives an ostensive translation of the sentence 'S is P'. Later I shall claim that this is because to do the one is to do the other with a certain intention. It does not follow that to analyse the fact *The economic man always buys in the best market* is to analyse the sentence 'The economic man always buys in the best market'. To suppose that it does follow is to fail to recognize the distinction between saying that analysis *is* translation and saying that it is a *logical construction out of*, i.e. *may be philosophically analysed into*, translation. It is nonsense to talk of analysing sentences.

I. IDENTIFYING PHILOSOPHICAL ANALYSIS

We want illustrations of the distinction between philosophical analysis on the one hand and material and formal analysis on the other, and of the equivalent distinction between Ostentation[2] on

---

[1] I think Mr. Black has both these in mind when he speaks of 'logical analysis'. Miss Stebbing uses 'metaphysical analysis' and 'directional analysis' for 'philosophical analysis'. 'The Method of Analysis in Metaphysics', *Proc. Aris. Soc.*, N.S., xxxiii, and *Logical Positivism and Analysis*.

[2] 'Ostentation' may be read 'capital ostentation' or 'new-level ostentation', and 'ostentation' may be read 'small ostentation' or 'same-level ostentation'. The *capital* symbolism is not an aimless affectation; it fights a tendency to suppose that Ostentation and ostentation are different species of the same genus.

the one hand and material and formal ostentation on the other.

1. THE DISTINCTION BETWEEN MATERIAL ANALYSIS AND PHILOSOPHICAL ANALYSIS. The scientist gives material analyses when he begins by 'defining his terms'. Thus the economist gives a material analysis of *wealth* if he defines it as *what is useful, transferable, and limited in supply;* and of *interest* when he defines it as *the payment made by a borrower for the use of a loan for, say, a year.*[1] He would not be giving a material analysis of *wealth* if he defined it as *riches;* nor of *interest* if he defined it as *usury:* these definitions do nothing to render explicit the connotation of the words defined.[2] To give a material analysis is to give an *analytic* definition.

When the psychologist says '*I am in awe of you*' means '*I fear and admire you*' he is giving a material analysis of the fact those sentences express by giving a more *ostensive* but still *same-level* translation of the first sentence. '*The average man is in awe of the medical man*' means '*The average man fears and admires the medical man*' is also a same-level ostentation. On the other hand '*The average man is in awe of the medical man*' means '*Most men (individual) are in awe of any medical man (individual) whom they meet*' is a new-level ostentation. To give a rule for translating sentences about any abstraction into sentences about what it is an abstraction from is to give a new-level ostentation (i.e. an Ostentation) of the sentences and a philosophical analysis of the facts they express.[3] Thus rules for translating sentences about the biological rabbit, the psychological individual, and the economic man into sentences about rabbits and men give philosophical analyses.

When Mr. Woodger tries to go a step further[4] and to treat rabbits like the biological rabbit, by translating sentences about rabbits into sentences about *rabbitish* sense-patterns, he is giving a philosophical analysis of rabbit-facts and answering the question 'What is the ultimate nature of rabbits?' When the psychologist is trying to reduce individuals to their experiences he is doing the same.[5] When the economist translates sentences about

---

1 Marshall, *Principles of Economics*, p. 73.

2 See traditional rules for definition. Material analysis must not be confused with physical or chemical analysis of things.

3 This is a very unostensive definition of an important species of philosophical analysis.

4 Woodger, *The Quarterly Review of Biology*, 1931.

5 The reduction of individual things is a step further, one may safely bet, than we shall ever be able to go, however sure we may be that there is such a step.

the representative firm into sentences about firms and these into sentences about individuals and these into sentences about experiences we have a still longer Ostentation process. We pass down a series of categories from an abstraction of the second order to one of the first order, thence to a thing, and finally to particulars.

A specially illuminating contrast between material ostentation and Ostentation is found in Ethics. The well-known question about the analytic definition of 'good' is not a question of philosophical definition but of scientific (i.e. material) definition comparable to the definition of 'comic' or of 'floating capital'. Thus to assert that 'good', as applied to states of affairs, means 'arouses approval', is to give a material definition of 'good'. On the other hand to assert that 'good', as applied to individuals, means 'his states are usually good' in the sense applied to states, is to give a philosophical definition. Here a predicate suitable in one category (a predicate-phrase intelligible with one kind of subject-phrase), is reduced to (translated into) one suitable to (intelligible with) another.

2. THE DISTINCTION BETWEEN FORMAL ANALYSIS AND PHILO-SOPHICAL ANALYSIS.— Illustrations of the distinction between formal same-level ostentation and Ostentation are provided by the logician when he says, for example, that 'Every dog is dangerous' can be translated into 'Something is a dog and dangerous and it is not the case that something is a dog and not dangerous'; and when he adds that all universal affirmative sentences can be translated on these lines he is giving a rule for the ostentation of all sentences of a certain class. The famous translation of 'The thing which has S and P' into 'Something has S and P and it is not the case that something else has S' is again a reformulating of a sentence and thus the formal analysing of the fact it expresses.

'Two horses passed him' means 'A horse passed him and then another' might be supposed to be a material analysis of two. But it is not; it is a formal analysis. For 'two' is not an adjective but functions like 'every' and 'the'; they enable us to express in one sentence what would otherwise require several.

On the other hand 'Two plus two equals four' means 'Any conjunctive sentence "Two S's are P and two other S's are P" can always be written "Four S's are P"' is a philosophical analysis in that it provides an Ostentation of 'Two plus two equals four' (a sentence in which 'two' is no longer used as a *quantifier*).

We may apply all three sorts of analysis to 'Two men are good'.[1] (1) 'A man is good and another man is good' (formal analysis). (2) 'A *mannish* pattern of states contains a high proportion of good ones and another *mannish* pattern does so also' (philosophical analysis).[2] (3) 'A *mannish* pattern of states contains a high proportion of states likely to cause approval and another does also' (material analysis).

Lastly I would draw your attention to the idealized example of Ostentation provided by Mr. Black and to the two examples worked out in the rest of this paper, namely (1) the Ostentation of '*S is P* is a general fact' and (2) the Ostentation of 'X is giving a philosophical analysis of the fact *S is P*'.

II. ANALYSING PHILOSOPHICAL ANALYSIS

1. PRELIMINARIES. 1.1. *The analysis of analysis.* For our purposes material and formal analysis are best spoken of together as same-level analysis or analysis,[3] and philosophical analysis as new-level analysis or Analysis.[4]

We have found three kinds of defect in sentences — one for the scientist, one for the logician and one for the philosopher. These defects are partly due to a desire for brevity. Roughly speaking the first consists in giving symbols double work, the second in using special abbreviating devices, and the third in using sentences of small scale. (The analogy has its dangers but — (1) a map may represent a railway and a river which marches with it by a purple line instead of by a blue line for one and a red line for the other; (2) instead of separately representing each church in a town it may show the sign for a church with a number against it indicating how many churches; (3) a map may use an adequate multiplicity of symbols for what it does purport to represent and yet be on too small a scale for certain purposes — putting dots for towns instead of for buildings.) For the present we may call the first and second defects *material and formal inexplicitness*, and the third a defect of *scale*.

[1] I am indebted to Mr. George Paul for this example.
[2] Good is used differently from goods.
[3] Read 'small analysis'.   [4] Read 'capital analysis'.

To remove either of the first two defects is to give a same-level analysis or analysis; to remove the last defect is to give a new-level analysis or Analysis. More explicitly: (i) *X is giving an analysis of the fact*[1] *that S is P means X is translating the sentence 'S is P' into a sentence which is more ostensive* i.e. *more explicitly displays the structure of the fact which 'S is P' displays.* (ii) *X is giving an Analysis of the fact that S is P means X is translating the sentence 'S is P' into a sentence which more explicitly Displays the Structure of the Fact which 'S is P' Displays.*

These statements require explanation in two respects. First, what is meant by 'more explicitly displays the structure of the fact which "S is P" displays', i.e. what is ostentation? Second, what is the significance of the capitals in 'more explicitly Displays the Structure of the Fact which "S is P" Displays', i.e. what is Ostentation?

1.2. *display and Display.—* It will be well to say first what is common to the use of 'display' and 'Display'. Hence the rules which I now give for the use of the word 'display' apply also to the use of 'Display'.

When we utter a sentence we do so because we wish to point out a fact.[2] In ordinary languages it is understood that certain internal features of the sentence — its form, the words it contains, and the arrangement of these words — intimate the internal features of the fact; in particular, it is understood that the form of the sentence intimates the form of the fact, the elements or words in the sentence the elements in the fact, and the arrangement of the elements in the sentence the arrangement of the elements in the fact.

When a sentence, S, intimates the form of a fact, F, by *identity* of its form with the form of F and by *each* element in F being *named* by a word in S and by the arrangement of the elements in F being *the same as* the arrangement of their names in S, then

---

[1] I do *not* mean by a 'fact' a configuration which may or may not *occur* or *exist* (cf. Black, *Analysis*, March, 1934, p. 39). This is the old *genuine* proposition in disguise. Of course it is possible to give a philosophical analysis of a false proposition *S is P*; but this is to say what would be the analysis of the fact which the sentence 'S is P' would locate if it did locate a fact. Hence if I wish to make my definitions of analysis cover the analysis of false propositions and at the same time to avoid making them cumbersome, I should just substitute 'proposition' for 'fact' in the above definitions — without allowing genuine propositions for a moment.

[2] Sometimes, of course, we are unsuccessful, in which cases we may be said to 'state a false proposition'.

let us say that S (1) completely and (2) perfectly explicitly and (3) directly displays F. Often sentences fall short of this. Some are incomplete, i.e. fail to name all the elements in their facts, e.g. 'Arnold is in love . . . (with someone)'. These give rise to gossip. Some are imperfectly explicit. They give rise to analysis. And then some which are perfect still suffer from a more subtle defect and are not Perfect. They give rise to Analysis, i.e. philosophy.

1.3. *Incompleteness.*– For three reasons it will be well briefly to consider incompleteness. By so doing we shall (1) distinguish displaying a fact from expressing a fact (2) work out an example of philosophical analysis (3) distinguish incompleteness from that more subtle defect of being on an inadequate scale which we wish to analyse.

Any sentence made up from proper names (grammar-book sense) adjectives, verbs and prepositions completely displays a fact. The sentences which incompletely display facts are those in which common nouns and an article are used. Each is derived from a complete sentence by substituting hiatuses, i.e. words like 'something',[1] for one or more of the proper names in the complete sentence. Thus 'Arnold hit Bob' completely displays the fact *Arnold hit Bob.* 'Arnold hit . . . (somebody)' incompletely displays *Arnold hit Bob* and *Arnold hit Bill* and etc. – as many facts as there are things which Arnold hit. And 'Something is a dog and dangerous and it is not the case that something else is a dog' incompletely displays *This is a dog and dangerous, that is a dog and dangerous,* etc., and also, as we shall see, certain negative facts. It will be seen that a sentence *incompletely* displays a fact when it does not intimate *all* the elements in that fact. A sentence can completely display only one fact but it can incompletely display any number.

When a sentence completely displays a fact it expresses it. But we must not say of a sentence which incompletely displays a fact that it expresses that fact. We cannot say that 'Arnold is in love' expresses the fact that Arnold is in love with Amelia, even if Amelia is in fact the person with whom he is in love. For 'Arnold is in love' does not tell us nearly enough to justify

---

[1] 'Something' is called a hiatus because its function in, e.g. 'Arnold hit something' could be fulfilled by a well-marked gap in the written sentence or a pause in the spoken sentence.

our saying that it expresses the fact that Arnold is in love with Amelia. It is customary however to say of an incomplete sentence such as 'Arnold is in love' that it expresses a general, i.e. incomplete, fact. This is just a misleading way of saying that it incompletely displays a fact. And if we spoke only in the best style we should never use the expression 'incomplete fact'. Obviously there is a sense in which 'incomplete fact' is a self-contradictory expression; it is self-contradictory if in it 'fact' is used in the way it is when we speak of the fact that Arnold is in love with Amelia. There are not two species of fact, one complete, the other incomplete; there are sentences which completely display facts and there are sentences which do so incompletely. Incomplete facts are philosophically analysable into facts (complete), and sentences which contain hiatuses, and the relation *incompletely displays*. 'The fact *S is P* is complete' means 'The sentence "S is P" completely displays a fact (complete)'. 'The fact *S is P* is incomplete' means 'The sentence "S is P" incompletely displays a fact (complete)'.

Whatever is said about the incomplete fact F could be said by speaking about the sentence 'F' which incompletely displays a fact (complete). Thus the sense in which incomplete facts have form and elements is definable in terms of the sense in which complete facts have form and elements. We cannot say that *Arnold hit somebody* has three elements *Arnold*, *hit* and *somebody* — there is no such person as somebody. On the other hand we cannot say that it has just two elements like *Arnold is happy*. This leads us to say something mysterious like 'It contains two elements and a variable element', or 'It has three elements but one is missing'. These mysterious utterances can be translated 'The sentence "Arnold hit somebody" displays a fact (complete) with three elements but one of these it fails to specify'. Again, to say that Bill is an element in the fact *Something hit Bill* is to say 'Bill is an element in a fact (complete) incompletely displayed by "Something hit Bill" and (unlike Arnold) is specified by "Something hit Bill".'

We so define 'displays' that it is nonsense to talk of a sentence displaying an incomplete fact; for a sentence is said to display a fact only when it intimates form and elements in the sense appropriate to complete facts.

Incompleteness is a defect from the point of view of the gossip, but not from that of the logician or of the philosopher. So let us say when a sentence S intimates the form of F by identity so that it contains a name or a hiatus for each of the elements in F and intimates to a corresponding degree their arrangement, that S *perfectly explicitly*, though perhaps incompletely, displays F. And let us say that the more explicitly a sentence displays a fact the more ostensive it is. 'Arnold prefers something to something else' or, better, 'Arnold prefers x to y' though it incompletely displays *Arnold prefers Beatrice to Belinda* displays it perfectly.

Many sentences however fall short of even this ideal. Their shortcomings may be either material or formal. This brings us to:

1.4. *The analysis of ostentation.* — It follows from what has been said that to remove these shortcomings from a sentence is to give an ostentation of it. The shortcoming is material when the several elements in the fact are not severally named or hiated by elements in the sentence, e.g. when 'awe' stands for both *fear* and *admiration*.

The shortcoming is formal when though the several elements in the fact are severally named or hiated the fact is nevertheless of more complex form than the sentence. This happens when a quantifier such as 'every', 'the', 'one', 'two', etc., is used. For example, 'Two men fell' means 'Something human fell and something else human fell'. A quantifier is used in order to express in one sentence what would otherwise require a second containing the same words as the first together with such words as 'not', 'other(else)', 'same'.[1] The removal of the formal shortcoming from a sentence 'F' is the formal analysis of the fact F. Thus to translate 'Every S is P' into '(a) Something has S and has P and (b) it is not the case that something has S and lacks P' is to give a formal ostentation of 'Every S is P' and thus a formal analysis of the fact it expresses. And it is now easy to see why we say that this consists in re-writing 'Every S is P' in a form more

---

[1] 'Dogs exist' is non-ostensive in a particularly vicious way because it looks as if it is a universal affirmative 'Everything canine exists', when it really means 'Something (is) canine'. This is an example of ostentation without increase in words. It should be noted that it is not an example of Ostentation since dogs are elements of the fact which 'Dogs exist' displays and of the fact which 'Something is canine' displays. 'He is dreaming of dogs' requires special treatment.

nearly identical with the form of the fact it displays. For the totality of facts 'which 'Everything which has S has P' displays has (i) a positive part, *This has S and P, that has S and P,* and (ii) a negative part, *It is not the case that this has S and lacks P, it is not the case that that has S and lacks P, it is not the case that that has S and lacks P,* etc. Clearly our new positive-negative sentence is much more nearly identical in form with this positive-negative totality than was the old sentence 'Everything which has S has P'.

To sum up. In section 1.1 we said that to give a same-level analysis of F is to translate 'F' into a sentence which more explicitly displays F. We now know what this means.

2. THE ANALYSIS OF OSTENTATION. We come now to that more subtle defect which renders even a perfect sentence not Perfect, the defect which is more and more removed in Ostentation. We may best begin by considering not the meaning of 'Ostensive' but the meaning of 'S is an Ostentation of S''.

2.1. *'S is an Ostentation of S'' does not mean 'S is an ostentation of S''.* A sentence may be quite ostensive without being Ostensive. (A map may use quite an adequate multiplicity of conventions for what it does purport to represent and yet be on too small a scale for certain purposes.)

If we re-write 'Every nation invaded France' as the sentence 'Some nations invaded France and it is not the case that there was a nation which did not invade France' we obtain, as we have seen, a sentence which perfectly explicitly displays the structure of the totality of facts which 'Every nation invaded France' inexplicitly displays. Nevertheless the philosopher who asks 'What is a nation?' is expressing dissatisfaction with our analysis because it is still 'in terms of nations'. It is easy to see the sort of improvement which such a philosopher desires. He would be better pleased if we translated 'Some nations invaded France and some did not' into 'There were groups[1] of people each with common ancestors, traditions and governors such that the members of each group selected from among themselves soldiers and these soldiers forcibly entered the land owned by Frenchmen'. This, of course, is not quite the correct translation of 'Some nations invaded France and none did not', but it is sufficiently nearly

---

[1] The word 'group' could be removed by writing 'There were individuals with common ancestors, etc., and there were other individuals with common ancestors, etc.'

correct for us to see that a correct translation in terms of individuals could be given. Let us pretend that 'Every group of individuals with common ancestors, traditions and governors forcibly entered the land owned by Frenchmen' is the correct translation. What is the improvement in the 'individual'-sentence which makes us call it an Ostentation of the 'nation'-sentence? Once more – What makes S an Ostentation of S'? We have seen that it is not that S is more ostensive than S', and in seeing this we have seen that *it is not that S contains more words than S'* and thus has a multiplicity more nearly equal to that of the fact it displays.[1] Usually a more Ostensive sentence does contain more words, but this is not always true and *a fortiori* will not provide us with a definition. 'The word "lions" (is an) incomplete symbol' is an Ostentation of 'Lions (are) logical constructions' but it contains no more words. And ' "Arnold hit someone" incompletely displays a fact' contains no more words than does ' "Arnold hit someone" displays an incomplete fact'. Besides mere ostentation usually involves more words.

2.2. *'S is an Ostentation of S'' does not mean 'S is more complete than S''*. For the Ostensive is a translation of the ostensive and therefore conveys exactly the same amount of information as does the ostensive.[2]

2.3. *'S is an Ostentation of S''* does mean *'The elements of the fact which S displays are more ultimate than the elements of the fact which S' displays'*. This is easily seen. England, Germany, France are elements of the fact displayed by 'Every nation invaded France' – the elements of the facts displayed by 'nation'-sentences are nations. Tom, Fritz, etc., are elements of the fact displayed by 'Every group of individuals with common ancestors, traditions, and governors forcibly entered the land owned by Frenchmen' – the elements of the facts displayed by 'individual'-

---

[1] Though this answer is most importantly wrong, it is not so utterly wrong as I here pretend.

[2] Contrary to what Mr. Black says, the analysandum and the analysis are identical in meaning, and therefore the latter is not more determinate. What Mr. Black has in mind is this: 'England invaded France' completely displays in *its* sense. A sentence which shall equally completely Display what 'England invaded France' Displays will be more complete than 'England invaded France'. But this new sentence is not the Ostentation of 'England invaded France', but is *the complete form of* that Ostentation. I believe that Mr. Black's way of putting the point in terms of degrees of determinateness is just the sort of muddled way of speaking that the theory of logical constructions is designed to prevent and the philosopher wishes to eliminate.

sentences are individuals. And individuals are more ultimate than nations. Sense-data and mental states in their turn are more ultimate than individuals. Similarly, judgments (meaning particular events in individual minds) are more ultimate than propositions[1] and sentences and facts (complete) than incomplete facts, and your credit and my credit than Credit, and Bob's belief that you can fulfil your promises to pay than your credit.

There are other ways of saying that the elements of a fact F' are more ultimate than those of a fact F. We may say that the elements of F are *reducible* to those of F', or we may say that they are *logical constructions out of* those of F'. A consideration of examples will show that if x is reducible to y then (i) to say something of x is to say something, though not the *same* thing, of y (ii) it is not true that to say something of y is always to say something of x (iii) to say the same thing of y as was said of x is to speak not falsely but nonsensically. For example, if we reduce a chair to a set of sense-data, then to say that I sat on the chair is to say something about the sense-data but not, thank goodness, that I sat on them.

When S is an Ostentation of S' then not only are the elements of the fact it displays more ultimate than those of the fact S' displays; its form also is more ultimate. This may be expressed by saying that the fact a less Ostensive sentence displays is *secondary* to that which a more Ostensive sentence displays. Hence 'S is an Ostentation of S'' will mean 'The fact which S' displays is secondary to the fact which S displays'.

From this it looks as if non-Perfection, unlike incompleteness and non-perfection, is not a defect in the relation between S and the fact it displays but is a defect in that fact itself, namely its secondariness to another fact.

But this account of non-Ostensiveness is merely true. What we want is a thoroughly Ostensive account of non-Ostensiveness. There are signs that we lack this. For the secondary facts are and yet are not identical with the facts to which they are secondary. This paradox indicates that we must push the analysis of Ostentation a stage further. This I propose to do by defining S' displays$_n$ a secondary fact$_n$ by S' secondarily displays$_1$

---

[1] See Broad, *Examination of McTaggart's Philosophy*, Vol. I, p. 58.

*a fact*₁ where the suffixes indicate modifications in sense. Let us work this out.

3. FURTHER ANALYSIS OF OSTENTATION. Analysis, up to this point, has helped in the identification of Ostentation but it will do so no further. Fortunately, it may now be assumed that there is no difficulty in recognizing Ostentation. Use is made of this assumption in taking its analysis a stage further by analysing *more ultimate* and *secondary*. This analysis we have seen must be such as to resolve a certain paradox.

3.1. *The paradox that the facts displayed by a non-Ostensive sentence S' and its Ostentation S, though not two, are not identical.* If S is an Ostentation of S' then it is a translation of S', i.e. expresses the same fact, i.e. displays equally precisely¹ the same fact or facts. Thus if you say 'Every group of individuals with common ancestors, traditions and governors forcibly entered the land owned by Frenchmen' you will merely repeat yourself if you add 'Every nation invaded France'.

On the other hand, if S is an Ostentation of S', then the fact which S' displays is secondary to that which S displays and therefore they are not identical. Thus the elements of the fact displayed by our 'individual'-sentence are Tom, Fritz and Jean, while the elements of the fact displayed by 'Every nation invaded France' are different, being England, Germany and France. Further, the form of the one fact is not the form of the other and therefore they are not identical.

We must then find some definition of 'more ultimate' and 'secondary' which removes this paradox by showing how the fact *Every nation invaded France* is not identical with *Every group of individuals with common ancestors, traditions and governors forcibly entered the land owned by Frenchmen*, while yet there are not two facts, the nation-fact and then, besides, the individual-fact.

3.2. *The solution of the paradox, and definition of 'secondary' and 'more ultimate'.* It will be remembered that we have met this sort of paradox before; indeed it is a Reduplication Paradox.² We saw that though the incomplete fact *Something fell* is not identical with the complete fact *This fell* it yet does not make a second fact. This paradox we removed by reducing the incomplete fact to

¹ Intimates just as much the form, elements and arrangement of the same fact or facts.
² *The* kind of paradox in analytic philosophy.

(*a*) the complete fact plus (*b*) the sentence 'Something fell' plus (*c*) a relation between the sentence and the complete fact, the relation of *incomplete* display. The same methods will serve us here. I therefore now introduce the required relation of *secondary*, i.e. *indirect*, display.

The significant features[1] of 'Every nation invaded France' fix the significant features of 'Every group of individuals with common ancestors, traditions and governors forcibly entered the land owned by Frenchmen' and thus it intimates *indirectly* the form, elements and arrangement intimated by the 'individual'-sentence. Thus if the 'nation'-sentence had been 'Every nation invaded Germany' then the 'individual'-sentence would have had to intimate different elements and if the 'nation'-sentence had been 'France invaded every nation' then the 'individual'-sentence would have had to intimate a different arrangement. The 'nation'-sentence intimates indirectly what the 'individual'-sentence intimates directly.

Although the 'nation'-sentence does not even try to intimate the form of the individual-fact by having an *identical* form and does not even try to *name or hiate* its elements, nevertheless the form and arrangement of the 'nation'-sentence play a part in intimating the form and arrangement of the individual-fact and the words the 'nation'-sentence contains intimate what are the elements of the individual-fact. Because of this the 'nation'-sentence may be said to *indirectly display* what the 'individual'-sentence directly displays.

There are two relations with which indirect display might readily be confused. (1) *S indirectly displays F does not mean S inexplicitly displays F.*[2] Doubtless there is a sense of 'tries for identity of form' in which an imperfect sentence such as 'Every dog is dangerous' may be said to intimate form without trying for identity of form. But this is not the sense I have in mind when I say that an indirect sentence does not try for identity of form. I should say that 'Every dog is dangerous' though it fails to display form by identical form does try to do so, and that consequently although it displays inexplicitly it does not display

---

[1] i.e. what words it contains and in what order as opposed to being written large or small, in blue or red ink.

[2] This is not so wrong as I now make it appear.

indirectly. It may be a badly drawn map of the fact of which 'Something is a dog and dangerous and it is not the case that something is a dog and not dangerous' is a well drawn map, but it is on the same scale and if the latter is life-size it is so also. On the other hand 'Every nation invaded France' is not on the same scale as 'Every group of individuals with common ancestors, traditions and governors forcibly entered the land owned by Frenchmen'. It is this defect of scale[1] which makes it correct to say that the 'nation'-sentence indirectly displays the individual-fact. This must not be confused with its inexplicit display of the nation-fact. True, when S' indirectly displays F it lacks identity of form with F, but this is not because it tries for identity and fails, but because it does not try.[2] Thus do I draw attention to the special sort of lack of identity involved in the special sort of display which I call 'indirect display'.

(2) It must not be supposed that S' *indirectly displays F* means (a) '*F*' *is a translation of S'* (so that '*F*' *displays what S' displays*) but (b) '*F*' *is not identical with S'* (so that it displays indirectly what '*F*' displays). Thus it would not be correct to say that 'Every nation invaded France' *indirectly* displays what 'Toutes les nations envahirent la France' displays. It *directly* displays what the French sentence directly displays. For the two sentences are on the same scale so that what the French sentence names the 'nation'-sentence names and the form which the French sentence shows by identity of form the 'nation'-sentence also shows by identity of form. The 'nation'-sentence directly displays the nation-fact which the French sentence directly displays and *also* indirectly displays the individual-fact which the 'individual'-sentence directly displays.

---

[1] This analogy is more appropriate for some kinds of indirectness than for others. Thus it is hardly appropriate to describe the indirectness of '"Something fell" displays an incomplete fact' as a defect of scale. It is, however, true that any sentence which indirectly displays appears to *multiply entities*, cf. Mace, *Mind*, January, 1931.

[2] There is a criterion for deciding whether a sentence is trying for identity of form with a fact. When 'F_1' is trying for identity of form with F, then the elements of the fact F_1 are the elements of F, even though 'F_1' is imperfect and uses disreputable expressions like 'two' and 'three'. When a sentence 'F_2' does not even try for identity of form with F, then the elements of the fact F_2 are less ultimate than those of F. This is not an analytic definition of *not trying for identity of form* and thus of *indirect display*. Such an analysis would be circular, since we shall analyse *more ultimate* in terms of *indirect display*. I shall not *analyse* indirect display at all; I *identify* it for you as the relation involved in such and such a way in the analysis of *more ultimate*. As *more ultimate* has already been identified my remark is useful, though not analytic.

It is clear from this last example that when 'F''' displays F indirectly then it displays another fact F' secondary to F and, conversely, when 'F''' displays two facts F' and F and the former is secondary to the latter, then it indirectly displays F. This enables us to define *F' is secondary to F* by *The sentence 'F'' displays indirectly what the sentence 'F' displays directly.*

This definition reduces secondary facts to sentences which indirectly display facts. For to say of a secondary fact that it is secondary is to say of the sentence which expresses it that it indirectly displays a fact; and, in general, when F' is secondary to F then whatever one says about F' just is a statement about the sentence 'F''', the fact F, and the relation between them of indirect display. This is the sense in which there are not two facts F and F'. On the other hand, though to say something about F' is to say something about 'F''' and F and indirect display, it is not to say the *same* thing as was said of F'. This is the sense in which F and F' are not identical. These are the senses in which *Every nation invaded France* and *Every group of individuals with common ancestors, tradition and governors forcibly entered the land owned by Frenchmen* are not two facts and yet are not identical. We may now write:—

F is an Analysis of F'
= 'F' is an Ostentation of 'F'''
= The elements and form of the fact which 'F''' displays are less ultimate than those of that which 'F' displays
= The $fact_n$ which 'F''' $displays_n$ is secondary to the $fact_{n-1}$ which 'F' $displays_{n-1}$
= 'F''' $displays_{n-1}$ indirectly the $fact_{n-1}$ which 'F' displays $_{n-1}$ directly

It is worth noting that (a) a secondary fact is reducible and its elements are reducible, and (b) a secondary fact is not secondary on account of being reducible to other facts — this is true of incomplete facts. A fact is secondary when it is reducible to another fact or facts in the special way indicated above, i.e. to sentence-facts, and *indirect display*. (c) The use of 'element' in which incomplete facts have elements is secondary to (new sense appropriate to phrases and sentences) the use in which complete facts have elements. But the elements of incomplete facts are not reducible to the elements of complete facts.

We have defined less ultimate elements in terms of indirect display. The mistake has often been made of reversing this procedure as follows: F' is a secondary fact means 'F'' indirectly displays a fact, say F. 'F'' indirectly displays F means 'F'' names a set of elements of F and exhibits their arrangement but these elements are not ultimate: i.e. they are themselves facts having elements and arrangement which 'F' fails to name and exhibit.[1]

This view is correct in that it reduces secondary facts$_n$ to sentences indirectly displaying$_{n-1}$ facts$_{n-1}$ and thus avoids the belief that secondary facts are a species of fact. And it does not make the crude mistake of identifying secondary facts with facts of the second order, i.e. facts about facts. But it does reduce secondary facts to facts of the second order. And this is a mistake.[2] Every Nation invaded France is not a fact about facts but about nations.

With our definitions not only secondary facts but also secondary elements are persuaded to vanish; not only are apparent species of fact reduced to uses of 'fact' but also apparent species of element are reduced to uses of 'element'. A fact can have many sets of elements; this is true in that there are many degrees of indirectness with which sentences may display it. A fact can have only one set of elements, since it is its elements arranged in a certain order; this is true in the sense that we cannot in the same use of 'element' say of a fact that it has this set of elements and this other set of elements.

3.3.   The ultimate definition of 'S is an Ostentation of S''. We have said S is an Ostentation of S' means S' displays$_n$ a fact$_n$ secondary to the fact which S displays$_{n-1}$; and that this means S' indirectly displays$_{n-1}$ the fact$_n$ $_{-1}$ which S directly displays$_{n-1}$ (Difference of suffix indicates difference of sense). This definition is practically[3] correct but it is not quite ultimate, i.e. Ostensive. For 'displays$_{n-1}$ a fact$_{n-1}$' may in its turn call for Ostentation. Thus it has been

[1] See for example, Susan Stebbing, 'Method of Analysis in Metaphysics', Proc. Aris. Soc., N.S., xxxiii.

[2] See John Wisdom, Mind, April, 1931, p. 212, and Psyche, 1933, p. 173, and A. J. Ayer, Analysis, November, 1933, p. 2.

But Ayer here makes the very mistake against which the analytic method is directed. For he argues from the mistakenness of the analyses offered by English philosophers of atomic facts to their non-existence or the senselessness of 'atomic fact' as used by English philosophers.

[3] It is made sufficiently general by putting 'displays$_{n-m}$' for 'displays$_{n-1}$'.

suggested that sentences about individuals are in their turn translatable into sentences about experiences. Then we should have a series of sentences S_n, S_{n-1}, S_{n-2}, . . . displaying more and more directly a fact F. Such a series would have a last term. For any sentence S_r in the series displays$_r$ a fact$_r$ only in the sense that it indirectly displays$_{r-1}$ a fact$_{r-1}$; and there must come a sense of 'displays a fact' which is not defined in terms of another. When 'displays a fact' is being used in this ultimate way we will write it 'displays$_1$ a fact$_1$, i.e. 'Displays a Fact', i.e. 'Displays the Form, Elements and Arrangement of a Fact', i.e. 'Displays the Structure of a Fact'. This gives us: *S is an Ostentation of S'* means *S Displays more directly the Fact which S' Displays indirectly.* And now it is clear that indirect Display is a special species of non-Explicitness of Display – not the in-Explicitness of Display caused by the use of 'every', 'two', etc., but the non-Explicitness of a sentence which does not try to be Explicit.[1]

To give an ultimate philosophical analysis of the proposition *S is P* is to give a translation of the sentence 'S is P' which quite directly Displays the Fact which 'S is P' indirectly Displays. When a sentence tries to Display it is Ostensive and when it is successful it is Perfect.

MR. BLACK'S QUESTIONS

I now try to outline answers to some of Mr. Black's questions. There are excuses for departing from his order.

A. '*For any given statement, is there a unique route for its analysis?*' (i) There are different kinds of Ostentation – that applied to 'Every nation invaded France' differs from that applied to '*Albert struck something* is an incomplete fact'. (ii) Not only may different facts be displayed with different kinds of indirectness, the same fact may be also. (iii) Nevertheless I fancy that given that S_1 is an Ostentation of S_n then there is only one Ostentation-route between S_1 and S_n; there may be any number of intermediate stations; but there are no loop ways, one through S_2 and another through $_2S$, where S_2 and $_2S$ indirectly display in different ways.

---

[1] We have seen that indirect Display is not non-explicit display, p. 12. Nevertheless the incompleteness or inexplicitness with which a sentence displays is reflected in the way it Displays. Thus shall we be able to frame definitions of incomplete and inexplicit display.

The field of ambiguities and some species of *display* may be suggested in the following diagram.[1]

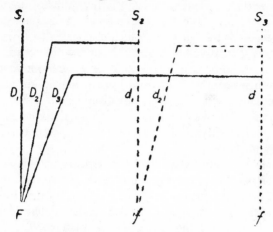

Smaller letters indicate greater secondariness.

Higher suffixes indicate greater indirectness.

Different placing of a suffix indicates different species of Display.

The S's are sentences.

F, f, f, are facts more and more secondary.

D_1, D_2, D_3 (against unbroken lines), are relations of Display more and more indirect.

d_1, d_2 (against broken lines), are relations of display in a secondary but first grade sense.

d (against dotted line) is a still more secondary relation of display.

The diagram is not completed for $_2S$ and $_3S$.

B. '*In what respects other than the more explicit formulation of a system of categories is a philosophical analysis of any given statements, different from a logical expansion of the same statement?*' If I understand correctly Mr. Black's use of the phrase 'the more explicit

---

[1] Suppose a language is such that a certain fact may be displayed more and less completely and more and less indirectly in two ways. Then the sentences displaying that fact may be set out in a 2-dimensional manifold, thus: Degrees of completeness may be indicated by horizontal order; degrees of indirectness by distance from the centre; one way of displaying by the upwards direction and the other way of displaying by the downwards direction. In general, the sentences displaying completely, incompletely, directly, and indirectly and in n ways a fact may be set out in an $\frac{n}{2} + 1$ dimensional manifold.

formulation of a system of categories', my answer is 'In none'.
I welcome Mr. Black's way of putting the matter. For though
it is in a sense very philosophically unilluminating because it is
so very far from Ostensive, nevertheless it is philosophically
useful, because it puts in *familiar* terminology what I have put in
more nearly Ostensive but regrettably unfamiliar terminology.

C. It is in some sense true that 'the direction chosen by
Ostentation is such as to increase immediacy of knowledge of,
or acquaintance with, the facts constituting successive stages in
the analysis'. But we are acquainted with the elements of the
lower-level facts in a different *sense* (as opposed to *degree*) of
'acquaintance'.

D. '*How is the system of categories used in analysis determined,*
e.g. *are the mutual connections necessary connections?*' (i) I am not
very sure what the first part of this question means. In so far as
we may speak of *the* system of categories, it is determined by the
accidents determining the development of language.

Mr. Black believes that the exhibition of the categories,
i.e. the Ostentation of a sentence, reveals presuppositions. This
is the old and untrue story that philosophy is a search for ultimate
premisses. *What* presuppositions are revealed by "Nation"-*sentences can be Ostensively translated into* "individual"-*sentences?*

(ii) As to the second part of Mr. Black's question, namely
Are the mutual connections between the categories necessary? They are
linguistically necessary. *Nations are of a less ultimate category than
individuals*, i.e. *Nations are reducible to individuals*, is a linguistically
necessary proposition like *Two plus two equals four*.[1] The explanation of this answer requires an explanation of necessity which I
have found myself unable to put shortly enough to include here.
I can only say that *Nations are reducible to individuals* is a linguistically necessary proposition because given the usage of 'nations'
and 'individuals' (a contingent fact) then to add that nations are
reducible to individuals is to assert a necessary consequence —
that is, to repeat oneself.[2] For, as we have seen, *Nations are*

[1] To assert that every nation invaded France and then to add that every group of
individuals with common ancestors, traditions and governors invaded the land owned by
Frenchmen is to make a proposition which is repetitive in the sense in which *Two men
fell and two more fell and four men fell* is.

[2] I am here indebted to Dr. Paul Weiss, 'Entailment and the Future of Logic', *Proc.
7th Internat. Cong. Phil.*, p. 143, and to Dr. Wittgenstein, though I make neither responsible for anything suggested here.

reducible to individuals though apparently a fact about nations is really about the relative usage of 'nation' and 'individual'.

SUMMARY

1. A sentence may incompletely display facts. With this defect the gossip is concerned. It can be removed only by more knowledge.

2. A sentence may be inexplicit (*a*) as to the elements (*b*) as to the form of a fact. These defects are removed (*a*) in the scientist's definition of terms and (*b*) in the logician's re-formulation of sentences. Such ostentation causes and is caused by greater explicitness in apprehending the structure of a fact.

3. A sentence may completely and/or perfectly explicitly display a fact and yet be unsatisfactory because that fact is secondary.

A sentence which displays a secondary fact always also indirectly displays in a more ultimate sense a less secondary fact and ultimately but still more indirectly a primary fact, i.e. a Fact. The fact$_n$ which a sentence displays$_n$ is not identical with the fact it Displays and yet we cannot say that there is the Fact and in addition the fact$_n$. This difficulty is removed when we see that ' "S is P" displays$_n$ a fact$_n$,' just means '*S is P*' *Displays indirectly at n removes a Fact.*

To translate S$_n$ which indirectly displays a Fact into S which less indirectly Displays that Fact is to give an Ostentation of S$_n$. The labour of Ostentation is usually undertaken with the intention of gaining a more explicit apprehension of the Structure of a Fact. Ostentation carried out with this intention is philosophical analysis.[1]

---

[1] 'Analysis' may be used for 'Ostentation with whatever intention' and 'philosophy' for 'insight into Structure however obtained'. It is in this sense that analysis is the, or only *a*, means to philosophy (analytic) and not identical with it.

PHILOSOPHICAL PERPLEXITY
(*Proc. of the Aris. Soc. Vol. XVI*)

1. *Philosophical statements are really verbal.* – I have inquired else-where the real nature of philosophical requests such as 'Can we know what is going on in someone else's mind?' 'Can we really know the causes of our sensations?' 'What is a chair?' and of philo-sophical answers such as 'We can never really know the causes of our sensations', 'A chair is nothing but our sensations', or 'A chair is something over and above our sensations', 'The goodness of a man, of a picture, of an argument is something over and above our feelings of approval and over and above those features of the man, the picture or the argument, which "determine" its goodness'. There is no time to repeat the inquiry here and I have to say dogmatically:

A philosophical answer is really a verbal recommendation in response to a request which is really a request with regard to a sentence which lacks a conventional use whether there occur situations which could conventionally be described by it. The description, for example 'I know directly what is going on in Smith's mind', is not a jumble like 'Cat how is up', nor is it in conflict with conventional usage like 'There are two white pieces and three black so there are six pieces on the board'. It just lacks a conventional usage. To call both 'Can 2 + 3 = 6?' and 'Can I know what is going on in the minds of others?' nonsensical questions serves to bring out the likeness between them. But if one were to deny that there is a difference between them it would be an instance of that disrespect for other people which we may platitudinously say, so often damages philosophical work. A disrespect which blinds one to the puzzles they raise – in this instance the puzzle of the philosophical *can* which somehow seems between 'Can 2 + 3 make 6?' and 'Can terriers catch hares?' Com-pare 'Can persons be in two places at once?' 'Do we have uncon-scious wishes?' 'Can you play chess without the queen?' (W).[1]

---

[1] Wittgenstein has not read this over-compressed paper and I warn people against supposing it a closer imitation of Wittgenstein than it is. On the other hand I can hardly exaggerate the debt I owe to him and how much of the good in this work is his – not only in the treatment of this philosophical difficulty and that but in the matter of how to do philosophy. As far as possible I have put a W against examples I owe to him. It must not be assumed that they are used in a way he would approve.

Even to say that 'I know directly what is going on in Smith's mind' is *meaningless*, is dangerous, especially if you have just said that 'There are two white pieces and three black so there are six' is meaningless.

It is not even safe to say that 'I know directly what is going on in Smith's mind' lacks a use or meaning and leave it at that. For though it has no meaning it tends to have a meaning, like 'All whiffey was the tulgey wood', though of course it is unlike this last example in the important respect that it does not lack a meaning because its constituent words are unknown. Nor does it lack meaning because its syntax is unknown. This makes it puzzling and makes it resemble the logical case. It is clear that for these reasons it would be even more illuminating and more misleading to say that 'God exists' and 'Men are immortal' are meaningless — especially just after saying $2 + 3 = 6$ is meaningless.

2. *Philosophical statements are not verbal.* — I have said that philosophers' questions and theories are really verbal. But if you like we will not say this or we will say also the contradictory.[1] For of course (*a*) philosophic statements usually have not a verbal air. On the contrary they have a non-verbal air like 'A fox's brush is really a tail'. (W). And their non-verbal air is not an unimportant feature of them because on it very much depends their puzzlingness.

And (*b*) though really verbal a philosopher's statements have not a merely verbal point. Unlike many statements the primary point of uttering them is not to convey the information they convey but to do something else. Consequently all attempts to explain their peculiar status by explaining the peculiar nature of their subject-matter, fail. For their subject-matter is not peculiar; their truth or falsity, in so far as these are appropriate to them at all, is fixed by facts about words, e.g. Goodness is not approval by the majority, because 'The majority, sometimes approve what is bad' is not self-contradictory. But the point of philosophical statements is peculiar. It is the illumination of the ultimate structure of facts, i.e. the relations between different categories of being or (we must be in the mode) the relations between different sub-languages within a language.

[1] I do not wish to suggest that Wittgenstein would approve of *this* sort of talk nor that he would disapprove of it.

The puzzles of philosophical propositions, of fictional propositions, general propositions, negative propositions, propositions about the future, propositions about the past, even the puzzle about psychological propositions, are not removed by explaining the peculiar nature of the subject-matter of the sentences in which they are expressed but by reflecting upon the peculiar manner in which those sentences work. Mnemonic slogan: It's not the stuff, it's the style that stupefies.

3. *The divergence of point from content.* – The divergence of point from content which is found in necessary and near necessary propositions can be explained here only briefly.

Suppose a decoder, though still utterly ignorant of the meaning of both of two expressions 'monarchy' and 'set of persons ruled by the same king', has after prolonged investigation come to the conclusion that they mean the same in a certain code. He will say to his fellow-decoder ' "Monarchy" means the same as "set of persons ruled by the same king" '. The translator, and the philosopher also, may say the same. They all use the same form of words because what they say is the same. But the point of what they say is very different. The decoder's point can be got by anyone who knows the meaning of 'means the same as'; the translator does what he wants with the sentence only if his hearer knows the meaning either of 'monarchy' or of 'set of persons ruled by the same king'; the philosopher does what he wants with the sentence only if his hearer already uses, i.e. understands, i.e. knows the meaning of, *both* 'monarchy' and 'set of persons ruled by the same king'. This condition makes the case of the philosopher curious; for it states that he can do what he wants with the sentence only if his hearer already knows what he is telling him. But this is true in the required sense. The philosopher draws attention to what is already known with a view to giving insight into the structure of what 'monarchy', say, means, i.e. bringing into connection the sphere in which the one expression is used with that in which the other is. Compare the man who says 'I should have the change from a pound after spending five shillings on a book, one and sevenpence-halfpenny on stamps and two and twopence-halfpenny at the grocer's, so I should have eleven shillings and twopence'. This is Moore's example and I beg attention for it. It is tremendously illuminating in the

necessary synthetic group of puzzles and in a far, far wider field
than this, because it illuminates the use of 'means the same' — a
phrase which stops so many. When on first going to France I
learn the exchange rate for francs, do I know the meaning of
'worth 100 francs' or do I come to know this after staying three
weeks?

The philosopher is apt to say 'A monarchy is a set of people
under a king' rather than ' "Monarchy" means the same as "a
set of people under a king" '. By using the former sentence he
intimates his point. Now shall we say 'A monarchy is a set of
people under a king' means the same as ' "Monarchy" means
"a set of people under a king" ' or not? My answer is 'Say which
you like. But if you say "Yes" be careful, etc., and if you say
"No" be careful, etc.'

If we decide to describe the difference between the two as a
difference of meaning we must not say that the difference in
meaning is a difference of subjective intension, nor that it is a
difference of emotional significance merely. For these are not
adequate accounts of the difference between the two — and not an
adequate account of the difference between the use of '3 plus 5
plus 8' and the use of '16'.

4. *Philosophy, truth, misleadingness and illumination.* — Now that
we have seen that the philosopher's intention is to bring out
relations between categories of being, between spheres of language, we shall be more prepared to allow that false statements
about the usage of words may be philosophically very useful
and even adequate provided their falsity is realized and there is
no confusion about what they are being used for.

The nature of the philosopher's intention explains how it is
that one may call a philosophical theory such as *A proposition is a
sentence,* certainly false, and yet feel that to leave one's criticism
at that is to attend to the letter and not the spirit of the theory
criticized.

The nature of the philosopher's intention explains also how it
is that one cannot say of a philosopher's theory that it is false
when he introduces it in his own terminology, while yet one
often feels that such theories are somehow philosophically bad.
Thus (W) suppose the word 'sense-datum' has never been used
before and that someone says 'When Jones sees a rabbit, has an

illusion of a rabbit, has an hallucination of a rabbit, dreams of a
rabbit, he has a sense-datum of a rabbit'. One cannot protest that
this is false, since no statement has been made, only a recommendation. But the recommendation purports to be enlightening
and one may well protest if it is, on the contrary, misleading.
This particular recommendation is liable to suggest that sense-
data are a special sort of thing, *extremely* thin coloured pictures,
and thus liable to raise puzzles, such as 'How are sense-data related
to material things?' We can abuse a philosopher as much as we
like if we use the right adjectives. *Good is an ultimate predicate* is
useless, *A proposition is a subsistent entity* is useless and pretentious,[1]
We can never know the real cause of our sensations is misleading.
And we can praise him although he speaks falsely or even nonsensically. People have considered whether it is true that 'an
event is a pattern of complete, particular, specific facts and a
complete, particular, specific fact is an infinitely thin slice out of
an event'.[2]

You may say 'How absurd of them since the statement is
nonsense'. Certainly the statement is nonsense and so, if you
like, it was absurd of them. But it was better than saying it was
nonsense and ignoring it. Suppose I say 'The thoroughbred is a
neurotic woman on four legs'. This is nonsense, but it is not
negligible.[3]

5. *Provocation and Pacification.*— So far, however, little or
nothing has been said to explain what sort of things make a
philosophical statement misleading and what make it illuminating.
Only a short answer is possible here.

In the first place there is the misleading feature which nearly
all philosophical statements have — a non-verbal air. The
philosopher *laments* that we can never really know what is going
on in someone else's mind, that we can never really know the
causes of our sensations, that inductive conclusions are never
really justified. He laments these things as if he can dream of
another world where we can see our friends and tables face to

---

[1] Neither of these theories is entirely useless. They are for one thing good antitheses
to the naturalistic error.

[2] *Problems of Mind and Matter*, p. 32.

[3] The matter can be put in terms of truth and falsehood. A philosophical theory
involves an explicit claim, an equation, and an implicit claim that the equation is not
misleading and is illuminating. The explicit claim may be false and the implicit true on
one or both counts, or vice versa.

face, where scientists can justify their conclusions and terriers can catch hares. This enormous source of confusion we cannot study now.

Secondly philosophical statements mislead when by the use of like expressions for different cases, they suggest likenesses which do not exist, and by the use of different expressions for like cases, they conceal likenesses which do exist.

Philosophical theories are illuminating in a corresponding way, namely when they suggest or draw attention to a terminology which reveals likenesses and differences concealed by ordinary language.

I want to stress the philosophical usefulness of metaphysical surprises such as 'We can never really know the causes of our sensations', 'We can never know the real causes of our sensations', 'Inductive conclusions are never really justified', 'The laws of mathematics are really rules of grammar'. I believe that too much fun has been made of philosophers who say this kind of thing. Remember what Moore said about 1924 – words to this effect: When a philosopher says that really something is so we are warned that what he says is really so is not so really. With horrible ingenuity Moore can rapidly reduce any metaphysical theory to a ridiculous story. For he is right, they are false – only there *is* good in them, poor things. This shall be explained.

Wittgenstein allows importance to these theories. They are for him expressions of deep-seated puzzlement. It is an important part of the treatment of a puzzle to develop it to the full.

But this is not enough. Wittgenstein allows that the theories are philosophically important not merely as specimens of the whoppers philosophers can tell. But he too much represents them as merely symptoms of linguistic confusion. I wish to represent them as also symptoms of linguistic penetration.

Wittgenstein gives the impression that philosophical remarks either express puzzlement or if not are remarks such as Wittgenstein himself makes with a view to curing puzzlement.

This naturally gives rise to the question 'If the proper business of philosophy is the removal of puzzlement, would it not be best done by giving a drug to the patient which made him entirely forget the statements puzzling him or at least lose his uneasy feelings?'

This of course will never do. And what we say about the

philosopher's purposes must be changed so that it shall no longer seem to lead to such an absurd idea.

The philosopher's purpose is to gain a grasp of the relations between different categories of being, between expressions used in *different manners*.[1] He is confused about what he wants and he is confused by the relations between the expressions, so he is very often puzzled. But only such treatment of the puzzles as increases a grasp of the relations between different categories of being is philosophical. And not all the philosopher's statements are either complaints of puzzlement or pacificatory. Philosophers who say 'We never know the real causes of our sensations', 'Only my sensations are real', often bring out these 'theories' with an air of triumph (with a misleading air of empirical discovery indeed). True the things they say are symptoms of confusion even if they are not of puzzlement. But they are also symptoms of penetration, of noticing what is not usually noticed. Philosophical progress has two aspects, provocation and pacification.

6. *Example of the pointless doubts: (a) how misleading they are.* — Let us consider this with examples. Take first the philosopher who says to the plain man: 'We do not really know that there is cheese on the table; for might not all the sense evidence suggest this and yet there be no cheese — remember what happened at Madame Tussaud's'.

Our assertion with confidence that there is cheese on the table or our assertion that we know that there is cheese on the table raises at last these three puzzles: (1) *the category puzzle*, which finds expression in 'We ought not to speak of a cheese (of the soul) but of bundles of sense-data'; (2) *the knowledge puzzle*, which finds expression in 'We ought not to say "I know there is cheese on the table" but "Very, very probably there is cheese on the table"'; (3) *the justification puzzle*, which finds expression in 'Empirical conclusions are not really justified'.

We cannot here speak of all these. We are considering (2) the *knowledge* or *pointless doubt* puzzle. There are a group of pointless doubt puzzles including the following: 'We don't really know that there is cheese on the table'; 'We ought to say only "It is probable that there is cheese on the table"'; 'It is improper to say

---

[1] See 'different level' in *Proc. Aris. Soc.* Supp. Vol. XIII, p. 66.

"I know that there is cheese on the table" '; 'It would be well if we prefixed every remark about material things with "probably" '.

All these suggestions are misleading – they all suggest that it has been discovered that we have been over-confident about material things. They should have slightly different treatment but I have only just *realized* this multiplicity. Let us take the puzzle in the crude form 'Couldn't there be no cheese here although all the sense-evidence suggests there is?'

Wittgenstein explains that this sentence though of the verbal form we associate with doubt and though it may be uttered with the intonation, expression and gestures we associate with doubt is not *used* as a sentence expressing doubt. To utter it is to raise a pseudo-doubt. People say 'We ought not to say "There *is* cheese on the table" but "Probably there is cheese on the table" or "The sense-evidence suggests ever so strongly that there is cheese on the table". For whatever we do we never observe a cheese, we have to rely upon our senses. And we may be suffering from a joint hallucination of all the senses or a consistent dream. Remember how people are deceived at Madame Tussaud's. And we may see and touch cheesy patches, smell cheesy smells, obtain cheesy pictures from cameras and cheesy reactions from mice and yet the stuff to-morrow be soap in our mouth. And then to-morrow we shall say "Yesterday we were mistaken". So our "knowledge" to-day that there is cheese here is not real knowledge. Every one ought really to whisper "Possibly hallucinatory" after *every* sentence about material things however much he has made sure that he is right'.

What those who recommend this should notice is how not merely unusual but pointless a use of words they recommend. As language is at present used, I raise my hungry friends' hopes if I say 'There is cheese on the table', and I damp them if I add 'unless it is hallucinatory'. But this additional clause has its effect only because I do *not always* use it. If a parent adds 'be very careful' to everything he says to a child he will soon find his warnings ineffective. If I prefix every statement about material things with 'probably' this doubt-raiser will soon cease to frighten hungry friends, that is cease to function as it now does. Consequently in order to mark those differences which I now mark by saying in one case 'Probably that is cheese on the table' and in another case 'I know that is cheese on the table', I shall have to introduce a new notation, one to do the work the old did. 'To do the work the old did!' that is, to claim what I formerly claimed with 'know!'

It may now be said 'In the ordinary use of "know" we may know that that is cheese on the table, but this knowledge is not real knowledge'.

This gives the misleading idea that the philosopher has envisaged some kind of knowing which our failing faculties prevent us from attaining. Terriers cannot catch hares, men cannot really know the causes of their sensations. Nothing of the kind, however. For when we say to the philosopher 'Go on, describe this real knowledge, tell us what stamp of man you want and we will see if we can buy or breed one' then he can never tell us.

It may now be said, 'No, no, the point is this: There is some inclination to use[1] "know" strictly so that we do not know that insulin cures diabetes, that the sun will rise to-morrow, because these propositions are only probable inferences from what we have observed. There is some inclination to use "know" only when what is known is observed or is entailed by something known for certain. Now you do not know in this sense that you will not have to correct yourself to-morrow and say "I was mistaken yesterday, that was not cheese", since nothing you know for certain to-day is incompatible with this. And if you do not know but what you may have to correct yourself to-morrow you do not know that you are right to-day.'

But what is meant by 'certain'? I should claim to know for certain that that is cheese on the table now. And as the objector rightly points out this entails that I shall not have to correct myself to-morrow. I therefore know in the strict sense that I shall not have to correct myself to-morrow.

It will be said that it is not *absolutely* certain that that is cheese on the table. But I should reply that it is.

It will be said that it is not *senseless to doubt* that that is cheese on the table, not even after the most exhaustive tests. I should reply that it is.

But, of course, by now I see what the sceptic is driving at. It is not senseless to doubt that that is cheese on the table, in the

[1] Another form would be: 'It is proper' as opposed to 'usual' to use 'know' so that, etc.

sense in which it is senseless to doubt 'I am in pain', 'I hear a buzzing' – not even after the most exhaustive tests – indeed the exhaustive tests make no difference to this. For, in this sense, it is not senseless to doubt that that is cheese on the table provided only that 'He says that that is cheese but perhaps he is mistaken' has a use in English. You see, 'He says he is in pain, but perhaps he is mistaken' has no use in English. Hence we may be 'absolutely certain' that he is not mistaken[1] about his pain, in the very special sense that 'He is mistaken' makes no sense in this connection.

Thus the sceptic's pretended doubts amount to pointing out that, unlike statements descriptive of sensations, statements about material things make sense with 'perhaps he is mistaken'. And the sceptic proposes to mark this by an extraordinary use of 'know' and 'probably'. He proposes that we should not say that we know that that is cheese on the table unless it is entailed by statements with regard to which a doubt is not merely out of the question but unintelligible, i.e. such that where S is P is one of them then 'S is P unless I am mistaken' raises a titter like 'I am in pain unless I am mistaken'. 'That is cheese on the table' is not such a statement and so of course it does not follow from such statements – otherwise a doubt with regard to it would be unintelligible, i.e. it would be absolutely certain in the strict, philosophic sense.

The sceptic's doubts become then a recommendation to use 'know' only with statements about sense-experience and mathematics and to prefix all other statements with 'probably'.[2]

This is very different talk and much less misleading. But still it is misleading unless accompanied by the explanation given above of the astounding certainty of statements about sense-experience. Even with the explanation the suggestion is highly dangerous, involving as it does a new and 'manner – indicating' use of the familiar words 'know' and 'probable'. Without the explanation it suggests that there is a difference in degree of certainty between statements about material things and statements about sense-data, a difference in certainty dependent upon

---

[1] Of course he may be *lying*.

[2] Compare the tendency to use 'what ought to be done' irrevocably. People who do this lament thus: 'What one ought to do is always for the best, but unfortunately we never know what we really ought to do'. Others lament thus: 'We can know what we ought to do but unfortunately this does not always turn out for the best'.

their subject-matter, in a sense analogous to that in which we say 'I am certain about what happened in Hyde Park — I was there — but I am not certain about what happened in Spain — I was not an eye-witness'. This suggests that I know what it would be like to be an eye-witness of cheese, but am in fact unfortunately obliged to *rely upon the testimony of* my senses.

Now the difference between statements about sense-experiences and statements about material things is not at all like this. The difference is not one of subject-matter (stuff) but of a different manner of use (style). And statements about sense-experiences are certain only because it makes no sense to say that they may be wrong.[1] Notice the connection between 'He says he is in pain but I think he is mistaken' and 'He cries "Ow!" but I think he is mistaken'. The difference between sense-statements and thing-statements cannot be adequately explained here. And consequently the full misleadingness of such a use of 'probably' as is recommended in what we may call the last form of the pseudo-doubt, cannot be adequately explained here.

But I hope I have said enough to bring out in good measure the misleadingness of saying such things as 'O dear, we can never know the causes of our sensations', and even 'It would be philosophically excellent to put "probably" before all statements about material things'.

7. *Example of the pointless doubts: (b) how importantly illuminating they are*. — But though the recommended use of 'probably' would be pointless as a cautionary clause and would thus be extremely misleading, the recommendation to use it so is not pointless, is not prompted wholly by confusion, but partly by penetration. The philosopher says to the plain man 'You do not really know that that is a cheese on the table'. We have pacified those who are opposed to this statement by bringing out the sources of their reluctance to agree with it. But the philosopher must pacify everyone and we must now pacify those philosophers who are pleased with it, and complete the pacification of those who are puzzled by it, being tempted to deny it and at the same time tempted to assert it. What *is* the point behind the misleading statement 'We can never know statements about material things'? The answer has been given already by the method of forcing refor-

---

[1] This, I realize, stands very much in need of pacifying explanation.

mulations. But we may now approach the answer by a different route. Under what circumstances are such things usually said?

It is when after considering hallucinations, illusions, etc., one wishes to emphasize (1) the likeness between such cases and cases in which there was 'something really there', and to emphasize the continuity between (a) cases in which one says 'I think that is cheese on the table', 'I believe that is a real dagger', 'Probably that is a snake, not a branch' and (b) cases in which one says 'That *is* cheese on the table', 'I found that it *was* a snake'; and to emphasize (2) the unlikeness between even so well assured a statement as 'This is my thumb' and such a statement as 'I see a pinkish patch', 'I feel a softish patch', 'I am in pain'.

It is not at all easy at first to see how in being revocable and correctable by others the most assured statement about a thing is more like the most precarious statement about another thing than it is to a statement descriptive of one's sensations. Ordinary language conceals these things because in ordinary language we speak both of some favourable material-thing-statements and of statements about our sensations, as certain, while we speak of other statements about material things as merely probable. This leads to pseudo-laments about the haunting uncertainty of even the best material-thing-statements and pseudo-congratulations upon the astounding certainty of statements about our sensations.

We are all, when our attention is drawn to those cases so often described in which it looks for all the world as if our friend is standing in the room although he is dying two thousand miles away, or in which we think we see a banana and it turns out to be a reflection in a greengrocer's mirror, we are all, in such cases, inclined to say 'Strictly we ought always to add "unless it is a queer looking stick and not a banana, or a reflection or an hallucination or an illusion" '.[1] We do not stop to consider what would happen if we did always add this. Horrified at the deceptions our senses have practised upon us we feel we must abuse them somehow and so we say that they never *prove* anything, that we never *know* what is based on them.

The continuity and the difference which are concealed by ordinary language would be no longer concealed but marked if we used 'probably' in the way recommended. But what an unfor-

[1] Then every statement would be tautologous but *absolutely* certain!

tunate way of obtaining this result! And in what a misleading way was the recommendation made! I do not really know that this is a thumb. The huntsman's coat is not really pink. A fox's brush is really a tail. (W).

8. *Other Examples.* – Now many other examples should be given. 'What is a mathematical proposition?' 'Do inductive arguments give any probability to their conclusions?' These other puzzles should be re-created; the temptations to give the answers which have been given should be re-created. But this cannot be done in this paper. Without bringing up the puzzles and temptations the following accounts are half dead, but I offer them for what they are worth.

Take 'The laws of mathematics and logic are really rules of grammar'. With this instructive incantation people puzzle themselves to death. Is it or isn't it true? And if false what amendment will give us the truth? If not rules then what? The answer is 'They are what they are, etc. Is a donkey a sort of horse but with *very* long ears?' People are puzzled because of course it isn't true that the laws of mathematics are rules of grammar (more obvious stiil that they are not commands). And yet they cannot bring themselves to lose the advantages of this falsehood. For this falsehood draws attention to (1) an unlikeness and (2) a likeness concealed by ordinary language; (1) an unlikeness to the laws of hydraulics and an unlikeness in this unlikeness to the unlikeness between the laws of hydraulics and those of aeronautics; for it is an unlikeness not of subject-matter but of manner of functioning – and (2) a likeness but not an exact likeness to the functioning of rules.

Again 'Inductive arguments do not really give any probability to their conclusions' gives the misleading idea that the scientists have been found out at last, that our confidence in our most careful research workers is entirely misplaced, their arguments being no better than those of the savage. Nothing of the kind of course. What is at the back of this lament is this: In ordinary language we speak of Dr. So and so's experiment with a group of 100 children whose teeth improved after six months extra calcium' as having very much increased the probability of the proposition that bad teeth are due to calcium deficiency. We also say that my having drawn 90 white balls from a bag which we know to contain 100 balls, each either white or black, has very much increased the probability of the proposition that all the balls in that bag are white. We even speak numerically in connection with empirical probability – we not only argue *a priori* and say 'There were six runners, there are now only five, we still know nothing of any of them, so it is now 4–1 against the dog from trap 1' but we also argue empirically and say 'It was 5–1 against the dog from trap 1; but I hear a rumour that each of the others has been provided with a cup of tea, and I think we may now take 4–1 against him'.

The similarity in the way we speak of these cases leads us when asked how empirical arguments give probability to their conclusions to try to assimilate them to the formal cases, balls in bags, dice, etc. But when this attempt is made it begins to appear that the investigation of nature is much less like the investigation of balls in a bag than one is at first apt to think.

At the same time is revealed the shocking continuity between the scientist's arguments by the method of difference and the savage's *post hoc ergo propter hoc*,[1] between the method of agreement and the reflexes of rats, and struck by the difference and the continuity and how they are concealed by ordinary language we provoke attention to them with 'Even the best established scientific results are nothing but specially successful superstitions'. We say this although we have made no shocking discovery of scientists faking figures, although the scientist's reasons for his belief in insulin still differ from my landlady's reasons for belief in Cure-all, in exactly the way which, in the ordinary use of language, makes us call the one belief scientifically grounded and the other a superstition. Similarly we may say, having seen a butterfly die or been told the age of an oak 'The strongest of us have really only a short time to live'. We say this although we have made no discovery of impending disaster, or we may say 'Man is nothing but a complicated parasite' when we watch the arrival of the 9.5 at the Metropolis.

CONCLUSION

The plain man has come to expect of philosophers paradoxical, provoking statements such as 'We can never really know the

[1] See Keynes, *A Treatise on Probability*.

causes of our sensations', 'Causation is really nothing more than regular sequence', 'Inductive conclusions are really nothing but lucky superstitions', 'The laws of logic are ultimately rules of grammar'. Philosophers know that the statements are provocative; this is why they so often put in some apologetic word such as 'really' or 'ultimately'.

These untruths persist. This is not merely because they are symptoms of an intractable disorder but because they are philosophically useful. The curious thing is that their philosophical usefulness depends upon their paradoxicalness and thus upon their falsehood. They are false because they are needed where ordinary language fails, though it must not be supposed that they are or should be in some perfect language. They are in a language not free from the same sort of defects as those from the effects of which they are designed to free us.

To invent a special word to describe the status of, for example, mathematical propositions would do no good. There is a phrase already, 'necessary yet synthetic'. It is, of course, perfectly true that mathematical propositions are 'necessary synthetics' — it should be true since the expression was made to measure. True but no good. We are as much inclined to ask 'What are necessary synthetic propositions?' as we were to ask 'What are mathematical propositions?' 'What is an instinct?' An innate disposition certainly. But philosophically that answer is useless. No — what is wanted is some device for bringing out the relations between the manner in which mathematical (or dispositional) sentences are used and the manners in which others are used — so as to give their place on the language map. This cannot be done with a plain answer, a single statement. We may try opposite falsehoods or we may say, 'Be careful that this expression "mathematical proposition" does not suggest certain analogies at the expense of others. Do not let it make you think that the difference between mathematical propositions and others is like that between the propositions of hydraulics and those of aeronautics. Do notice how like to rules, etc., and yet, etc.'

If you will excuse a suspicion of smartness: Philosophers should be continually trying to say what cannot be said.

METAPHYSICS AND VERIFICATION
(*Mind Vol. XLVII*)

'THE meaning of a statement is the method of its verification.' Some philosophers bring out this principle with confidence and satisfaction; others are utterly opposed to it and cannot understand how anyone can be so wrong-headed as to insist upon what so little reflection shows to be so palpably untrue. This conflict is of the greatest importance in philosophy to-day, and it is easy to see why. The Verification Principle is the generalization of a very large class of metaphysical theories, namely all naturalistic, empirical, positivistic theories. While its opposite, which I venture to call the Idiosyncracy Platitude, is the generalization of all common-sense, realist, transcendental theories. The verification principle is the generalization of such theories as: A cherry is nothing but sensations and possibilities of more; A mind is nothing but a pattern of behaviour; There are no such things as numbers, only numerals, and the laws of logic and mathematics are really rules of grammar; Beauty is nothing but the features in respect of which a thing is beautiful, and the feelings these arouse. According to the idiosyncracy platitude every sort of statement has its own sort of meaning, and when philosophers ask 'What is the analysis of X-propositions?' the answer is that they are ultimate, that 'everything is what it is and not another thing' (Butler, quoted by Moore on the title-page of *Principia Ethica*). This principle is the generalization of theories such as: Ethical propositions involve value predicates and are ultimate; Psychological propositions are not reducible to physiological propositions, they are ultimate; Mathematical propositions are necessary synthetic propositions – an ultimate sort of proposition; Statements about nations are not to be reduced to statements about individuals, they are about a certain sort of concrete universal.

There are not other answers to these metaphysical questions. Consequently most or all metaphysical conflict finds expression in 'Shall we or shall we not accept the principle that the meaning of a statement is the method of its verification?' and sometimes 'Is the verification principle true?' I do not at all wish to suggest that we cannot get on with metaphysical questions without first dealing with this question. On the contrary if I were forced to consider either first the verification principle and then other metaphysical theories or first the other theories and then the principle, I should much prefer the latter plan. In fact an intermediate plan is best — first an examination of easier metaphysical and nearly metaphysical questions, then a mention of the verification principle, then an attack upon the more difficult theories, then a more thorough investigation of the verification principle, then a return to the theories. . . .[1]

But now suppose someone were to ask 'Is the verification principle true?', what would you do? I myself should at once ask for the question to be put in the wider, less answer-fixing form 'Shall we accept the verification principle?' For I believe the other form misleads us as to the general nature of the question asked. I believe that this is of the utmost importance because I believe that once its general nature is apparent the question 'Is it true or not?' vanishes into insignificance while its important metaphysical merits and demerits will have become apparent in the process.

What I have in mind is this. Many different things are covered by the expressions 'accepting a theory', 'holding a view'. 'Shall we become Fascists?' 'Are you a Surrealist?' 'Is art the production of significant form?' 'Does 1 plus 1 make 2?' 'Does 378 multiplied by 56 make 21,168 or 21,268?' 'Is cancer due to a germ?' 'Do you think there is another giant panda in Tibet?' To accept the theory that cancer is due to a germ is different from accepting the theory that it is due to a chemical poison. But this is a difference *in* the theories, not in the sort of theories they are; and it is not the sort of difference I have in mind and call a difference

---

[1] On the whole the process of thought has been from the more specific theories to the more general, from the doctrine that analytic propositions are verbal to the doctrine that all necessary propositions are verbal, and from this and such theories as those mentioned above to the verification principle, rather than deductively downwards from it. I admit that in the writings of those supporters of the principle who are positivists (I have in mind such writings as those of Ayer and Schlick) there is to be found ground for Dr. Ewing's accusation that the procedure has been from the principle to the specific theories. Such a procedure, once the verification principle has been recommended by the specific cases, is perfectly satisfactory in a way I shall try to explain. But when the verification principle is regarded as an equation and the 'deductions' treated as deductions (calculations) then such a procedure leads to what it has led to — insistence and contra-insistence without end—deadlock.

in general nature. A difference in general nature is such a difference as we draw attention to when we say 'To become a Fascist is not a purely intellectual process like becoming convinced of the germ theory of cancer', or such a difference as we indicate when we say 'A man who says that 1 plus 1 makes 2 does not really make a statement, he registers a decision'. We often use the words 'not really a statement'[1] when we wish to draw attention to a difference in general nature, a difference in style of functioning as opposed to difference in subject-matter. People are inclined to say 'The statements of fiction are not really statements and so it is silly to ask whether they are true; and even poetical statements such as "A woman is a foreign land" are not really statements, and aren't really true or false'. Now there are differences of this sort *within* the range of statements which are on most occasions unhesitatingly called statements and to which it is quite usual to apply the expressions true or false. When this is so, the differences in general nature are apt to be overlooked. And sometimes overlooking them produces an inappropriateness in what we do when asked whether they are true. We act like one who when asked whether it is true that 'the stars are rogues which light the wanderer home' says he doesn't know and looks up books on astronomy.

It is, in my opinion, the neglecting of this sort of difference which has prevented the solving, the *dissolving* in Wittgenstein's[2] phrase, of metaphysical problems and of the problem of the verification principle in particular.

Well, shall we accept the verification principle? What is it to accept it? When people bring out with a dashing air the words 'The meaning of a statement is really simply the method of its verification', like one who says 'The value of a thing is really simply its power in exchange',[3] in what sort of way are they using words? What is the general nature of their theory?

---

[1] See A. H. Gardiner, *The Theory of Speech and Language*, p. 185.

[2] Wittgenstein has not read this paper, and I warn people against supposing it a closer imitation of him than it is. On the other hand, I can hardly exaggerate the debt I owe to him and how much of the good in this work is his — not only in the treatment of this philosophical difficulty and that, but in the matter of how to do philosophy. I have put a W against some examples which I owe to him. It must not be assumed that they are used in a way he would approve.

[3] Indeed one might put the verification principle in the form 'The meaning of symbols is really simply their power in prediction'.

The answer is 'It is a metaphysical theory'. True, it is a peculiar metaphysical theory as appears from the fact that we are inclined to say: it is not so much a metaphysical theory as a recipe for framing metaphysical theories; it is not a metaphysical theory, it is a mnemonic device for getting from metaphysical theories which have been illuminating in easy metaphysical difficulties to theories which shall work in harder cases, a mnemonic device reminding us how to meet objections to positivistic theories; it is a recommendation to so use 'mean' that S means the same as S' provided they are verified in the same way, where this recommendation is not for the purpose of metaphysically illuminating the use of 'meaning' but for another metaphysical purpose, namely the illumination of the use of expressions which on the recommended use of 'meaning' will be said to mean the same. It is this 'altruism' which makes the verification principle a peculiar metaphysical theory.[1] But it is the *likeness* of the verification principle to metaphysical theories which I now want to emphasize and explain. It is like not only to such theories as 'A mind is really simply a pattern of behaviour', 'Goodness is a matter of causing approval', but also to such theories as 'We never really know that what we see is real and not a dream', 'We never really know what is going on in another person's mind', 'Nothing is really the same from moment to moment', 'All words are vague'. It is to emphasize this likeness that I call the verification principle a metaphysical theory. I should be prepared to argue that there is nothing incorrect in calling it this. But that is neither here nor there. What we are concerned with is its metaphysical nature. And to illuminate this I say that it is a sort

[1] The non-altruistic theory connected with it is 'The meaning of a statement is a functional feature of it, not an object, like the Hampton Court Maze, of which it is the plan', or 'The meaning of a statement is a matter of its uses'. The comparison of this with the verification principle would help to deal with many conflicts in which one philosopher says that S means the same as S' while another says it does not. For often these arise because one is using 'meaning' in accordance with the verification principle so that only certain functions count in estimating the meaning of a sentence, while the other is using it so that other functions count. Thus one may count only the conditional predictive functions of a sentence so that 'You will be stone deaf to-morrow' means the same to a deaf man as to one who can hear, because the predictions about what each will do *if* given the Seashore tests are the same. But the unconditional predictive power is different; the man who can hear will listen to a noise and say 'No more of this'. And if the unconditional predictive power is counted in estimating meaning then the sentences do not mean the same to a deaf man as to one who is not. This, worked out, throws much light on the puzzles connected with the soul's survival of the body and the ego-centric predicament.

of metaphysical theory; and for our purpose it does not matter whether it is a sort of metaphysical theory (*a*) in the way that a hackney is a sort of horse, or (*b*) in the way that a motor cycle is, because it is a sort of tireless horse on wheels. If (*a*) my statement is correct; if (*b*) it is not. But this correctness is of no importance.[1] For I make the statement to draw attention to certain likenesses, and whether they suffice or no for the proper application of 'metaphysical' does not affect their existence. I say that the verification principle is a metaphysical principle because I want (1) to draw the attention of those who accept it to the deplorably old-fashioned clothes in which it presents itself. Indeed it resembles not only positivistic theories but also the worst transcendental theories by appearing in the disguise either of a scientific discovery removing popular illusion, or of a logical equation (incorrect) from which deductions may be made. No wonder our conservative friends cannot accept it. I want (2) to draw the attention of those who reject it to the fact that because they are taken in by its disguise they fail to recognize the merits which like other metaphysical theories it conceals. Both those who accept it and those who reject it do not realize what they are doing because they do not notice that it is disguised. But metaphysics reveals the hidden, plucks the mask of appearance from the face of reality — and we shall now see what a metaphysical theory really is and thus the general nature of the verification principle.

To say that the verification principle is a sort of metaphysical theory would be extremely illuminating if we had already an adequate grasp of the ultimate nature of metaphysical theories, but lacking this we must go on. It is possible to go on in either of the two following ways: We may examine the nature of the verification principle and thus throw light on the nature of other metaphysical theories, or we may examine the nature of other metaphysical theories and thus throw light on the nature of the verification principle. Let us adopt the latter plan and work from the specific to the general. Then applying our results in a direct examination of the verification principle we shall obtain a review of the whole of metaphysics, because the

---

[1] Except while it is thought to be; like the doctor's highly coloured medicine or the reserve ratio of the Bank of England. People believe it is important that the reserve ratio should not fall below 9 to 1, say; and because they believe this, it *is* important.

verification principle is the generalization of one set of answers
to metaphysical 'questions while its opposite is the generalization
of the opposing answers.[1]

I. What is a Metaphysical Theory?

1. *The metaphysician is a profound scientist?* Metaphysical
theories were at one time presented as super-scientific discoveries.
They are still presented so as to be mistaken for these. Consider
the verification principle[2] itself and Wittgenstein's remark in
a lecture, 'We are inclined to think that there must be something in common to all games, say, and that this common
property is the justification for applying the general term "game"
to the various games.'[3] But this way of presenting metaphysical
theories went out of fashion. Something was lost when this
happened, because, for one thing, the scientific theory prevented
people from regarding metaphysics as analysis, a matter of how
words are used. In a sense, like poetry, metaphysics is synthetic
because it reveals something which is hidden in a way in which
logical definitions never do. It is worth seeing something of why
the scientific theory of metaphysics gained such a hold.

It did so because it is so tempting to exhibit the metaphysician
as an extra cautious scientist. A scientist or sophisticated person
may doubt whether a rabbit has come from a hat or a table risen
from the floor, when an ordinary or unsophisticated person will
swear these things have happened. But if the phenomena can
be regularly repeated, photographed, seen by all, smelt by dogs,
scared by cats, then even the scientist will say 'We now know for
a fact that these things happen'.

There are, however, people who might still refuse to say 'We
know a rabbit came', 'We know the table rose'. A madman
might refuse, a *Times* correspondent might refuse,[4] (for he never

---

[1] I make no apology for the ambitiousness of this plan. The view is there. I am
aware that someone with more space, time and ability than I have, could make it clearer.

[2] Dr. Ewing actually takes the verification principle to be an empirical statement.
Mind, Vol. XLVI, No. 183, p. 349.

[3] The great value I attach to what Wittgenstein says here, appears later, pp. 80-92.

[4] If only we had noticed how much liker is the philosopher's doubt to that of *The Times*
correspondent than to that of the madman! *The Times* correspondent is as energetic as
anyone in building armaments, and the philosopher as confident as anyone when seating
himself on a table. Hence Wittgenstein's expression 'pseudo-doubt'.

says that a certain power has so many troops at such and such
a place but always only that this would appear to be so). And
a philosopher might refuse. But the philosopher or metaphysician
is easily distinguished from the others, not so much by his appearance as by his subsequent talk. He will say, 'We don't know
that the table moved because we don't know whether there was
a table there at all. We don't know that we are not constantly
being taken in by an arch-deceiver, a super-illusionist who runs
without a hitch a continuous show of prodigious length: so we
can never be certain. After all there is no difference in kind
between a fleeting glimpse and an hour's scrutiny. And if seeing
does not suffice, does seeing and touching? or seeing, touching
and smelling? Are 5 independent witnesses required to prevent
talk of infectious hallucination or would 237 be necessary?
Further observation may increase probability but probability is
not knowledge. Knowledge man never obtains; not from the
time he reaches for a golden ball and learns it's the moon till when
he dreams of Paradise and wakes in Camden Town'.

Again, a doctor may be sceptical of the value of a new drug
although you tell him ten people took it and soon improved.
He says that perhaps they all changed their diets in a certain
way when they took it, or that perhaps it was suggestion; or
he says that with so few cases it may have been a coincidence.
But if thousands of people, some with faith and some without,
some from cold climates, some from warm, some . . . all improve
then even a very scientific doctor will admit the value of the
drug. It is only the philosopher who says 'But it *may* still be
coincidence. Where do you draw the line[1] and say, "Now we
know it was not coincidence, now we know that quinine has an
effect"?'

Again, consider the series of questions: 'Do flowers feel?'
'Does the amœba feel?' 'Does a worm feel?' 'Does a dog feel?'
Here the ordinary man says 'Yes', and the scientist may say 'No'.
The philosopher proceeds, 'Does a baby feel?' 'Does your friend
feel?' and he says that we do not know that they do. Then there
is the series which begins with the policeman asking whether
you are sure that this is the man you saw hanging round the
garage, and ends with the philosopher asking whether you are

[1] This phrase is a common metaphysical weapon of great power.

sure that the woman who comes down to breakfast each morning looking like your wife is always the same woman. It is all this sort of thing which leads people to think of the philosopher as a super-scientist. Nor is it only the epistemological metaphysical theories which are associated in this way with science. For through the epistemological theories the ontological theories also are associated with it. Instead of asking 'Do we know that there are Siamese cats?' we may ask 'Are there Siamese cats?' And instead of asking 'Are there Siamese cats?' and answering 'There are none really, only dogs which look like cats,' we may, because there are such appearances of Siamese cats as there are, ask instead 'Are Siamese cats really cats?' or 'What are Siamese cats really?' Similarly, there being such appearances of chairs as there are, instead of asking 'Are there chairs?' and answering 'There are none, only families of sense-data', we may ask 'What *are* chairs really?' and answer 'They are really families of sense-data'. There is an intermediate form of words namely, 'There are cats but only in a Pickwickian sense', 'There are chairs but only in a Pickwickian sense'. Propositions about cats and chairs will then be said to be phenomenally true.

2. *Logical Theory of Metaphysics.* The metaphysician is a profound logician engaged on an a priori *science of definitions?* This new formulation 'What is a chair?' was of the utmost importance. For though one may use this form of words 'What is an X?' in asking for fresh factual information, like the wife of an instrument-maker who, though she knows anemometers well by sight, may suddenly ask 'Jack, what *is* an anemometer?', one may also use it in a very different way, the way Socrates explained he was using it when he asked 'What is virtue?' From his explanation it is clear that he was asking for a logical definition.[1] Consequently if, in order to avoid the hint of ridiculousness in the question 'Are there such things as chairs?' we ask 'What are chairs?' then we use a form of words which at once suggests an analogy between the philosopher and, not the scientist, but the logician.

Now as science grew and people saw better how it is based on observation and experiment there grew a suspicion of anyone who professed to have obtained new factual information by

[1] There are reasons for saying that he was really wanting a metaphysical 'definition'.

anything but empirical methods. There were sneers at the philosophers who were represented as employing arm-chair, *a priori* methods. The deplorable affair of Hegel and the planets was not forgotten. Besides, philosophers could not agree, were in fact in a deadlock—at each other's throats.

To this situation came Moore and Russell, Moore from a study of Plato and Aristotle, and Russell from the world of logic and mathematics. They revolutionized philosophy for many of us by reinterpreting the philosopher's 'What is an X?' as a request for logical analysis. This is too well known to need support by much quotation. Russell wrote[1] '... every philosophical problem, when it is subjected to the necessary analysis and purification, is found either to be not really philosophical at all, or else to be, in the sense in which we are using the word, logical'. Moore writes, 'I am not at all sceptical as to the truth of such propositions as "the earth has existed for many years past" ... But I am very sceptical as to what, in certain respects, the correct *analysis* of such propositions is'.[2]

This theory of metaphysics provided a response to the metaphysical challenge 'If a metaphysical theory isn't empirical, what is it?' (How often is this club used to induce us to accept some simplifying lie.) Like all good big ideas it seemed the simple, natural thing to say, the moment someone said it. And it proved itself by breaking up the deadlock. The theories of descriptions and numbers, and the theory of classes, were all pieces of logical analysis and they worked like charms on many hitherto incurable philosophical complaints. The proof of the unreality of space, the ontological argument for the existence of God and the extra entities in the universes of discourse all went up in smoke, though from the fictional entities there lingered still a peculiar smell. Thus these analyses showed themselves to be what philosophers needed, what they were really asking for. But there were little clouds upon the horizon. (1) Unless the positivistic analyses were correct the epistemological difficulties 'How do we know that chairs and other minds and value predicates exist?' could be

---

[1] *Our Knowledge of the External World*, p. 33.
[2] *British Contemporary Philosophy*, Vol. II, p. 216. Mention should be made of the careful analytic work of Sidgwick, and of McTaggart's insistence on getting the meaning of a question clear, in spite of the fact that McTaggart defended to the last the possibility of an *a priori* investigation of the nature of existence.

answered only by Intuitionism (special way of knowing), Scepticism (we don't know), Dogmatism (we know somehow — never mind how). (2) Unfortunately in the most fundamental cases the positivistic analyses could never be got both complete and correct. This encouraged people to say what Broad and sometimes Russell were inclined to say, namely that the philosopher gave the analysis not of all the plain man does say but of all he has any right to say.[1]

We shall see how these points are connected with the nature and fundamental defects of the analysis theory.

3. *The metaphysician looks for the definition of the indefinable.*

3.1. *The meaning of this statement.* To say that metaphysics is analysis is unsatisfying in certain respects. To begin, with people are apt to ask, 'And what is analysis?' Just as when James says that an emotion is nothing but a complex of sensations[2] people are apt to ask, 'And what is a sensation?' (then the fun begins). Again, 'A nation is nothing but the individuals which make it up' may lead to the question 'What are individuals?'

These responses are hardly complaints, and are therefore to be contrasted with those prompted by 'A nation is a society of a certain sort', 'An instinct is an unacquired disposition involving consciousness'. These definitions are apt to make people say, 'But that is *just* what I want to know. What is a society? What is a disposition?' Unlike these, the question 'And what is analysis?' is not a complaint that we have not provided the right stuff, but a request for the same again. It can be called a complaint against incompleteness if you like, but if so, it must be distinguished from the complaints (*a*) of another sort of incompleteness and (*b*) of incorrectness, to which we must now attend.

For 'Metaphysics is analysis' is apt, in the second place, to provoke the challenge 'Not all analysis is metaphysics. Now *which* sort is?'

We are reminded at once of how people respond to 'Statements about nations are just statements about individuals'. They are apt to say 'Ah! Now which statements about individuals

---

[1] Russell said this with regret, but Broad I think always felt that the plain man had something in the way of a surprise coming to him from the philosopher; and he was right, though not as to its nature.

[2] He should have said 'of actual and possible sensations' on the lines of this sort of answer to 'What is a chair?'

are about nations? Complicated ones, no doubt. But be more specific. Take any statement about a nation and tell us which statements about individuals make it up'.

Now there are two reasons for which people make this challenge. (1) They may make it because they hold that statements about nations are not statements about individuals nor compounds of such statements, or are so only in a very extended sense. (2) They may be satisfied that nation-statements are individual-statements, perhaps in a somewhat stretched sense, but wish to ask what distinguishes those individual-statements which are nation-statements from those which are not — like one who is not troubled about the sort of entity a cow is, but feels he doesn't know what the essence of the distinction between cows and other things of the same sort is, because he feels sure this is a matter of shape or colour or upper incisors or something, while yet nothing of this seems *essential*.

But let us attend first to the matter of the genus or general nature of metaphysics. I want to contend that metaphysics is not analysis or, if you like, that it is so only in a dangerously extended sense. The extension has been illuminating in the past, but it *is* an extension and as such it may, and in fact now does, mislead.

Questions of this sort as to the general nature of metaphysics, analysis, mathematics, ethics, poetry, fiction have been made more difficult by defining these subjects as respectively classes of metaphysical, analytic, fictional, etc., propositions, and then asking to what genus these classes of proposition belong. It is better to describe mathematics, analysis, metaphysics, poetry, as sorts of game played with words as pieces, the usual significance of which must of course be understood by the players, and then to define metaphysical, analytic and fictional questions and sentences by reference to the purposes they serve in the game.

Now I contend that metaphysics is not analysis, and that metaphysical questions are not requests for analyses, even though they are expressed in forms of words which may be used in the analysis game to ask for analyses, and that metaphysical answers are not analyses though they may be forms of words used in the analytic game to state analyses. Of course one could say instead that the questions are requests for analyses and the answers analyses, only all with a hidden purpose, just as one may say that 'What is the meaning of good?' when asked by a philosopher, is a verbal question but with a hidden purpose, instead of saying that it is not really a verbal question. To say that analytic statements are verbal is useful if one wishes to get rid of the idea that they differ from statements about words in the way that statements about dogs differ from statements about cats or statements about colour differ from statements about shape and size. One might express this by saying that to say that analytic propositions are verbal is useful in getting rid of the idea that they differ from ones that are not analytic in being about a new species of thing or 'in subject-matter'. I shall use the last expression although it involves deciding arbitrarily not to describe the sort of difference there is between analytic and verbal statements as a difference in subject-matter. The excuse for doing this is that for every statement about abstract entities – propositions, characteristics – there is a verbal statement which makes the same factual claims though its meaning is different. I have explained this point elsewhere,[1] but it is of such importance that I must explain it briefly here.

If I say that 'good' means 'approved by the majority', in so far as I make any factual claims they are justified by what people would say, that is, are verbal; but my purpose, or primary intention, in saying so, is not verbal. Suppose a Chinaman is decoding an English message, and does not know the meaning either of 'vixen' or of 'female fox', but says after investigation, ' "vixen" means the same as "female fox" '. He says this though he knows his hearer also does not know the meaning of either expression. Suppose now Smith says ' "vixen" means "female fox" ', because he believes his hearer knows the meaning of 'female fox' but not of 'vixen'. Suppose now someone says, 'A vixen may be defined as a female fox'. The factual claims involved in the statements are the same. But the purposes they serve are very different, and this makes us speak differently about their meanings. A hearer understands the Chinaman's statement though he understands neither 'vixen' nor 'female fox'; but only if he understands one

---

[1] *Psyche*, Vol. XIII, 166-9; *Mind*, Vol. XLII, pp. 195-6. And Ayer explains this clearly: *Aristotelian Society*, Supp. Vol., XVI, p. 167. The extraordinary thing is that he does not see that he has answered his own question of p. 172, line 1.

of the two does he understand Smith, and only if he understands the meaning of both does he understand or, if you like, fully understand the philosopher. Hence statements about propositions and characteristics such as 'He asserted the proposition that Africa is hot', 'She is chic', can be turned into statements about words 'He uttered the sentence "Africa is hot" ', 'She is what the French call "chic" ', if, and only if the verbal statements are so used that we say that a man understands them only if he understands not merely the expressions 'the sentence "Africa is hot" ' and 'what the French call "chic" ' but also understands the sentence 'Africa is hot' and the word 'chic'.[1]

It follows that to say that analytic statements, such as 'Phœnixes are birds which renew themselves from their own ashes', are verbal statements, emphasizes their likeness to the statements of translators and decoders and their unlikeness to scientific statements such as 'Phœnixes do not drink before sunset'. At the same time it slurs over a serious unlikeness between analytic statements and those of translators and decoders, an unlikeness which is emphasized if one insists on the platitude that they are not verbal, but are of their own peculiar sort.

Now I wish to emphasize the unlikeness between metaphysical questions and answers and analytic ones. So I say that metaphysics is not analysis, metaphysical questions not requests for analyses, and metaphysical answers not analytic definitions, or, if you like, not *merely* analytic (compare 'not merely verbal').

Of course if 'Metaphysics is a sort of analysis' is taken like 'A motor cycle is a sort of horse though it can neither gallop nor jump' then it is not incorrect — how can such statements be incorrect? — and it is illuminating, but it is dangerously apt to mislead. It is apt, for example, to mislead people into rejecting statements of the sort 'Nation-statements are individual-statements', 'Analytic statements are verbal', as not to the purpose,

[1] (a) To deny this results in the extreme paradox '*All* statements are verbal'. (b) This is part of the explanation of the necessity of necessary statements. For such statements connect abstract things and are therefore purely verbal in a way in which 'He asserted Africa is hot' is not; that is, they are purely about the use of the expressions they connect. And what they assert must be known to the hearer if he understands them. Hence, if he denies them, the speaker says the hearer does not understand. This is characteristic of necessary statements. Logically necessary statements are checked by the actual usage of language and to this extent may be called true and false. Metaphysically necessary statements only have *excuses* in the actual use of language and so can only be called 'excusable' and 'inexcusable'.

because they are wrong in analysis. It is apt, for example, to make people reject such a statement as 'Metaphysical questions are analytic questions' as not to the purpose in metaphysics, because it is wrong in analysis.

I do not reject 'Metaphysics is a sort of analysis' as not to the purpose in metaphysics because it is incorrect in analysis, but I bring out its dangers in metaphysics by bringing out its incorrectness in analysis.

It will be noticed that one who asserts as an analytic proposition that metaphysics is analysis cannot defend it on the lines I have just indicated.[1] He will have to defend it on the lines that it is correct as an analysis. In disputing this I shall be doing what I want to do, bringing out how it misleads as metaphysics.

If the metaphysician really wants analysis it is a curious thing that nearly every formula for giving definitions which is submitted to him he rejects, either on the ground that the definitions it yields are not sufficiently profound to be called metaphysical, or on the ground that the definitions it yields are not definitions because they are incorrect.

If when a metaphysician asked 'What is a penny?' we were to reply 'A coin, English, etc.' that would be no good to him. Even if we said 'A material thing which, etc.' we should only have succeeded in stating the essence of the problem which he put in the misleadingly specific form 'What is a penny?' On the other hand, if we reply: 'Pennies are just bundles of sensations' or, in order to avoid tiresome objections, 'Statements about pennies are just statements about sensations', then the metaphysician complains that there are no statements about sensations which mean the same as any statement about a material thing.

The metaphysician is like a man who, meeting an old friend in disguise, asks us 'Who is this?' and then if we merely sponge the old friend's face and straighten his tie, says 'Still I don't know who it is', while if we pull off the false beard and the wig, he says 'But this is not now the same man. The man I asked you about had a beard and a wig'. Nothing satisfies him. Or rather — and the change is important — nothing in the way of analysis satisfies him.

[1] Unless he maintains that 'What is the ultimate nature of a metaphysical question?' unlike all other questions of this form, is not a request for analysis.

Now I contend that this is because it is not what he wants. When a man tells me he would love to ride a horse but, no matter what animal I offer him, says 'Not *that* one', then I think he does not really want to ride. Especially if, when offered a motor cycle, he takes it with alacrity. Of course, you may say if you like that I did not find the right horse. Or you may say that he wanted a perfect horse and then explain that a perfect horse is impossible, since, unless its speed was unlimited, we might at any time wish it could go faster, while if it could always go faster when we wanted, then, like an aeroplane, it would shrivel space and thus be unable to conquer distance.

And this *is* what is said about the metaphysician – that we have not found the analysis of what he wants analysed, or, in other cases, that what he wants analysed is ultimate, unanalysable. I am content to accept the latter statement but not the former.

Instead of saying 'The man who said he wanted a horse really wanted a motor cycle' one might say 'He wanted a horse but *needed* a motor cycle' or 'What he wanted *primarily*, apart from his wrong idea about what he wanted, was a motor cycle'. Now many metaphysicians, nowadays, put their requests in the form 'What is the analysis of X propositions?' and because of this we may feel it best to say that they want analysis but need something else. On the other hand in view of the fact that other people with no axe to grind in the way of a theory of metaphysics ask very like questions in the older form 'What is the ultimate nature of so and so?' and are then satisfied by judicious *description*, we may feel it best to say 'What metaphysicians want, or really want, is not definition but description'.

3.2. *Proof that the metaphysician looks for the definition of the indefinable.* The metaphysician's request is the limit to which a series of requests for analysis approaches. Now requests for analysis approach nearer and nearer to requests for the impossible. This appears if we consider for a moment what has sometimes been called 'the paradox of analysis'.

It is sometimes claimed that analysis is impossible for the following reasons: To analyse p is to translate the sentence 'p' into another which expresses a proposition of different structure, form and elements from p. But any proposition which has not the form and elements of p is not the same proposition as p. Hence any sentence which expresses a proposition having a structure different from p does not express the same proposition as 'p', i.e. does not mean the same as 'p', i.e. is not a translation of 'p' and hence does not provide an analysis of p.

Now of course analysis is possible. It is done. Universal affirmative propositions are not ultimate; they can be analysed into propositions which are not universal affirmatives. But a consideration of the paradox of analysis enables us to see on what the possibility of analysis depends. Universal affirmatives are analysable because we do *not* mean by 'universal affirmatives' 'the propositions expressed by English sentences of the sort "All S is P" or *any* which mean the same, no matter what devices they employ'. True, we do not mean by 'universal affirmatives' 'those propositions which are expressed by *English* sentences of the form "All S is P" '. They can be asserted in French. But we do mean by 'universal affirmatives' those propositions which are expressed by sentences using devices having a use like 'All' or 'Every' or 'Tous les'. Consequently we do *not* say of a man who says 'There were lions there, but there was not one which attempted to harm him', that he asserts a universal affirmative proposition. At the same time in the sense of 'same proposition' required by 'mean the same' in the sense of 'mean the same' required by 'translation of', we should say of a man who says 'There were lions there, but there was not one that attempted to harm him', that he asserts the same proposition as one who says 'All the lions there made no attempt to harm him'. In general: X propositions are analysable into non-X propositions, only if the differences we require between two sentences in order to say that one expresses an X proposition and the other does not, do not conflict with the resemblances we require in order to say that two sentences mean the same.

We are tempted on the one hand to use 'mean the same' so narrowly that if two sentences, though they convey the same information, function otherwise very differently, e.g. express propositions of different form, then they do not mean the same. Directly we do this, it becomes impossible to analyse propositions of one form into propositions of another.

And we are continually tempted to define 'X propositions'

(the ones we want analysed), as 'those which are often dressed in English sentences of kind "X", but *may* be dressed in *any* sentences which mean the same'. Directly we do this it becomes impossible to analyse X propositions into non-X propositions.

We do not always yield to these temptations, so analysis is possible. Thus if I mean by 'a fictional proposition',[1] such a proposition as you or I now make if we assert that Mrs. Bardell had fainted in Mr. Pickwick's arms, then one can analyse fictional propositions into non-fictional as follows: If A asserts of some author's character, S, that S had a property P then X means 'In the accepted text it is written that S had P'.

But it easily happens that we yield to the temptations without knowing it and then analysis becomes impossible without our knowing it. Thus suppose I mean by a fictional proposition 'such a proposition as an author expresses when he says of one of his characters "S had P"'. Now here any sentence which could be said to mean the same as the one the author used would have to fulfil the same sort of imaginative, non-informative, purpose; and 'fictional proposition' in the sense now in question is so used that any sentence used with the same sort of imaginative purpose would be said to be a fictional proposition. Hence it is impossible to analyse fictional propositions in this sense. That is, in this sense fictional propositions are ultimate.

Now it is my contention that this happens again and again in metaphysics: that is, that 'X proposition' is used so widely and 'mean the same' so narrowly, that the only correct answer to the question 'Are X propositions analysable into others?' is that they are not. This is frequently obscured by the fact that the expression 'X proposition' has a narrower use than that given it by the metaphysician with whom we are speaking, while nevertheless, that narrower use is so profound that definition of it is fairly called philosophical and even metaphysical.

These claims can be supported only by looking at metaphysical questions and answers and the reactions people have made to these. Let us now do this.

3.21. *Formal Puzzles*: (*a*) *Numerical propositions*. People have asked 'What is the nature of numerical propositions?' meaning not mathematical propositions but such propositions as 'Two

[1] See Ryle, Braithwaite and Moore, *Aris. Soc.*, Supp. Vol. XII, pp. 18-70.

men were murdered, three women drowned'. Russell[1] offers
the analysis: 'Not three people are interested in mathematical
logic' may be expressed in the form: 'If x is interested in mathematical logic, and also y is interested, and also z is interested,
then x is identical with y, or x is identical with z, or y is identical
with z'. And this satisfies some people. Their being satisfied
does not prove that their question was not profound enough
to be called philosophical or even if you like metaphysical. But
I do want to claim that some who use the same form of words
would not be satisfied, would say that they were asking a more
general question involving a wider use of 'numerical proposition'.
They would say that Russell's new formulation, which comes to
'Something is interested in mathematical logic and something not
identical with it is interested in mathematical logic',[2] still expresses
a numerical proposition, and thus does not provide an analysis
of numerical propositions into non-numerical propositions but
only sponges their faces.

We should say of a man who was dissatisfied with a definition
of instinct as a disposition that he was concerned with a more
general, more profound, more really metaphysical question
than one who was satisfied with it. Both used the same form of
words, 'What is an instinct?' but the one who is dissatisfied
with the answer in terms of dispositions was really only using
this form of words to ask a deeper, more metaphysical question,
'What is a disposition?' And I want to claim that we should
say the same of the man who was dissatisfied with Russell's definition.

I am well aware that Russell's definition of numerical propositions has important claims to the title 'philosophical' and even
'metaphysical' which the definition of 'instinct' in terms of
'disposition' has not, and that therefore the question to which
Russell's definition is an answer has such special claims. My
point is that beyond Russell's question is another which has still
better claims. For there are and have been people dissatisfied,
in the special way indicated, with Russell's definition, saying that
it was not sufficiently profound. What did they want?

---

[1] *Our Knowledge of the External World*, p. 207.
[2] This is a slip. The latter expression means 'At least two people are interested in
mathematical logic'. J. W. 1952.

Joseph, in discussion some fifteen years ago, said that Russell's definition was circular in that his new definition involved the notion of plurality and was thus in essence still a numerical proposition. It was said at that time that he had not grasped the point of Russell's definition and, as I have said, I do not wish to deny the logical, even the philosophical value of Russell's definition. It removed the impression that numbers were a special kind of quality applicable to groups. On the other hand those who derided what Joseph said were metaphysically blind, in that they could not feel the inclination to ask his wider, profounder question.

Let us look at this profounder question carefully. It differs from Russell's not merely in that some answers which would satisfy Russell would not satisfy the profound metaphysician, but in that no answer or, rather, no answer in terms of a definition would satisfy the metaphysician who asks it. For he asks that we should analyse numerical propositions into non-numerical propositions. And yet it soon comes out that for him, if a proposition involves the notion of plurality, it is a numerical proposition, and that a proposition involves the notion of plurality if it involves the notion *other than*. Now no proposition involving the notion *other than* can be analysed into one which does not. Further, if we take any numerical proposition p_1 it will, as everyone admits, involve plurality and thus the notion *other than*. Hence if p_1 is analysed into p_2, p_2 will involve the notion *other than* and thus plurality; and thus *on the metaphysician's use of* 'numerical proposition' p_2 will again be numerical. Hence the class of propositions to which the metaphysician refers by 'numerical' cannot be analysed into propositions not in that class. Which is what Joseph wished to show.

How natural it is to proceed as the metaphysician does may be brought out more plainly as follows: The metaphysician asks that numerical propositions shall be defined in terms of non-numerical propositions. At the same time he very naturally defines numerical propositions, not as those which are expressed by English sentences of the sort, 'Two S are P ', 'Three S are P', etc., nor as those which are expressed by these English sentences and their French, German, etc., translations, but as those expressed by the English sentences and *any* sentences, whatever devices

they may involve, which stand for the same propositions, mean
the same. Nothing could be more natural, but the result is a
self-contradictory request. For to analyse numerical propositions
is to translate sentences which stand for numerical propositions
into others which do not. But if a new sentence, S_2, is a translation of one, S_1, which stands for a numerical proposition, then S_2
will mean the same as S_1 and therefore, with the metaphysician's
use of 'numerical proposition', the proposition it expresses will
not be non-numerical. Hence with this use of 'numerical proposition' numerical propositions are ultimate. I prefer to put
this by saying that the description 'analysed numerical propositions into others' describes no process, or the description 'translated sentences expressing numerical propositions into sentences
which do not' describes no process. The descriptions describe no
process not merely in the sense in which 'completed the old course
at St. Andrews in 25' describes no process which has been or will be
carried out, but in the sense in which 'squared the circle', 'found
a perfect movable pulley in which W did not balance $\frac{1}{2}$W', 'found
a leopard without spots and a purple Union Jack' describe no
process.

It might be thought that there is a more drastic answer which
would help the metaphysician. If a child were to ask us 'What
does "Two men were murdered" mean?', part of what we should
do to explain would be to say 'Well, if Alf and Bill were
murdered, or Charles and David, then two men would be
murdered'. And then, anxious to prevent the idea that only
Alf and Bill, Charles and David, would count, we might add
'and so on'. So we might suggest that 'Two men were murdered'
means 'Either Alf and David were murdered or Charles and Bill
were murdered, or . . . and so on'. The metaphysician would say:
'When you say "and so on" is this short for a list you could put
down? Then your translation does not mean the same as the
original. But if it means "or any other man and another" then
your translation is only another form of Russell's, and you have
again given us a numerical proposition involving the notion
other than'. Or the metaphysician may object that the 'specimen'
facts, e.g. 'Alf and Bill were murdered', themselves involve
plurality.

Thus once more it appears that any sentence which means

the same as the original will again be said to express a numerical proposition. No wonder that numerical propositions are ultimate.

3.21. *Formal puzzles: (b) Generality.* It is the same with general propositions such as 'Something moved'. People complain that there is no finite list of propositions of the sort 'Smith moved' which disjunctively combined mean 'Something moved'. We may say if we like that there is an infinite list which does, and this brings out an important feature of the relationship between 'Smith moved' and 'Something moved'. This feature we can also bring out by saying 'The *more* specific propositions we put in our list, the *nearer* does a disjunction of them come to meaning the same as the general proposition'. But when we say that an *infinite* disjunction would give the meaning, we mean not only the fact just mentioned, but also the fact that however long the list is it will *not* give the meaning unless we call a list with 'and so on' at the end a definition.

Or again people complain that the 'specimen' facts, e.g. 'Smith was murdered', again involve generality because 'Smith' is a disguised descriptive phrase. The suggestion is that all would be well if we could analyse these into statements about our present sense data such as 'This is red'.

If these explanations are not definitions then there is no definition of general propositions into non-general.

It may now be said 'The conclusion you have reached about numerical and general propositions,. and incidentally about fictional propositions, is the perfectly familiar but utterly unhelpful one that they are ultimate'.

I am delighted to welcome this criticism. This is precisely what I want to say myself, that this answer 'Numerical propositions are ultimate' is quite inadequate, leaves the philosopher feeling that somehow there *was* something he wanted which he has been denied. As I have explained, I want to go further and generalize and say that whenever in answer to a metaphysician's question 'What are X propositions?' the answer is given 'They are ultimate' then that answer is (1) correct, but (2) inadequate.

3.22. *Category puzzles: (a) Time.* Let us now take an example from another class of metaphysical questions. These arise, not from the 'queerness' of the form of the class of propositions which is felt to be queer, but because of the queerness of the

category of what they are about. These are apt to present themselves in the form 'What is X?' 'What are X's?' where 'X' is a
name for the puzzling category, or a name for a species of that
category. We have for example, 'What are characteristics?
What are numbers? What are abstract, necessary propositions
about?' and we have 'What are chairs and tables? What are
material things?' 'What is a nation? Is it something over and
above the individuals of that nation?' 'What is Time?'

Suppose we offer an answer to the last on the lines suggested
by Moore.[1] We say, 'Well, when we speak about Time, what are
we talking about? Such facts as this — that lunch is over, supper
to come, that Smith's anger is past and so on. Let us call such
facts "temporal facts". Then "Time is unreal" can be *translated
into the concrete* (Moore's phrase) by "There are no temporal
facts" '. When we read this, we draw a breath of relief. This is
the stuff. With this translation into the concrete, we get 'the cash
value' (Broad), the predictive power, of the statement 'Time is
unreal'. What a contrast to the answer 'Time is an abstract
entity, super-sensible, having a sort of existence all its own'. For
the latter answer only tells us that time is not brown or yellow,
not big or little, not to be found in the bathroom, and like Space
only different. Such an answer only emphasizes what ordinary
language suggests that, besides the facts that lunch is over and his
anger past, there is the fact that Time is real. True, Moore did
not *find* a definition, but he showed how it was a mere accident
of language that we could not provide a definition and thus
remove an uneasy feeling about Time, just as we did when we had
the uneasy feeling that though the class of all men is not to be
identified with its members, yet there were not in addition to the
facts about men, e.g. that men exist, that all are mortal, facts
about the class of men, e.g. that it exists, has members, has
members which are mortal.

We may say here that Moore meets a philosophical request,
even, if you like, a metaphysical request, not indeed by finding
but by creating an analytic definition.

I do not wish to deny this any more than I wish to deny that
Russell did the same with his definition of number. They both
translated sentences which trouble us into others which do not.

---

[1] *Philosophical Studies*, p. 209

But of course there will be people dissatisfied with this answer. They fall into two very different classes. In the first place, some will say 'What is meant by "Time is real" is different from what is meant by "Either lunch is over, or my supper yet to come, or his anger is past, or something of that sort (i.e. and so on)". What I have in mind when I say "Time is unreal", is very different from what I have in mind if I say 'Either lunch is over or etc." ' And yet these same people, some of them, will not be satisfied by any definition which does not put 'Time is unreal' in terms of individual events. So they reject every definition either on the ground that it is incorrect or on the ground that it is not sufficiently profound. The nature of this difficulty in metaphysics and the light it throws upon its nature will appear later.

In the second place, there are people who will say that even the definition in terms of individual events or temporal facts is not sufficiently profound; they ask that the definition should be taken further. And if we say 'By temporal facts we mean such facts as "Smith's anger is past" and so on' they complain (a) against the 'specimen' fact as again involving time, or (b) against the phrase 'and so on'. It is soon clear that there is nothing to be done for them with regard to (a). We may try saying 'His anger is past' means 'He was angry and is not'.[1] But it is a hopeless game. The reply will be that 'He was angry' involves Time again. And of course it involves it if any sentence using a verb with a tense involves Time. And it is now apparent that this is how the metaphysician uses 'involves Time'. He cannot translate sentences which work like the ones with tenses into sentences involving only a timeless 'is' such as 'Red is a colour'. But this is what he wants. Nothing short of it will do, nothing else will be a reduction of temporal facts to non-temporal. No new language will help. Suppose we invent a new language with no time-indicating words such as 'was', 'will be' and no time-indicating endings such as 'ed'. Now the new sentences, if they are to provide translations, must do the work the old did; so there must be differences between those which correspond to the old 'was'-sentences and those which correspond to the old 'will be'-sentences. We might put them in different coloured inks

[1] Broad, *Examination of McTaggart*, p. 316; Wisdom, *Proc. Aris. Soc.*, Vol. XXIX, (1928-9), p. 92.

(compare Ramsey's writing negatives as positives upside down).
But then the new sentences would surely again express temporal
propositions.

I am well aware that there is nothing novel in the conclusion
that temporal propositions are unanalysable, and that this
unanalysability is not a matter of our being unable to do or find
the analysis but of the nature of the facts. Prof. Broad supports
far more fully and carefully than I have done this very conclusion
about temporal facts.[1]

I am so sorry that he advances his conclusion *tentatively*.
He says 'And so, *prima facie*, the temporal copula has not been
analysed away. Of course it may be answered that this objection depends simply on defects in the language that we speak.
It may be so. But I am more inclined to think...' What is
he in doubt about? He knows our own language well. His
own examination has shown that there are no sentences in English
which we should say do not stand for temporal propositions
which are nevertheless such that we can translate those which
do into them. We may bet anything that the same is true of
French and German. Is Broad asking whether, if we invented
an entirely new and very different system of symbols into which
we could translate temporal sentences, we should be satisfied —
should be willing to speak of having translated sentences which
express temporal propositions into sentences which do not?
There may be people who would be satisfied by this. Sometimes
metaphysical difficulty is removed by inventing a word when
it would not have been removed without such an invention.
We cannot say that Ramsey's writing negatives as positives
upside down was useless. On the contrary it distilled the problem
of negation into such purity that it vanished; but it did not
achieve its result by analysing negative sentences into non-
negative sentences. And this is what signifying tense by colour
would do. After the removal of 'not' it could not be complained
that the negative sentence was misleading in its shape. We may
doubt with regard to a particular person whether he would be
satisfied if such a new language were introduced, just as some
might be satisfied by a definition of 'two' in the symbolism of

---

[1] *Examination of McTaggart's Philosophy*, Vol. II, Part I, Chap. XXXV, especially pp.
271, 272, 304-7, 314, 315.

Principia Mathematica, while they would be dissatisfied with any in English. But we also know that there are many who would say that such people would be wrong to be satisfied.

By a study of how these difficult people use 'temporal sentence' we come to learn that they mean what anyone reading this will now be inclined to mean by it, namely any sentence conveying temporal information. By a study of how these metaphysically-minded people react to proffered definitions we can see that no peculiarity in the way the sentence performs its work, the images it raises, the feelings it arouses, will prevent them calling it a temporal sentence provided its cash value is the sort of cash value which 'He was angry' has, i.e. provided it is a translation of sentences with 'was' and 'will' and 'is now' in them, used as they are now used. We know, then, that they so use 'temporal sentence' that 'a translation of temporal sentences into ones which are not temporal' is a self-contradictory description. Suppose a man says he cannot find a perfect movable pulley in which W does not balance $\frac{1}{2}$W. By prolonged search I find a golden pulley so smooth that the highest-powered microscopes detect no deficiency in its surface, on which, nevertheless, W does not balance $\frac{1}{2}$W. But he explains that by 'perfect' he wished to exclude so dazzling a material as gold. From the fairies I obtain a gold which does not dazzle or from the angels a pulley in blue. But now he complains of the microscope, says that a larger one would reveal defects even if the pulley has been sent down from heaven. But even a heavenly microscope does not convince him. God no doubt possesses a microscope of His own which would reveal what no other does, namely, the defect which *must* be there because if the pulley were perfect W *would* balance $\frac{1}{2}$W.

Is it not apparent that the well-known facts, including the fact that the smoother we make pulleys the more nearly does W balance $\frac{1}{2}$W, have induced him to so use 'pulley' or 'perfect pulley' that for him balancing W by $\frac{1}{2}$W is part of the connotation of the expression, a necessary condition of a thing's being a perfect pulley? Some people nowadays would not call a loaf 'bread' if it failed to react to the chemical tests for starch, though others, whose usage of 'bread' has not been equally affected by science, would call it 'bread' provided it was otherwise satisfactory.

Surely we have come to know how this man uses 'perfect pulley'; and that in his usage the request for a perfect pulley on which W does not balance $\frac{1}{2}$W involves a description which describes nothing, is self-contradictory? There is no process of calculation by which we can show this to him, as we can show him that when he asks for the proof that 2345 multiplied by 3 equals 6935 he is making a request which is self-contradictory. But neither is there a process of calculation by which we can show him that a request for a proof that $1 + 1 = 1$ is a self-contradictory request.

He appears to ask for something because, though his description 'a movable pulley in which W does not balance $\frac{1}{2}$W' may be used as he uses it, there is, or we can easily imagine, a use in which such a description might describe something, 'Laws of nature broken; Scientist finds golden pulley, etc.' There is, or we can easily imagine, a use of 'Union Jack' in which one could find one in purple, green and yellow; you know what such a flag would be like – a Union Jack in purple, green and yellow. When a philosopher asks for the unattainable, the fact that he is doing so is frequently obscured by the existence of a 'contingent copy' of what he wants – like those which we find for the pulley and the flag. And the requests for analysis are no exception. The philosopher complains, perhaps, that we say that his request for the analysis of X propositions into non-X propositions makes no sense. 'On the contrary', he says, 'it is quite easy to explain what I want. You know what general sentences are, don't you? And you know what non-general sentences are, don't you? Well what I want is that the former should be translatable into combinations of the latter without the use of such expressions as "and so on" '. Now this describes a perfectly possible ideal. What is there to prevent our altering our use of English so that this should be the case? But this of course would *not* be what is wanted by the philosopher who is asking for the analysis of general propositions into non-general propositions. It only looked as if it were what he wanted because we allowed him to translate his request into 'Are general sentences translatable into non-general sentences?' and then forgot the reminder for the formal mode (*see* p. 463).

Had we remembered this we should have realized that what he asks is that general sentences *used as they are now used* should be translatable into non-general sentences *used as they are now used* and without the use of 'and so on' *used as it is now used.* And this is like asking that 20 shillings should have the value they now have and be equal in value to 20 half-crowns, meaning here again not just coins of the half-crown shape and size, but coins of half-crown value.

Here is another factor which prevents metaphysicians noticing how, as requests for definitions, their requests are self-contradictory.

Let us sum up our conclusion so far with regard to the question 'What is Time?' or 'What are propositions about Time or involving Time?'

(1) There are people who ask these questions and are satisfied by such a definition as Moore's or by the definition ' "Time is real" just means "There are events such as race meetings, collisions, wars" '.

(2) There are people who are dissatisfied with any definition of Time in terms of a class of temporal facts, because such definition does not give us statements which mean the same as statements about Time — destroy its unity, etc.

(3) There are people who are dissatisfied with any definition of Time in terms of 'temporal facts', because they are dissatisfied with a definition of 'temporal facts' as 'such facts as "Smith was angry" and so on' on account of the specimen fact still involving Time and on account of the expression 'and so on'.

It remains (*a*) to say something about the insatiableness of the request for an account of the notion 'and so on'; (*b*) to show that there is not some definition not in terms of temporal facts which would satisfy those hitherto unsatisfied. But these points will reappear in other examples and may be ignored for the present.

3.22. *Category puzzles: (b) Nations.* Both Professor Broad and Dr. Ewing[1] express themselves as *in doubt* whether statements about nations can be analysed into statements about individuals. But about what are they in doubt? We know that there is no statement of the form 'Every Englishman . . .' which means just the same as 'England has declared war'. We know also that if asked by a child 'What does "England has declared war" '

---

[1] Broad, *Examination of McTaggart*, Vol. II, p. 693; Ewing, *Idealism*, p. 435.

mean?' we should say 'Well, a great many people in England are hurrying to make shells and tanks and guns and gas, and a message has been sent by the man who manages these things for Englishmen to the man who does the same for the people they are going to fight, to say that now they are going to fight and so on'. And we should say that the child would after a while know what 'England has declared war' means. Or we might proceed thus: 'To say there is a nation in Arabia is to say that there are a number of people there *nationally* related' and this means 'that there are a great many people who perhaps all have the same king or queen or have all decided that a certain two or three people shall rule over them, though of course this isn't necessary, they may have no governors but just be alike in . . .' We are reminded of a doctor trying to explain what paranoia is. We say 'he has no definition'. And this is what many people say about our efforts on behalf of the child. They say 'This is no definition; you have not given an analysis of what one says in, for example, "There is a nation in Arabia which never remains long in one place". You may have *explained* what you mean but you haven't defined it'.

Now some say our explanation is no definition because as one might say it is never completed unless you call adding 'and so on' completing a definition. Others might say 'Even if you could complete your infinite stories you would not have provided a statement which means the same as, for example, the simple statement that England is at war'. Some might be dissatisfied with what we have done on the ground that we have not gone far enough and told them what individuals are, so that we have not explained the nature of our 'specimen' facts. We may ignore these last people. They will be satisfied no doubt when we reach the philosopher's paradise where a man speaks only of his own sensations and only at the time he is having them. Here at last generality, uncertainty, and reduplication have disappeared, for here are found the perfect proper names, the incorrigible knowledge and the ultimate categories that we have sought so long.

But we must concentrate our attention (*a*) on those who say that statements about nations cannot be translated without loss of meaning into statements about individuals, though the tests for the truth of statements about nations may be the same as the tests for the truth of the long stories about individuals; (b) on those who allow that nation-statements may mean the same as individual-statements ending 'and so on', but complain that this is not a definition because it is not complete — that what they wanted has not been done because we have not completed a definition of what distinguishes those statements about individuals which are equivalent to statements about nations from those which are not.

It is the same when if asked 'What is a chair?' we reply 'A chair is a set of sensations *chairishly* related', or 'To say there is a chair here is to make a certain sort of statement about sensations'. People say '*What* sort?' It then appears that no statement about sensations ever entails a statement to the effect that a chair is present, or, if you like, that only at the point of infinity does one reach a statement in terms of sensations which entails a statement about a chair. And others object that even if one could complete the endless story (in other words apart from the objectionableness of 'and so on'), they would reject the definition. They say: 'A statement that a chair is here is categorical, and can never be equivalent to statements about what we should smell if we sniffed, what we should hear if we listened, etc. And surely an arch-deceiver is logically possible'. There is just no doubt that no more extensive knowledge of English or more ingenious use of the knowledge we have would ever enable us to produce something in terms of English expressions at present in use, which would be called by these people a definition of statements about chairs in terms of sensations. And some will remain dissatisfied even if we invent expressions such as 'chairishly' and explain the analogy with Moore's invention of 'temporal fact'.

It may be said 'You have not shown that those who allow that "There is a nation in Arabia" means the same as "There are individuals in Arabia who are nationally related" are insatiable. For if you provided a definition of "nationally" they would be satisfied. And the people who allow, as some would, that "There is a chair in the room" means "There are chairish sensations among our roomish sensations" would be satisfied if a definition of "chairish" could be provided'.

But this request for a definition of what it is for individuals to be nationally related as opposed to non-nationally related comes from another great class of unsatisfiable requests for analysis. The only definition in terms of individual statements which will mean the same as 'nationally' will involve the expression 'and so on'. The only possible definition of 'chairishly related' will also involve the expression 'and so on'; it will involve an infinite disjunction of conjunctions of statements about sensations. And it will be complained that it is just this infinity which is mysterious. It is true that if a person is satisfied about the category of chairs (or nations) then all that now puzzles him is the nature of the distinction between chairish groupings of sensations on the one hand, and non-chairish groupings on the other (between national groupings of individuals and non-national). But about this he may well be insatiable.

3.23. *Differentia puzzles.* Let us look at other examples of this sort of request which arises not from trouble about the *form* of a proposition nor from trouble about the *category* of its subject but from trouble about the *differentia* of its subject. Allowing that Henry is an individual, what makes him Henry and not Albert? Allowing that a cow is an animal, what is the nature of the distinction between a cow and a buffalo? It is no doubt, in the latter case, the possession of a common property; but what is this property? People say, 'We cannot define what it is to be a cow'. They often have at first the idea that what they are saying is that 'cow' is not definable in the way that 'brother' is.[1] Now it happens that 'cow' is definable in this way though one is apt to overlook it. For cows are female kine. But this definition is at once rejected by one who asks *metaphysically* 'What is a cow as opposed to a buffalo?' He says 'Ah! yes of course that sort of definition. But what is it to be kine? What is it to be female? Must animals if they are to be kine have horns? Must they chew the cud? Must they avoid canine ears? But none of this is essential. Is it then that they must *either* have the right horns, *or* chew the cud, *or* have the right ears? But this disjunctive character hardly suffices to constitute an animal a cow.'

---

[1] Wittgenstein has given me the impression that he thinks that our trouble here consists in wrongly fancying that all words are definable like 'brother'. But in the sense here involved 'brother' is also indefinable. What is true is that the trouble arises from our fancying that the only reductive explanation is through conjunctive definition of which the definition of 'brother' is a model.

At once we find ourselves in the situation of a man who wrote: 'We can say that horses are mammals, move on legs not wheels, are bred not built, and so on. But are these qualities essential? There is no selection of them which enables us to construct that "elusive quality of horsiness which we can detect only by acquaintance with the animal and watching it perform its functions"'.[1] This elusive quality becomes for Locke an unknown essence. He says 'He that thinks he can distinguish sheep and goats by their real essences, that are unknown to him, may be pleased to try his skill in those species called *cassiowary* and *querechinchio*'.[2] We can easily imagine people saying that we know of its presence by the intellect or *infer* it from the qualities we detect by the senses. Heaven knows how we justify the inference since we have *never* observed the essence in conjunction with the signs of its presence. Notice how a transcendental ontology is associated with scepticism, intuitionism and problematic inference of a *very* peculiar kind.

Now what is it that is wanted and is such that the failure to find it (1) is represented as ignorance and (2) leads to these entrancing tales about elusive essences? What is the essence of electricity? Do we not really know what it is for a wire to be electrically charged?

As usual, it is possible to offer a 'contingent copy' of what is wanted. If 'cow' like 'skewbald' and 'spotted' could be defined as a conjunction or disjunction of sensory adjectives without the use of 'and so on', this would be what is wanted. Now this is an understandable ideal provided it is not required that the words should function as they now do, i.e. stand for the qualities they now stand for. But, of course, this is required. And as the use of the word 'cow' is not related to the use of the sensory adjectives on this simple conjunction-disjunction model it is self-contradictory to ask whether, keeping the use of language unchanged, we can set out 'x is a cow' as a conjunctive-disjunctive function of a finite number of statements attributing sensory adjectives. It does not follow that it stands for another character to be inferred

---

[1] Notice that uneasiness about the doctrine that acquaintance with the animal enables us to detect a quality in addition to its colour, shape, etc., produces a half return to a positivistic doctrine that horsiness consists in these and the functions of the animal. If only this half return had been pursued. . . .

[2] *Essay concerning Human Understanding*, Bk. III, Chap. VI, Section IX.

from the sense characters, as 'has an enlarged liver' is to be inferred from 'looks yellow etc.' It is related to the use of them in its own way, a way with which we are perfectly familiar. There are sense characters which are characteristic of cows though they are not necessary conditions of a thing's being a cow, and others which are not. And we can go on explaining as long as we like which characters are characteristic and which are not.[1] Prof. Broad, many years ago, suggested a model which throws light on this. Someone said, 'I know perfectly well what "horse" means, but I cannot *analyse* what it means'. Broad said that it seemed to him that such words as 'horse', 'house', 'cow', are not analysable in the ordinary sense. He said that in the case of such words there are *n* characters such that if any *m* of these are present we say that a thing is a horse, a cow, etc., as the case may be. He said this with a view to helping those who said in a puzzled way, 'I know well what these familiar words mean. How then is it that I cannot give their analysis?' Broad explained that a thing's being properly called a cow, did not determine uniquely its having this or that character but determined it with such and such a degree of freedom.[2]

Of course this again is only a model. There is no finite list of sensory statements related to 'That is a cow', even on these more complicated lines. And it is just this infinity as usual which troubles people.

If a child asks us, 'What is a zebra?' we explain that it is rather like a donkey, has long ears and a mane which stands up, is rather less angular than a donkey and thus somewhat resembles a pony. Must it have long ears? Well no, but they usually have. They have, of course, hoofs like a donkey and they are nearly always striped. They eat grass, breed and so on, like donkeys.

Similarly if a child asks us what a tallboy is, or a chair, or what it is for people to form a nation.

In all these cases we can *explain*. We finish always with the expression 'and so on' to cope with the infinite. If it is said that this prevents our explanation being a definition, then we cannot find one because there is nothing which the inquirer

---

[1] And some more so than others. Just as some are more characteristic of St. Peter or Napoleon than others.
[2] See also Broad, *Exam. of McTaggart*, Vol. I, p. 125.

would call a definition no matter how hard we were to work with the words we have or how many new ones we were to invent.

Here then is another large class of metaphysical requests for analysis which like the others we have considered are distinguished from ordinary requests for analysis by the fact that they are requests that a certain class of statements should be exhibited as finite conjunctive-disjunctive functions of another 'fundamental' class, when this is impossible because the class of statements in question happens *not* to be a finite conjunctive-disjunctive function of those which are taken as fundamental. Some would allow that they are infinite functions of the fundamental statements; others would insist that not even the infinite functions mean the same as the statements to be analysed.

3.24. *Do the transcendental theories provide analyses?* It may now be objected 'You have reached the conclusion that if the philosopher is asking for an analysis then he is asking for the impossible, only because you have considered only the wrong analyses. You have considered analyses of general propositions into specific propositions, analyses of super-individual things such as Time, Space and nations into individual things, and of individual things into sensations. The right answer to the question "What are numerical propositions?" is that they predicate a peculiar kind of trans-individual quality applicable only to groups, or that they are analysable into general propositions together with the peculiar relation *other than*. General propositions are about a *variable entity*, neither Smith nor Jones, neither this nor that. Propositions about nations are about an entity which is not a person nor to be reduced to persons though it is in many ways like the persons which belong to it,[1] and its nature is known to us only through them. And Space and Time and a work of art, such as *Hamlet*, are again about entities which are "neither physical things nor minds nor sensa, neither particular existents nor abstract universals, neither substances nor mere qualities, relations, or states of substances, and therefore elude orthodox philosophical classifications. These things cannot be said to exist in the sense in which particular things and persons can be said to do and yet are essentially particular and not abstract universals" '.[2]

---

[1] Broad, *Examination of McTaggart*, Vol. II, p. 693.
[2] Dr. A. C. Ewing, *Idealism*, p. 433. He is not giving a theory of his.

Propositions about numbers, universals, or propositions are about what is objective, real and possible, but non-sensible, neither subjective nor palpable and spatial.[1] These objects do not exist but they subsist.

These theories are perfectly correct. They could not be otherwise since they proceed on the lines: The peculiarity of facts about classes, numbers, propositions and characteristics is that they are about *subsistent entities*. What are subsistent entities? Well, they are not chairs and tables. Indeed they are not known by the senses but by the intellect. Characteristics, for example, are subsistent entities, so are propositions, numbers and classes.

But the idea that there are questions to which these theories and the positivistic or reductive theories are alternative answers arises from a confusion. The question 'What are X propositions?' may mean 'What is the analysis of propositions with regard to propositions that they are X propositions, e.g. "*Something moved* is a general proposition"'; and it may mean 'What is the analysis of propositions which *are* X propositions, e.g. "Something moved"'. Now these theories provide answers of a sort to the first question but not to the second. If I ask 'What are propositions about instincts?' and someone says 'They are propositions about dispositions which, etc.' this is a definition which brings that class of propositions under a genus and mentions a differentia. But no one supposes that this enables me to translate sentences expressing propositions about instincts into sentences which are not propositions about instincts. Hence anyone who, wishing to do that, asks 'What is the analysis of propositions about instincts?' will be entirely dissatisfied and will say 'But what is a disposition?' Similarly, the people who ask 'What are numerical, fictional, general, national, material, propositions?' in that sense of these questions which we have been considering, will be dissatisfied if offered one of these definitions in terms of a transcendental constituent. He will at once re-express his questions in the forms, 'What is a variable entity?' 'What is a subsistent entity? and how do the numerical ones differ from others?' 'What is a particular universal?' Just as when I asked a plain man, 'What is the proposition $2 + 2 = 4$ about?' and received the answer 'Numbers', I asked at once 'What are

---

[1] Russell, *Our Knowledge of the External World*, p. 201.

numbers?' and received the answer 'Oh, I don't know, I can't answer that, 2 and 3 and 7 are numbers'. The transcendentalist likewise when asked 'What are these entities?' replies 'They are ultimate. Such things as nations, institutions, poems, the Exchequer are particular universals. Such things as characteristics, classes, propositions are subsistent entities'. That is, the transcendentalist agrees with the conclusion we have reached about *our* question, namely the conclusion that when the profound metaphysician asks, 'What is the analysis of X propositions?' then his request is a request for the analysis of the unanalysable. He agrees with us, too, that merely to say this is inadequate. Something must be done to explain why we should so persistently return to our vomit, the positivistic theories; and the explanation he offers is that the entities which the ultimate but 'difficult' propositions are about, are of a sort we have hardly recognized (Russell),[1] because they are not detected by the five senses and consequently they 'elude orthodox philosophical classifications' (Ewing). How this reminds us of the fictional entities upon which Russell poured so much scorn.[2] But at the moment we must emphasize our agreement with the negative aspect of the transcendentalist's conclusion, namely, that the metaphysician's requests for the analysis of X propositions into non-X propositions is a request for what is impossible.

And now the inadequacy of this conclusion is still more apparent because it is apparent that the transcendentalist theories are common-sense answers dressed up. The plain man, when asked what the proposition $2 + 2 = 4$ is about, and how we know it, replies 'It is about numbers and we know it in a special way, and "Red is a colour" is about colours'. The transcendentalist replies: 'Both propositions are about subsistent entities and we know them by intuition'. The plain man, when asked 'What is "There is a chair in this room" about? and how do we know it?' replies 'It is about a chair, of course, an article of furniture, and we know it by looking, by the evidence of our senses'. The transcendentalist replies 'It is about a material thing which is not to be identified with our sensations and we know it by direct but

---

[1] *Our Knowledge of the External World*, p. 201.
[2] *Introduction to Mathematical Philosophy*, p. 169. There is a difference. Fictional propositions in one sense are analysable into non-fictional.

not immediate knowledge,[1] or "in and through" our sensations, but the knowing of it is not to be identified with sensing, it is something more than this, and what is known by this process is something more than mere sensing reveals, or perhaps we infer the chair from what we know by our senses'.

The plain man, wishing to encourage us to believe in the soul, says 'You believe in the wind don't you, though you can't see it? Well, it is like that with the soul'. What the phenomenalist resents is the suggestion that it is not by our eyes and ears that we know of the existence of the wind, when there is one. This leads him to say 'The wind is nothing but slates off the roof and a smell from the gas-works. You speak like the Irish coachman who whispers to children that goats can see the wind'. But of course the wind isn't just that. Or is it just slates off the roof and/or a smell from the gas-works and/or a rustle in the leaves, the hurrying of the clouds and so on? Is it or isn't it?

Ordinary language suggests analogies which puzzle us. From the rapidity of Smith's pulse I infer that the malaria germ is in his blood, from the fall of the slates that Boreas is angry, from the powerful smell that there is a cheese near which is going bad. Transcendentalist language emphasizes and (usefully) collects these suggested analogies and thus increases these puzzles and distils them into more concentrated forms. Positivism suggests a way of removing them. The answer 'The classes of proposition which puzzle us are ultimate, unanalysable' insists that the positivist's way out will not do. But it leaves us where we were, except in the important respect that we can no longer imagine that definition will help us out. We are left giving the answer '"Smith is good" is about Smith and goodness, about an ego and a value predicate; it is not a statement about a body and how it behaves'. A realist philosopher might say 'You ask "Do we know the past and how, since it no longer exists to stand in any relation, cognitive or otherwise, to anything?" the answer is that we *do* know it, by memory'. But we do not need a philosopher to give us this answer. Again, after reading Zeno's arguments to prove that we cannot reach the end of a racecourse we do not need a philosopher to show

---

[1] Stout, *Mind and Matter*, p. 256. Here is an answer thoroughly common-sense in some respects and not in others.

us that we can and how. A mere 'plater' can do both quicker. But we know that there is another sense in which only a skilful philosopher can show us that we can and how. He will show us what is wrong with Zeno's puzzling argument – give us what we want.

We have seen, however, that in the case of the profound metaphysical questions we have looked at, definition is not what is wanted. They are of the form 'What are X propositions?' or sometimes 'What is the analysis of X propositions?' or 'Surely X propositions are not ultimate, what is their analysis?' We have found that in these cases 'analysis of X propositions into non-X propositions' describes nothing, so that to say that what we want here is definition of X propositions is to say nothing. On the other hand to say that what we want is this conclusion that analysis is impossible, takes no account of our use of the phrase 'Surely X propositions are not ultimate' and leaves us still unsatisfied. Nor is this dissatisfaction removed when it is explained how easy it is to pass from sensible requests for analysis to nonsensical ones because of ambiguities in 'X proposition' and 'mean'. For we feel that even when these confusions have been removed and we are clear that we are asking with regard to an ultimate class of propositions, 'What *are* these propositions?' still we are are asking for something. But what?

4. *The metaphysician may be described as seeking descriptions of a certain sort. But of what sort? and how do they help him?* The answer may be put in three ways:

(1) We might say that we are asking for analyses in a wider sense of 'analysis', a sense which does not require that if p_1 is analysable into p_2 then the sentence 'p_1' and the sentence 'p_2' mean the same. This is Mr. Duncan-Jones's suggestion.'[1] It has two important merits: (i) It emphasizes the continuity of metaphysics with analysis. (ii) It hints that our trouble lies in the fact that we sometimes are more inclined to say that two sentences express the same proposition (stand for the same fact) than we are to say that they mean the same.

It will, however, be objected that this altering of the use of words does not meet the case. The question was, e.g. 'Can

---

[1] I cannot make him responsible in any way for the use I have made here of what he writes in, 'Does Philosophy Analyse Common Sense?' *Aris. Soc.* Supp. Vol. XVI.

general propositions be analysed into non-general propositions?' and the trouble was that we were inclined both to say Yes and to say No. Now it is no use saying 'In a new sense "yes", in the old sense "no"', because the question was 'In the old usual sense of analysis, can general propositions be analysed into non-general propositions?' We have shown that they cannot be unless a definition with 'and so on' in it is counted as a definition. But is this a definition in the old sense or isn't it? The answer 'It would be in a new sense' is no more use here than it is when I ask 'Is a cassiowary a goat?' or 'Did Smith exercise reasonable care or didn't he?' You might as well say when asked whether a dog has gone round a cow who keeps her horns always towards him 'He has in a sense'.

(2) We might say: 'In a new sense of "meaning" the metaphysician asks, "Do general sentences mean the same as some collection of non-general sentences? Does the statement 'There is a nation in Arabia' mean 'There are a number of individuals in Arabia who are nationally related'?" He is confused by the old sense of meaning and so does not realize that the answer to his question is emphatically Yes'. But again there will be the objection that the question asked was in terms of the old use of meaning. We come on cases where it is difficult to tell whether two sentences mean the same, express the same proposition, stand for the same fact or not. 'Now', it will be said, 'there is no use in saying that there could easily be a sense in which the answer would certainly be "Yes" or a sense in which the answer would certainly be "No". For what we want to know is whether in the usual sense of "mean the same" they do or do not mean the same. And when people allow that "There is a penny on the table" means the same as "If you look you will see a brownish circular or elliptical patch, if you ... and so on" but inquire whether this is a definition, then it is no use saying "There could easily be a sense of definition in which it would be a definition". And this answer is also no use in dealing with disputes between philosophers as opposed to disputes within the breast of a single philosopher'. We shall see later how far there is use in saying this and how far there is not.

(3) We might say: 'What the metaphysician asks for when he asks "What are X propositions?" is not a definition but a

description, and when he asks whether X propositions can be analysed into non-X propositions he is asking for a *description* of the relations between them. He is apt to think that he is asking for a definition because in many cases to give a definition of X propositions has been the best way of giving a description. When the philosopher says analytic propositions are a sort of verbal proposition, this must not be taken as a definition but as a description throwing light upon the nature of analytic propositions and their relations to verbal propositions. By this means he describes a man asserting an analytic proposition just as one may describe, to a Red Indian, a man riding a motor cycle as a man riding a horse on wheels.

'And similarly to say that a metaphysical statement is a sort of analytic statement but not quite because it is a sort of description, is to give a description of a metaphysical statement and of a metaphysician'.

Two objections may be made. First, it will be said: 'The metaphysician asks "Are general propositions to be identified with some combination of non-general propositions or not?" "Are analytic propositions to be identified with verbal propositions or not? Can the one class be defined in terms of the other, or not?" You say "They are not to be so identified with each other but the one can be described by reference to the other as rather like the other" This is like the man who when asked whether a llama is a goat or not, replies, "No, but a llama may be described as a sort of goat"' We can recognize in these objections the objection made to the first two accounts of what it is the metaphysician really wants.

There is a second complaint which may be raised against the first and second accounts of what the metaphysician really wants, namely, that they do not give an analysis (new sense) of the new sense of 'analysis', or the meaning (new sense) of the new sense of 'meaning', and that therefore they do not analyse (new sense) or give the meaning of (new sense) 'metaphysics'. Similarly it may be objected that our description of a metaphysician is *inadequate*. It may be said 'You say the metaphysician describes ultimate classes of proposition, or describes the use of ultimate classes of sentence. But even if this is accepted you have not defined the metaphysician; for not all descriptions of ultimate classes of propositions or sentences are metaphysical. Now which sort are? Until you have told us this, you have not told us what metaphysics is'.

We are, by now, familiar with this sort of complaint. It is necessary to repeat that the request 'What is a metaphysician?' is not a request for definition. We can *explain* what the *felidæ* are. We do this 'internally' by explaining that leopards, lions, lynxes and cats are *felidæ*, and 'externally' by explaining that dogs, monkeys and even Siamese cats are not. We can explain what a pony is by giving a false definition, 'A horse under 14 hands high', and then explaining how this is not quite correct. Likewise we can explain what a metaphysician is 'internally' by explaining that positivists and 'ultimatists' are metaphysicians, and 'externally' by explaining that grammarians, logicians and poets are not. Here again we may in each case begin by a false definition 'Metaphysics is grammar', 'Metaphysics is logic', 'Metaphysics is poetry', and then explain why this is not so, drawing attention to such statements as 'Life is a tale told by an idiot', 'The world was made by God', 'Thou canst not stir a flower without troubling of a star', 'All relations are internal'.[1]

However, it may still be complained that the definition is *inadequate* in that the descriptions the metaphysicians give are connected in some way which has not been brought out by showing that metaphysics is not science, not logic, not grammar, not poetry.

We may say, remember the 'internal' part of our description. The metaphysician is concerned with those descriptions of ultimate classes of fact which bear on the great groups of puzzles which we have considered.

It may now be said, 'Yes, but how do the descriptions bear on the puzzles? Bring out now the nature of the puzzles in such a way that it is clear how the descriptions bear upon them'.

It is now clear that if we go on to make our description more adequate we shall be dealing also with the first complaint, namely How does the answer 'General propositions may be described as a sort of infinite disjunction of specific propositions' bear upon the questions, 'Can general propositions be identified with specific propositions?' 'Are the facts which correspond to them

[1] Locke, Bk. III, Chap. VI, Section V.

identical?' 'Do the sentences which express them mean the same'? The answer put briefly is this: (a) The metaphysical questions, 'Are X propositions to be identified with Y propositions?' 'Do X sentences mean the same as Y sentences?' 'Do they stand for the same facts?' arise and present difficulty not only because the expressions involved are ambiguous but also because they are 'vague', especially the expressions 'mean the same', 'express the same propositions', 'state the same fact'. It is because of this that the descriptions are relevant. How the descriptions are relevant is obscure because the nature of the questions is misunderstood in a way in which the nature of questions which present difficulty because of the vagueness of their terms is constantly misunderstood.

(b) The case is further complicated by the fact that the use of the expressions 'have the same thing in mind when I say S as when I say S'', 'mean the same by S as by S'', 'express the same proposition by S as by S'', 'state the same fact by S as by S'', are connected in a way which forms a slide irresistible by any logician, and we are all somewhat afflicted that way. For there are not cases in which one would *unhesitatingly* say one of these and deny another. At the same time, there are cases where one hesitates more about one. than about another.

5. *Let us look again at 'primitive' metaphysical difficulties.* In order to see all this, let us look once more at metaphysical difficulties arising, and let us look at them arising in people before they have been influenced by having the nature of their difficulties 'explained' to them.

I remember someone saying to me, 'You ask me to write an essay about Negation. But what is the trouble about Negation?' I may confess that I was somewhat at a loss. After all, what could be simpler? 'It is Jones', 'It is not', 'Her coat was blue', 'It was not blue'. What is the matter with the negatives? Why prefer the positives?

Now this case presents with simplicity what we have seen so often. First, an attempt is made to deal with the difficulty by definition in terms of expressions, new or old, which certainly mean the same as the usual sentences for expressing negative propositions. Thus Ramsey suggests expressing negation by writing positive sentences upside down. This throws a light, but leaves a more refined question, leaves the shadow unreduced to the substance (W). Then we try saying ' "This is not a tiger" means "This is a leopard or a lion or a giraffe or a donkey" '. Then for accuracy we add 'and so on'. Then it is said perhaps that this is just a negative sentence in disguise, because the whole infinite force of the negative lies in the 'and so on'. Or perhaps it is said that this does not mean the same as the original negative sentence.

The failure of the positivistic answers leads to the conclusion that negative facts are ultimate, that we are tempted to identify them with positive facts because the special sort of element they contain is not detectable by the senses. But this again does not satisfy.

Now what desire produces these abortive efforts? It is this. No one minds admitting that there are negative sentences as well as positive ones, but everyone feels uneasy when asked whether there are negative *facts* as well as positive ones. Yet negative sentences have meaning, express propositions which are true. If these propositions are not identical with propositions expressed by positive sentences, then surely what makes them true must be not identical with what makes true the propositions expressed by positive sentences.

In general: The metaphysically-minded person feels that the actual world is made up solely of positive, specific, determinate, concrete, contingent, individual, sensory facts, and that the appearance of a penumbra of fictional, negative, general, indeterminate, abstract, necessary, super-individual, physical[1] facts is somehow only an appearance due to a lack of penetration upon our part. And he feels that there are not, in addition to the ways of knowing the non-penumbral facts, additional ways of knowing employed for ascertaining the penumbral facts. At the same time the penumbral do not seem to be identical with the non-penumbral and thus *do* seem to call for extra ways of knowing.

Now this feeling of taking the same reality twice over (McTaggart[2]), this feeling of superfluous entities (Russell[3]),.

---

[1] Sometimes he makes physical facts ultimate, sometimes facts about sense-data. This serious complication I ignore.

[2] *Nature of Existence*, Vol. I, p. 135.

[3] *Our Knowledge of the External World*, p. 107. Compare MacTaggart's unsatisfactory answer in terms of 'possessing the same content'. What is content?

this feeling of metaphysical double vision has been removed in certain cases by definition. We can imagine someone saying 'What is the average man? How do I know he exists?' and then both troubles being dissolved by the definition ' "The average man is 5 ft. 4 ins. high" means "The sum of the heights of individual men divided by their number is 5 ft. 4 ins." ' We can imagine someone saying ' "All vegetarians are temperate" does not mean the same as "No vegetarians are intemperate" ' and then having to say that we know that the one fact is always present when the other is because the propositions are connected by a necessary connection which we know by intuition. We can even imagine someone saying ' "Geoffrey is George's brother" does not mean the same as "Geoffrey is a man and his parents are George's" '[1] and then again having to talk of two facts and two propositions connected by a necessary relation. Or again we can imagine someone wondering how we know that when (1) there are two white goats and four black in a field then (2) there are six goats in the field or there exists a class *goats-in-that-field* which has six members. Definition removes these troubles. Take the last case. When we saw that the two sentences meant the same or that the meaning of the one included the meaning of the other, then the appearance of plurality was explained by the plurality of sentences, while the assurance of identity was justified in the single meaning made true by a single fact. And with the disappearance of the ontological puzzle the epistemological puzzle vanished also. No wonder the definition model fascinated.

But unfortunately, as we have seen, there are cases[2] where definitions cannot be found, where no ingenuity reveals non-penumbral sentences which we can feel sure mean the same as the penumbrals. And yet we cannot feel that the facts which make the penumbral true are anything but the positive, concrete, etc., non-penumbral facts which make up the actual world. Indeed there are cases where we know that there are no non-penumbral sentences which mean the same in the ordinary use of 'mean the same' as the penumbral, while yet some of us feel that there is no difference between the facts which make

[1] People sometimes say 'No two expressions really mean the same'.
[2] But for them, metaphysics would not exist.

those penumbral sentences true and those which make the non-penumbral sentences true. Some people come down on one side of the fence, some on the other. Thus Broad[1] argues from the fact that the question 'Fido behaves in all respects intelligently, but is he intelligent?' is not silly like 'Smith is rich, but is he wealthy?' to the conclusion that the question is synthetic like 'I have given Smith two ounces of arsenic, but will it kill him?' That is, he concludes that the sentences 'Fido behaves in all respects intelligently' and 'Fido is intelligent' do not mean the same, do not stand for the same proposition, do not stand for the same fact. To do this is to represent the question 'Smith still breathes, and he nods, smiles, and talks as usual, but does he really think and feel?' as like the question 'Smoke still comes from the chimneys, the lights go on in the evenings, but have the inhabitants fled?' Has Smith's soul left his body but arranged with the nervous system that appearances shall be kept up in its absence? Has his *rha* flown? And yet we feel that the question is *not* like this — yet surely it must be, for Broad's premisses are true and there is no logical slip.[2]

6. *Let us reformulate the difficulties.* These difficulties arise from a misunderstanding of the nature of the questions, 'Are X facts ultimate?' 'Are X facts reducible to Y facts?' Let us try reformulating them.

Instead of asking 'Are X facts reducible to non-X facts or to Y facts?' let us ask 'Are X propositions reducible to non-X propositions or to Y propositions?' And instead of asking this let us ask 'Do X sentences mean the same as any combination of non-X sentences or of Y sentences?' And instead of putting this back[3] into 'Do X sentences stand for the same proposition as any combination of non-X sentences or Y sentences?' let us ask instead 'Are X sentences used in the same way as some combination of non-X sentences or of Y sentences?' i.e. 'When we have an X sentence can we find a Y sentence which serves the same purpose?'

This reformulation is permissible of course, only when we remember that it means 'When we have an X sentence used in

---

1 *The Mind and its Place in Nature*, p. 614.
2 No logical slip between any *adjoining* steps one might say
3 For dangers of this, see Ayer, *Aris. Soc.*, Supp. Vol. XVI.

that way with which you are familiar, is there some combination of Y sentences used in that manner with which you are familiar, which serves the same purpose?'[1]

We have then the questions, 'When we have a general sentence can we find a combination of non-general sentences which serve the purpose it serves?' and 'When we have a nation-sentence, can we find a combination of individual-sentences which serve the purpose it serves?' and so on.

Compare these questions with the questions 'Does the paper pound serve the purpose which the sovereign served before the war?' 'Could anything which is not a bridle serve the purpose which a bridle serves?' 'The Red Indian with his single strip of hide can stop and turn his pony with it, so the practical, debunking person will say 'Yes', may even insist that it is a bridle, which of course is quite untrue. The instructor in equitation will say 'No' because he cannot obtain with it the balance and 'collection' he obtains with the bridle. Others hesitate, wondering which is right. But what sort of wondering is this, and what sort of right and wrong? We see at once that we have only to put the question in the plural, 'Which of the purposes served by a bridle does the strip of hide serve?' to see that the answer is a matter of describing these, and if after this it is asked 'Well, does it serve the same purpose?' the question is now obviously 'Shall we say "It serves the same purpose" or shall we not?'.

We can now see how to deal with the sovereign and the paper pound. Those who say the value of a thing is its power in exchange will say the paper pound does serve the same purpose. Others will say, 'No there was something about a sovereign which a dirty bit of paper can never do'.

And now let us take another case. People ask, 'If when a dog attacks her, a cow keeps her horns always towards him, so that she rotates as fast as he revolves, does he go round her?' We may imagine them offering reasons 'He does go round her, because he goes all round the place where she is standing, that is, he encircles her. Therefore he goes round her'. 'But', it may be protested, 'he never gets behind her, therefore he doesn't go round her'.

[1] This is again open to misinterpretation but reference to p. 463 will prevent it.

Suppose the disputants now appeal to you and ask 'Which is right?' or 'Which do you think is right?' There is at once an inclination to answer, 'There is a sense in which he does and a sense in which he does not go round the cow'. But this is untrue. There are not in English two uses of 'go round' in one of which the answer is 'Yes' while in the other it is 'No'. Had there been, the question would hardly have produced difficulty.[1] But the answer is not useless because it brings out how easily there might have been a use of language in which we should have had an answer ready, and thus hints that the question is a matter of language. It is, however, *very* necessary to explain what sort of a question about language it is.

This appears if we set out the right way to deal with the question. One should say: You speak as if you are asking a question about the dog and the cow. But you know the facts about them. And what is more you know the answer to the question, 'What would ordinarily be said in such a case when the question is put "Did the dog go round the cow?"' For you know that people would hesitate and some insist, though with a certain bravado, that he did and others that he did not. In asking me this question you are treating me like a judge of the High Court who is considering a question of law not of fact, e.g. 'Was it in the case described reasonable and probable that someone would try to cash the cheque which Mr. Smith made out so carelessly? Was it? or was it not?' Now I can of course give a decision if that is what you want. But you want more than that. You want me to sum up and bring out the features of the case which incline one to say that the dog went round the cow, and those which disincline one to say this. In this particular case, unlike other cases of the sort, this can be done fairly easily. For the features which incline one to say that the dog went round the cow are summed up in the statement 'He circled round the place where she stood', while those which disincline one to speak so can be summed up in the statement, 'He did not change his position with respect to the parts of the cow'. Now you will notice that you who wished to say that the dog went round and your opponent who wished to say that it

---

[1] We might say 'Metaphysical difficulties have been so hard to remove because of the illusion that ambiguity is the only bar to logic'.

did not, had between you already described these features although at the time you regarded yourselves as giving reasons for its being right or wrong to say that the dog went round the cow. So you see you had already done what you wanted done though, because you mistook the nature of your question, you did this in a misleading way. Had you put your question in the form, 'Which of the features which we expect to find in a case when told that A has gone round B do we find in the case of the dog and the cow?' you would not have found yourself in difficulties.

Let us return to the question: 'Given such a sentence as "There is cheese here" does this mean the same as any string of sentences about what we should see if we looked, smell if we sniffed, etc? Is there any sensation-sentence which means the same, expresses the same proposition as, stands for the same fact as, the cheese-sentence?'

Here again, as we have seen, there is an inclination to say 'There is a sense of "meaning" in which the answer is "Yes" and a sense in which the answer is "No" '. But there are not two such uses of 'meaning' in English. If there had been, the difficulty would have been removable in the way it is when someone says of a mare that she is a horse while someone else says she is not.

Here again the proper answer is: 'You are not asking anything about cheeses, you know about them, what they are made of, and so on. But what is more, you are not asking what would be said here nor what the language experts would say here. No expert in heaven or earth could help you. What you are asking for is a decision and the reasons for it *in the sense in which reasons can be offered for a decision* – by counsel for the plaintiff and counsel for the defendant. But these as a matter of fact you have already set out – the positivists have set out the "reasons" for deciding in favour of saying that the sentences mean the same, the "ultimatists" have set out the reasons against saying this'.

There are cases of metaphysical dispute, however, where the answer should not be quite as above. Suppose A says that poetry which does not rhyme is not really poetry, while B says it is. Now in so far as the question is one of logic as to whether being poetry entails rhyme, B is right, because language is in fact so used as to make him right. But A is of course well aware that this is how language is used and is not denying what he knows to be true. But they think they are contradicting each other, and are thus wrong. If now A asks, 'Don't you agree with me?' one can only explain those features of one's attitude to their dispute which incline one to say, 'I agree with A' and those features of their dispute which incline one to say, 'I agree with B'. (For neither the answer 'I agree with A', nor the answer 'I agree with B' is correct though neither is incorrect.) Now this explanation will involve an explanation of the nature of the dispute, and this will involve describing what leads A to say what he does and what leads B to say what he does.

Similarly in metaphysics. Broad shows how as a matter of logic, 'Fido is intelligent' does not mean the same as 'Fido behaves intelligently'. But he has not grasped what those who deny this are doing. And since they advance their thesis as the contradictory of his, it is not to be wondered at that he should not have grasped what they are doing. On the other hand surely it is apparent that even when they have to allow that the two sentences do not mean the same, they are not going to be convinced that they were wrong. No proof that taken as a statement in logic what they say is false convinces them. The younger child who has been insisting against his pedantic elder brother that a fox has a tail may not be convinced that he was wrong even when an adult convinces him that experts and others do not say that a fox has a tail (W).

The situation is often complicated by the fact that the following steps seem impeccable: 'What I have in mind when I say S, e.g. "Smith can do successfully all the tests for colour blindness and *never* fails in ordinary life either" is not the same as what I have in mind when I say S', e.g. "Smith can see red and green and all the colours". Hence S and S' do not mean the same. Hence they do not stand for the same proposition. Hence they do not stand for the same fact'. As we have seen, the argument may be reversed. Now as a matter of fact, the features of the use of two sentences which incline us to use the expression 'stand for the same fact' are not quite the same as those which incline us to use 'put the same ideas into our mind'. Hence it sometimes happens that we get from certain features of the use of two sentences a strong inclination to say that they do *not* mean the same, derived from a strong inclination to say that we have not the same things in mind when we utter the one as when we utter the other, and at the same time a strong inclination to say that they *do* mean the same, derived from a strong inclination to say that they do not stand for different facts. And when this happens we may be induced to say that S and S′ stand for different facts when but for faith in this logical ladder we should never have done so; and we may be induced, by tipping the ladder the other way, to say that two sentences mean the same when we should never otherwise have done so.

It is this ladder or slide which, together with a wrong way of speaking about meaning and the assumption that the only purpose of indicative sentences is to state facts, that leads us to look for fictional facts to fit the fictional propositions required by the significance of fictional sentences. Here the assumption that the sole function of indicative sentences is to state facts reaches the limit of absurdity. It will be noticed that this assumption is the Verification Principle. Having seen its falsehood in the case where the factual functions of an indicative are zero, we are ready to look for non-factual functions in cases where the factual functions are not zero, in ethics, in mathematics, in psychological statements, in metaphysics, and thus in the principle itself. A flood of light is thrown on the numerous philosophical disputes arising from the fact that sentences may agree in factual function while they do not in other functions. But it must be remembered that this method is far from fool-proof because the hardest problems are those in which there is an inclination both to say that two sentences *stand for the same fact* and to deny this, e.g. psychological and behaviour sentences (worst of all), analytic and verbal sentences, material thing and sensation sentences (less acute). And such a conflict, as we have seen, can be met only by explaining its nature, that is by explaining that the dispute is resolved by setting out what has induced each disputant to say what he has said.

To sum up: The metaphysician is concerned with certain fundamental ontological and epistemological reduplication questions: Are X facts to be identified with Y facts? How do we get from knowledge of the latter to knowledge of the former?

Usually, even as questions of logic, there is no right or wrong answer to these questions. I should be inclined to say this in every case where the question is in the form in which reduplication is most intolerable, namely, 'Are X facts nothing but Y facts or are they something over and above Y facts?' Sometimes in the form in which reduplication is less intolerable, namely, 'Do X sentences mean the same as Y sentences' (taken as a question of logic) there is a correct answer 'No'.

But in either case the metaphysical dispute is resolved by explaining what induces each disputant to say what he does. This is done as follows: First explain the nature of the question or request; (a) Negatively — remove the wrong idea that it is a question of fact whether natural *or logical*; (b) Positively — give the right idea by showing how, as in other disputes of this unanswerable sort, the questions are really requests for a description of (1) those features of the use of the expressions involved in the questions which incline one to answer 'Yes', and of (2) those features of their use which incline one to answer 'No'. In the case of ontological questions such as 'Are X facts to be identified with Y facts?' 'Do X sentences mean the same as Y sentences?' 'Does the sentence S stand for the same fact as the sentence S'?' the expressions involved are of course (a) the expressions 'X facts', 'Y facts', 'X sentences', 'Y sentences', 'The sentence S' and so on, and (b) the *connectives* 'stand for the same fact', 'mean the same' and so on. In the case of epistemological questions, expressions such as 'know', 'rational', take the place of the connectives.

Second provide the descriptions that are really wanted.

Fortunately when the nature of the questions has been explained, then the nature of the 'answers', 'theories' and 'reasons' which they have been 'offering' and 'advancing' becomes clear to the disputants. And then it becomes clear how much of the work of providing the descriptions has been already done, though under the disguise of a logical[1] dispute. Thus the metaphysical paradoxes appear no longer as crude falsehoods about how language is actually used, but as penetrating suggestions as to how it might be used so as to reveal what, by the actual use of language, is hidden. And metaphysical platitudes appear as

---

[1] At one time under the disguise of a contingent or natural dispute.

timely reminders of what is revealed by the actual use of language and would be hidden by the new. To take an example which we have ourselves come upon: Some have said 'Analytic propositions are verbal', others have said 'They are not', and, in supporting these 'views', they have between them done all that is primarily asked for by one who asks 'Are analytic propositions verbal or are they not?'

Thus it appears how it is that, to give metaphysicians what they want, we have to do little more than remove the spectacles through which they look at their own work.[1] Then they see how those hidden identities and diversities which lead to the 'insoluble' reduction questions about forms, categories and predicates, have already been revealed, though in a hidden way.

[1] It should again be remembered how much of this is due to Wittgenstein.

A CRITICAL NOTICE

Science and Ethics. By C. H. WADDINGTON AND OTHERS

(*Mind Vol. LII*)

THE first 11 pages are an essay by Dr. Waddington, the next
36 pages are comments by thirteen authors with replies by Dr.
Waddington, the next 38 pages, entitled 'Some psychological
considerations', are by Dr. Karin Stephen, Mrs. Klein, Miss Roths-
child and Dr. Waddington, the next 10 pages are a correspondence
between Professor Dingle and Dr. Waddington, the next 12 pages
entitled a Marxist critique, contain Professor Bernal's criticism and
Dr. Waddington's reply, the next 15 pages contain final comments
by the Bishop of Birmingham, the Dean of St. Paul's, Professor
Chauncey D. Leake and Dr. Waddington. Finally, there are some
notes on the contributors and an index.

Dr. Waddington has three purposes: (1) to contend that ethical
statements, such as 'You oughtn't to kill', are empirical generalizations like 'You oughtn't to take less than 7 mg. of vitamin C
daily'; (2) to emphasize and increase our grasp of the connection
between ethics and psycho-analysis; (3) to contend that 'in the
world as a whole, the real good cannot be other than that which
has been effective, namely that which has been exemplified in the
course of evolution' (p. 18).

1. In saying that ethical statements are statements and statements of scientific fact Dr. Waddington opposes, first, those who
say that ethical statements are exclamations and/or exhortations,
and secondly, those who say that they are self-evident truths stating
a necessary synthetic connection between, on the one hand, such
things as cruelty, content, and exhilaration, and on the other hand,
goodness and badness, which are detected by a moral sense or intuition. He less explicitly opposes the latter because, finding it
impossible to produce a formal definition of goodness in terms of
naturalistic characters, he cannot venture to say definitely that
the good or evil of a state of affairs is a matter of *what* that state
of affairs is and of how we feel and shall feel towards it. This combination of a transcendental ethical ontology with his positivistic

epistemology works havoc. (See Broad's notes on the symposium between Waddington and Ewing, *Proc. Aris. Soc.*, May 28th, 1942.) I shall assume that if Waddington had been acquainted with recent work on how one thing may be a matter of other things without being formally definable in terms of them then he would have constantly said what he sometimes finds himself obliged to say, namely, that goodness *is* a matter of natural characters.

Though less dogmatic than Professor Bernal in his little sermon (p. 114) Dr. Waddington is almost equally innocent. To deal with the intuitionist doctrine of ethics it is necessary not only to make fun of it but also to remove the difficulties and admit the limitations of positivistic accounts. Dr. Waddington in rejecting the rhetorical doctrine and the analytic doctrine (Dr. Karin Stephen, p. 79, lines 8 and 9) makes this impossible. Yet Sidgwick, Moore and others cannot be ignored. No doubt their thinking, like that of poor Broad, is vitiated by the fact that their 'concepts are non-developmental' (p. 51) or are 'anthropomorphic abstractions such as Will, Conscience or Desire' (Bernal, p. 120). It would be kind, however, to explain a little *how* it is vitiated so that those of us who are still so anthropomorphic about men may the sooner go to where we are going, or should I say, the sooner reach that realistic ethos and superior social environment towards which the dynamic processes of evolutionary change are even now inevitably conducting us.

If someone says of a baby, 'He's his father to a T', while another says, 'No, no, he's his mother all over', then one expects to find each right in some ways and to find that some of the ways in which the one is right make the other that far wrong, and that anyway the baby is quite a lot just like himself and not like his parents. It is the same when someone tells me that a giant panda is just a little bear while another says, 'No, he just a big guinea-pig', while a third says, 'No, he isn't anything but himself, the living essence of all cuddly toys'. What makes one think well or ill of these paradoxes, hyperboles, exaggerations, simplifications, is an intricate tale. Certainly, it isn't only a matter of the degree of likeness between the things concerned. Even if the baby is much more like his father than his mother, if the likeness to the mother can be revealed to me by suitable talk then I may think better of

'No, it's his mother he's so like', just because this likeness doesn't leap to the eye but is subtle and profound.

'Ethical statements aren't statements but are commands, exhortations, exclamations'[1] is false but profound and, till recently, novel, though *strongly* hinted at by Hume. 'Ethical statements are statements, statements of fact' is of course true. They are statements of fact about what is good and right, i.e. about ethical fact. And mathematical statements are statements about mathematical fact. And both sorts of fact can be discovered. But to say all this is platitudinous and useless except in opposition, i.e. as corrective to falsehoods such as, 'They are exclamations'. For, as always in metaphysics, the difficulty lies *within* the expressions 'statement', 'fact', 'true', 'false', 'discover'.[2] It is not for nothing that we use the same words in ethical and aesthetic and mathematical procedure as we use in scientific procedure. But 'Ethical statements are statements' is a platitude and reveals nothing, for it reminds us only of a likeness our notation already emphasizes. It can be useful only in opposition to a paradox, i.e. in the way 'A man is a man and neither a monk nor a monkey' (with apologies to Forster) is useful.

In contrast to this, 'Ethical statements are statements of scientific fact, and in particular of psychological fact' is not a platitude and boring, but false and though not novel can still be illuminating if followed up in a novel way. I don't feel that we can say that Dr. Waddington does this, but he *does* make a suggestion as to how it could be done.

2. Dr. Waddington is anxious to increase our grasp of and emphasize the connection between ethics and psycho-analysis. It is the speaking out of this idea and the help which Dr. Stephen and Mrs. Klein give him in doing so which make this little book worth something, so it seems to me. The idea is still new though it has been put forward before to some extent, e.g. by H. V. Dicks when in *Clinical Studies in Psychopathology* (p. 109) he writes, 'Clearly the union of the opposites has been set as the highest goal of human achievement . . . a task to be fulfilled by the individual within himself — a process of psychological growth and unification — the

---

[1] See 'Ethical Words and Ethical Facts', Duncan-Jones, *Mind*, 1933.

[2] We can all remember those o-so-valid proofs that mathematical statements aren't commands nor rules of grammar because it is *true* that 375×2 equals 750 while neither commands nor rules *can* be true.

resolution of conflict, to give it its modern name. The discovery of oneself, the finding of the centre from which we cannot err, of the "still, small voice" of the "Golden Flower" ... of the thousand-petalled lotus, etc. etc. by whatever name this precious self-realization and acceptance has been called – this is nothing less than the aim of psychotherapy, within the limits of the patient's powers'.

This seems to me to be in a certain very important respect a better account of the connection between ethics and analysis than Dr. Waddington's. On page 10 he writes, 'the psycho-analytical discoveries, which are concerned with the development of the ethical systems of individuals, are the most profitable basis from which to begin an examination of the scientific basis of ethics'. This suggests that psycho-analysts discover generalizations and that then from these ethics may be deduced. This misrepresents the psycho-analyst who, like a mechanic or a teacher of dancing, is as much an artist as a scientist. And also it is the discoveries in analysis by the analysed rather than the discoveries from analysis by the analyst that are most importantly connected with ethics. And, finally, the 'discoveries' in analysis like discoveries of beauty in pictures or music are as much alterations in oneself and one's object as discoveries.

An account such as Dicks' suggests how a man in the course of analysis may suddenly say to himself, 'Why, this *is* ethics. I have been reading about it all my life, and sometimes when a difficult decision has been called for I have been forced to do ethics, but often the decision has been a matter of having to act one way or another – not a settling of things in myself.'

Of course working through an analysis is *not* doing ethics. But just as besides doing logic in the sense of setting out logical rules there is logical practice from which the rules are extracted as mnemonics, so besides ethics there is ethical practice from which, *much* less successfully, ethical rules can be extracted if that kind of thing amuses you. Now it is not so wrong to say that part of analysis is ethical practice. By 'logical practice' I mean estimating the value of arguments, offering and accepting arguments and sifting our reactions to arguments. By 'ethical practice' I mean accepting and rejecting persons, acts and feelings, and the sifting of those acceptances and rejections. I mean the asking and answering of such questions as, '*Is* Jack such a blackguard?' '*Ought* I to have done that?' 'Is it horrible of me to feel like I do when . . .?' This is what Hume called, significantly, our decisions of praise or blame.[1]

But even if we say that it is this which is done in analysis we shall still be apt to mislead. For just as in deciding whether a picture is good, and even in deciding whether a show is funny, we don't merely look again at the picture and sift *our* reaction to it but *also* count the reactions of *others*, especially Clive Bell, so in deciding whether it would be right to do so and so and whether it was right to do so and so we count the reactions of others. If, say what we will and say what they will, they differ from us still, then we say either that they use words differently or, in different circumstances, that though it is funny to us, or lovely to us, it isn't to them. And but for the extra regularity of nature in the matter of sweetness and redness and hotness and roundness we should do the same for them and say, 'It's red to us but not to others', or 'It's sweet to children but not to adults'. And just as the redness, the real objective redness, of a red flag is a matter of its redness to nearly everybody to-day and also to-morrow unless it's been dipped in ink, so is the beauty of a face, the niceness of a person, and the rightness of an act, a matter not only of how they seem to oneself but also of how they seem to others, and not only now but also when the bands stop playing.

To sum up in jargon: Real redness is constructed from redness to A and redness to B and redness to C and, etc. And redness to A is constructed from seeming now red to A, still seeming, e.g. on closer inspection, red to A. Likewise satisfactoriness is constructed from satisfactoriness to A, to B, to C. And really satisfactory to A is constructed from seems satisfactory to A, still seems satisfactory to A after listening to it again, or even now that he is sober, or, etc. Likewise rightness is constructed from really seems right to A, to B, etc., and really seems right to A is constructed from seems right to A at first blush, still seems right to A after review, comparison, etc. It is with the business of the transition from 'seems for the moment acceptable and right to A' to 'seems really right and acceptable to A' that one is concerned.

I remember how after I had been going to an analyst for about a

---

[1] *The Enquiry*, Appendix A.

month I was walking home and thinking over the sort of thing I had been doing and I said with surprise, 'Why, this *is* ethics'. It was because what I had been doing struck me as being just more of the sort of thing I should call thinking a thing over to see whether it seems right to me, whether I can 'accept myself' if I do it. And yet what I had been doing could also be described as going into how I felt towards doing this with those consequences, or that with those other consequences. To say that right is a matter of what at infinity still seems right to everybody and that what seems right to so and so is a matter of what he finally feels, is not to make right more subjective than red or round — (though it is *more* subjective). But it is a naturalistic and anti-transcendental *metaphysic* of ethics, i.e. ultimate description of ethical activity. It is opposed to the type of talk in, e.g. *Principia Ethica*, which suggests that goodness is related to those natural characters which make a thing good and our feelings to them like the power of a horse is related to those structural characters which cause that power and our feelings to them. The naturalistic type of talk suggests that on the contrary goodness is related to stopping on the way from Damascus[1] and cups of water and so on and our reactions to these, like the grace of a dancer to her movements and our feelings for these. Her grace *is* a matter of the patterns she gives to our eyes and the lift she gives to our hearts. So there is no problem of how we know she's graceful.

All this isn't new. Mill said that the desirable is the desired and he didn't mean all the nonsense he's been said to mean. He didn't mean that the desirable is what happens to be consciously desired at the moment. He meant that it is what is really desired. What is really desired is what is desired when *all* our inclinations towards it are faced and not some ignored, including desires not to have a desire for such a thing; in other words, our desire for X is a real desire when all our desires for all that is for us in X have been 'owned' and 'sifted'. What does this mean?

In ethical effort people take note of the voice or prick of conscience — of the immediate response, 'O no, mustn't do that'. But they do not always take this as final. They say, 'But there's no harm in it really, it's only my puritanical conscience', and a small Dionysian voice grows louder, 'It's foolish, but it's fun'.

[1] Karin Stephen, p. 79

They join in the frolic of the Restoration. And then they turn again and say, 'The Puritans had something after all', and take to driving in a victoria round Balmoral – only to leave it for a faster car and the dancing 'twenties and so on. Oscillation in deciding between philosophical doctrines goes hopelessly on until one gives up suppressing conflicting voices and lets them *all* speak their fill. Only then can we modify and reconcile them. It is so with other things.

The sifting of one's reaction towards doing such and such a thing having such and such consequences is like the sifting of one's reaction to a picture or an argument, or one's reaction (non-ethical) to a person. Professor Joad recently said to me, 'How much of our reaction to these pictures is nostalgia for France?' and again one may say, 'How much of my reaction to that man's argument was rhetorical or due to flattery, how much logical?' In this way one may say, 'How much of my reaction against a "blind" on a Saturday night is due to my puritanical upbringing?', or 'How much is it due to my father's being such a drunken misery-maker every Saturday night?'. And saying this alters the reaction. True, one says, 'I thought I disapproved a Saturday "blind" but I didn't really', but one might equally well say 'I used to disapprove a Saturday "blind" until I connected my reaction to Bill's "blind" to-night with my reaction to all father's "blinds" when I was three'. And there is much in analysis which isn't different in kind from this. It is still connecting. It is more extensive and it is finding, grasping, how much the past is hidden in the present. And this is best done not so much with what Proust calls the 'intellectual memory' which he says 'preserves nothing of the past itself', but in the way in which he found hidden in a madeleine and a cup of tea all those Sunday mornings and the streets and gardens of Combray, in the way he inhaled 'through the noise of falling rain, the odour of invisible and persistent lilac trees' from the Méséglise way'. It wasn't *dugouts* that Rivers' patient *feared*, or, if you like, it was dugouts, only in them was hidden for him that frightening and shameful moment when having just pawned the watch his mother and father had given him he found himself caught in a narrow passage by that figure of vengeance, a big, silent dog, straight from the landscapes of the surrealists.

Though it is especially the past it is not only the past that is hidden in a reaction to this or that now. 'Her voice is in the falling rain' even if she is still alive and even present. In a different way the future comes in too.

> 'Unborn Tomorrow and dead Yesterday,
> Who cares about them if To-day be sweet?'

The question would not have been asked if the answer hadn't been 'Everybody'. Nor would it have been asked had not everybody sometimes wished the answer to be 'Nobody'. Is it that to get a real response to the present we need something that will 'clear to-day of past regrets and future fears?' 'In vino veritas' they say. But the pubs mostly close at 10. Besides, though the Méséglise and Guermantes "ways" leave us 'exposed, in later life, to much disillusionment and even to many mistakes ... by the same qualities, and by their persistence in those of my impressions, to-day, to which they can find an attachment, the two "ways" give to those impressions a foundation, depth, a dimension lacking from the rest'. And in sifting one's reactions one may at first reject as infantile and compulsive what in a re-sifting one may accept though in a different degree and different way perhaps. 'How much is this nostalgia for France?' we may ask, and looking again at the picture see it rather differently, and then turning on ourselves once more we may say 'And why not nostalgia? Is it all to be rejected? Isn't the Primavera what it is, in part because in the face of the Flora are so many Springs?' It is not the mere fact that a reaction comes out of the past that makes it tyrannous — it depends on what past it comes from and what welcome it receives.

Ethical effort is the weighing of considerations and, as Aristotle said, there are no rules which will enable us to avoid this effort. The trouble is we are very apt to be dissatisfied with our weighing, the weights too often and too much change with every re-weighing. It is not that we want the weights never to change. And it is not so much abrupt and even frequent change that is the trouble — it is that oscillation which finds expression in 'I don't know *what* I really want' which is so distressing. It's all very well for the vocalist to advise

> 'Experiment
> And it will lead you to the light'.

No doubt if you wish your child to become a connoisseur in tea you will encourage him to try lots of teas. But then tea is cheap while murder, adultery and robbery are not. Besides that way, namely, seeing life, may be inadequate even with tea, and many men 'experienced with horses' are still bad with them. With your tea drinking child you will do your best in choosing the order in which he drinks the teas just as you would over the order in which he 'looks at' horses, pictures and arguments in order that he may develop with respect to these from the stage at which all are marvellous or all a bore to a stage in which he has greater discrimination. And, unfortunately, he may easily come to hate them all more and more as Mrs. Arnot Robertson came to hate ships, or become unable to like anything except Bach and Mozart or, worst of all, come to have a strong love *and* hate for all. This last is best avoided and best resolved by increasing his discrimination not so much of the objects to which he reacts as of his reactions to the objects. The mother says, 'How would *you* like it?' i.e. 'How much is your complaisance due to the fact that it's you who are pulling the cat's tail and not vice versa?' And in this she is *not* merely putting something into the child but *bringing out* the uneasiness which lurks in *him* just as it did when biting her breast he laid waste his world and with it himself.

There are other ways in which analysis is connected with ethics. For example, analysis isn't concerned only with what one really approves, really accepts in oneself, but also with what one really wants, fears, loves, hates. In deciding what to do, one of the things necessary is, of course, to estimate what consequences will follow and primarily what consequences in the way of how people, including oneself, will really feel, and that *not* in the way of approval or disapproval.

3. About the connection between what is good and what has been exemplified in the course of evolution. I heartily agree with Dr. Waddington's critics that most of what he says won't do at all and involves old muddles. But I would like to point out that on page 39 he says he means 'if the ethical system is to be derived from the nature of the experimental ... one of the most important data is the scientifically ascertained course of evolution'. If it were not for the words 'scientifically ascertained' this might easily mean '*One* of the criteria as to what a man or people really want is

what they tend to get hold of in the end' and then it would be right though not easily applicable except in simple matters like wine and cars.

Finally, do we value Socrates (p. 38), Van Gogh (p. 90), because of their contribution to the progress of mankind? Not on your life. Social progress be damned. It's the picture that counts.

PHILOSOPHY, ANXIETY AND NOVELTY
(*Mind Vol. LIII*)

EVERY philosophical question is really a request for a description of a class of animals — of a *very* familiar class of animals. That is my point, that the classes of animals are very familiar to us all. Consequently philosophical answers are descriptions of very familiar classes of animals — and because the animals are so familiar there is no question of the answers being wrong descriptions — but only of whether they are happy descriptions or not.

There are, of course, already descriptions of these animals, and when our minds are set in a certain way it may for a moment seem odd to us that anyone should want others. But then we may remember how, when our minds are set in a certain way, it may seem odd to us that anyone should wish to paint things at all, and then further seem still odder to us that he should want to paint them in some *queer* way when he has already painted them *beautifully*, with photographic faithfulness. And again, red roses are red roses and white ones white roses, and to say 'that the red rose is a falcon and the white rose is a dove' is going out of one's way to say what isn't true. So it is to say that poverty is a crime, or that everyone who looks at a woman to lust after her has already committed adultery with her.

Of course there is here no question of making an untrue statement of fact. What such statements involve is logical or verbal impropriety, i.e. the introduction of a new logic. But these improprieties are not without a purpose: they reveal what is known but hidden. They wouldn't reveal if they weren't novel; in other words, they wouldn't reveal if they weren't wrong. I should like to expand all this a little.

1. *As to why every philosophical question is a request for a description of a familiar class of animals.* The proof for ontological questions is as follows: 'What is philosophy?' means 'What is a philosopher?' 'What is a necessary statement, a mathematical statement, an ethical statement, a statement of fact?' means 'What are mathematicians, etc.?' 'What is memory?' means 'What are those persons doing who remember?' and this means 'What are those persons doing who say of someone that he is

remembering?' One who asks philosophically 'What are mathematicians?' points to two people talking mathematically with one another, and asks 'What are they doing?' He doesn't ask this like one who, seeing two men creeping on their hands on wet ground, asks 'What are they doing?' when the proper answer is 'Wait and see' or 'Stalking deer'. For it isn't that the philosopher doesn't know what the mathematician is going to do next. That he knows just as well as he knows what people are going to do when they set out the chess pieces. [In knowing so well what people *do* do in chess he comes to know what they *should* do; he comes to know what they are really wanting to do. He knows this very well for mathematics too, and for statements about animals and things such as 'There's no cake left'. But he doesn't know it so well for philosophers nor for proposers of scientific theories. Here it is more a matter of knowing very well what they do do but not being able to extract very well from this what they really wish to do. This is a complication which I am ignoring for the present.]

2. To repeat: *It isn't that the philosopher doesn't know how one who makes, e.g. a mathematical statement, is going to proceed, so when he asks for a description of mathematicians he is not asking a question of fact.* One who asks 'What is a semaphorist?' may be asking for the translation of an unfamiliar word. Or he may be asking 'What is one who so moves his arms doing?' and be asking a question of fact about the purposes of such a person, which question is answered by explaining the understanding that exists between the semaphorist and the man on the opposite hill who then speaks on a telephone. It isn't a question like that which the philosopher is asking when he asks 'What is a mathematician?'

3. *The philosopher's question is like that asked by a person who, very well knowing all that there is in semaphoring, asks 'What is it to semaphore?'* The answer is, 'It is to semaphore'. This is much more accurate an answer than 'It's shouting with your arms'. In other words the philosopher is not like one who having seen part of a performance wishes to know its subsequent or hidden parts. He is more like someone who having seen a complete performance by kangaroo rats playing in the moonlight turns and asks, 'What are they doing?' The answer is, 'Playing in the moonlight', or 'Well, you have seen'.

Of course there are differences. First, as we have already noticed, in the case of the rats there is no distinction between what it is they do do and what it is they wish to do. And again, though people don't semaphore perfectly, they mostly do it very well. The philosopher who asks 'What is a philosopher?' is more like someone who has gathered what he can of what people want to do when playing chess or tennis from watching people who don't do it very well. But this, as I said, is not a thing I want to emphasize here. For there is a quite different anxiety in philosophers as comes out in the fact that they ask, 'What is a mathematician?' 'What is one who asserts something about a material thing?' where no question of what it is that these speakers *really* want to do comes in, because mathematicians and train announcers are very successful with language so that what they do when they talk is what they really want to do.

4. *When, then, a philosopher asks, 'What are mathematicians and train announcers?' he must, in a sense, answer his question in asking it.* For he must carefully describe what the class of talkers he wants described actually do if he is to ask his question, 'How are they to be described?'

5. *Now of course this makes his question look nothing in a way in which it is not.* The fact is the philosopher wants *another* description and one of a special sort. And if we remember the answer, 'Talking with his arms', this will give us a hint as to how to describe what it is the philosopher wants. He wants a description which shall remove certain puzzles he feels about how we can claim to know certain things and whether these things amount to this and that which he feels we can claim to know or to something more which he feels we can hardly claim to know. In other words he wants a description of familiar kinds of talkers which shall bring out the epistemological and ontological relations between what they are doing. I am not here concerned to describe more fully what it is he wants.

6. *What I want to do here is to recall with emphasis that when two philosophers are talking about what, e.g. mathematical talkers and train announcers do, they both know perfectly well what they do. So the whole of what the philosophers do is deductive, deductive from the descriptions they both allow. If the deductions were complex, if they were lineally complex, there would be room for deductive anxiety. But*

they are not. The steps from the agreed, aseptic, descriptions to the philosophical conclusions or descriptions are childishly short.

7. *And yet Moore, for example, insists on knitting his brows* about what it is that one who says 'I have two hands' or '326 × 3 = 988' is doing. Is the former about a sense-datum to the effect that it is part of a hand? Is the latter a rule, a rule of grammar? Are ethical talkers perhaps not asserting anything which could be true or false?[1]

There is a simple proof that ethical talkers are asserting something which could be true or false. I will make the proof longer than is necessary so as to make it more impressive. A proposition is anything which is asserted, doubted or denied. (Definition. See almost any logic text-book.) One who says 'It was right of Brutus to stab Caesar' asserts something and not merely, if at all, that Brutus did stab Caesar. He is asserting in addition that this action of Brutus' was right. In other words he is also asserting what he would assert if he said 'It was right of Brutus to stab Caesar, if he did'. In other words, he is not only asserting the proposition that Brutus stabbed Caesar but also another proposition. (See definition.) [The proposition is the proposition that Brutus' act was right.] Now every proposition is either true or false. (Law of contradiction.) Therefore that proposition which one who says 'It was right of Brutus to stab Caesar' is asserting in addition to the proposition that Brutus did stab Caesar (assuming that he is asserting the latter) is either true or false. Therefore it is not true that one who asserted that it was right of Brutus to stab Caesar 'would be asserting nothing whatever which could conceivably be true or false, except, perhaps, that Brutus' action occurred'.

Again it isn't true that three hundred and twenty-six multiplied by three comes to nine hundred and eighty-eight. What one who gives a rule says cannot be true or not true. Therefore one who says '326 × 3 = 988' is not giving a rule.

Moore knows these proofs perfectly well of course. We all do. That's what makes them *so* boring.

8. *Take now what Moore says in his Reply about Lazerowitz's paper.*[2] Lazerowitz with great clarity and compactness explains that though taking a hurried glance at philosophers you might think that they were engaged on a scientific inquiry and that the

---

[1] *The Philosophy of G. E. Moore* (ed. by P. A. Schilpp), p. 544.
[2] *The Philosophy of G. E. Moore* (ed. by P. A. Schilpp), p. 675.

very good ones could tell you what happens when you remember
your breakfast, like a doctor can tell you what happens when you
digest it, they are not; and that though you might then think
that they were engaged on a logical inquiry as to, e.g. whether the
admitted features of philosophical discussion entail that it is or is
not logical discussion, they are not. In the course of doing this
he explains something of how what they are doing differs from
these two things which you might think it is. Then, searching for
a *mnemonic* description, summing up the things he has said, he tries
'Philosophers aren't making statements, factual or not, but are
making notational recommendations'.

What does Moore do? He thinks of the most typical case of
recommending a notation. It is, as we must all agree, that of a man
who (1) points out that though we in ordinary language would
not call a so and so a such and such, e.g. a tiger a cat, yet the
differences are unimportant or just such as in other cases we don't
count; (2) says in so many words 'We ought to call tigers cats'
and (3) means by this that we ought to do this as a regular thing.
Moore then says that philosophers don't do all that. Undoubtedly
he is right.

9. *I call Moore's procedure 'legalistic'.* I don't want to say that
a legalistic procedure never does good — especially in the hands
of someone so penetrating and utterly first-rate as Moore. On the
contrary, without it we could hardly do philosophy. It stops our
glibness, it forces us to realize that 'there's more to it than that'.
But if we never leave it, it leads to endless worrying, and philosophy becomes hopeless.

Moore's complaints, Moore's refutation, may make Lazerowitz
amplify and 'explain' his account of the likeness and unlikeness
between philosophical statements and verbal recommendations.
But is such 'amendment' wise?[1] I admit I've begun it in my
paper in the Moore volume. But I doubt the wisdom of what I
did. It only encourages people to think that we are trying to get
it right. And the legalists will never be satisfied with what we
say until it is reduced to a platitude.[2]

---

[1] The disastrous effects of qualms in an iconoclast are seen in Mr. Ayer's last book,
The Foundations of Empirical Knowledge. And people readily mistake mock qualms for
real ones.
[2] A good example is Stace's note on Whitehead's doctrine that everything is everywhere (*Mind*, January, 1943, p. 61, ll. 12-28).

By a legalistic procedure I mean the following: We are trying
to describe a newly-discovered but carefully-examined kind of
animal. We know all about this animal so there is no question of
telling ourselves untruths about it. Even so the legalist won't
allow us to stretch or narrow for the occasion the use of old
words in order to describe the new animal so as to give us a grasp
of its relation to other animals.

10. *We can meet this by describing the animals little point by little
point*, by ears and teeth and tails, by food and drink and mates
and miles per hour, by day and night, in winter and in spring. The
legalist can do this too. But why should we confine ourselves to
this? In other matters, in describing other classes of animals, we
adapt language to the occasion. Why not here?

11. *Besides, the detailed description doesn't give us* GRASP. *And
wishing for this, the legalist says 'If we looked harder still couldn't
we find the correct description in general terms?* He means a description in old general terms without alteration in their use, i.e.
keeping them old.

12. *We never shall. For this reason:*

(*a*) *There is already a system of general term descriptions* for talkers
and in particular for talkers in the indicative. Every classification
of facts or propositions generates such a system. Thus we have
contingent and necessary facts, and amongst the necessary facts
mathematical and non-mathematical ones and so on, and to any
class of proposition, π, there corresponds the class of those talkers
who in talking are asserting propositions in π.

(*b*) *But all this of course is nothing to the purpose.* These indeed
are the descriptions which have led to the ontological difficulties,
'Are there then all these different sorts of fact made up of different
sorts of entity?', and to the epistemological difficulties, 'How do we
know them?' These are the descriptions which so long kept us
hanging about those impenetrable coverts where universals lurked,
facts preyed upon events, and variables with logical constants
frolicked for ever down the rides of infinity.

(*c*) *At last Wittgenstein gave tongue and the quarry went away to
the notes of 'Don't ask for the meaning [analysis], ask for the use',
and the transformations of the formal mode* — transformations such
as these: 'X in saying that S is P is asserting a general proposition'
means 'X in saying that S is P is using the sentence "S is P"

generally'; 'X in saying that S is P is asserting a proposition
about mathematical entities' means 'X is using the sentence
"S is P" mathematically'; 'X in saying that S is P, e.g. that there's
a dagger in the air, is asserting a material thing proposition'
means 'X is using the sentence "S is P", e.g. "There's a dagger
in the air" materially, i.e. objectively'; 'X in saying S is P, e.g.
There's a dagger in the air, is asserting a proposition about a
sense-datum merely' means 'X is using "There's a dagger in the
air" subjectively'; 'S is P is an ethical proposition' means
' "S is P" is an ethical sentence', i.e. 'The sentence "S is P" is
used ethically'.

(*d*) *But the benefits of the new formal mode descriptions lie only
in this, that they leave us free to begin.* They leave us with the old
questions though wonderfully transformed. For they leave us
with the questions 'What do you mean by "ethically", "subjectively", "generally"?' And if when faced with this question we
are obsessed with the subject-matter idea, that is the idea that all
sentences in the indicative differ only in the way that sentences
about dogs and cats or even wind and water differ, then we shall
soon find ourselves back where we started, with unknowable
categories of reality for ever seeking to devour each other.

(*e*) On the other hand *if we permit ourselves to imagine vividly
the talkers and the occasions when sentences of the sorts in question
are used and then describe the talkers by setting down a lot of that about
them which makes us say that they are using sentences 'generally', 'ethically',* etc., including all their purposes, and therefore purposes other
than preparing their hearers for tigers or no cake, and all their
ways of supporting their sentences (not tied down by logic-book
models) *then we shall have descriptions of all talkers which, though
very long and still incomplete, involve nothing but talk, nods, smiles,
and surprises.*

(*f*) *Now again it may be asked, 'Is there no system of general
descriptions, are there no general words, which would enable us to
describe utterances well enough without this endless detail?* Does a
statistical description in terms of mean, mean deviation, inter-
quartile range, describe well enough the individuals we have
examined?' Well enough for what? Well enough for some things
but not for others. It all depends. Certainly there is a system of
general words for describing utterances – 'imperative', 'inter-

rogative', 'indicative', 'indicative used generally', 'necessarily', 'ethically', etc., in fact the system of words already mentioned.

(*g*) *But for removing philosophical puzzles these words won't do until it is too late to save our labours, for they won't do until the point-by-point descriptions have been given.* Even then if we go back to the old general words only we shall soon half lose what we have gained. Looking at the detailed pictures of utterances, we saw them all anew and in doing so saw how the old system of descriptions hid so many of their varieties of purpose and of logic; regardless of distortion they were crammed into boxes with labels on – no need to look inside.

(*h*) *It is not because it's bad that the old system won't do, but because it's old.* As we all know but won't remember, any classificatory system is a net spread on the blessed manifold of the individual and blinding us not to all but to too many of its varieties and continuities. A new system will do the same but not in just the same ways. So that in accepting *all* the systems their blinding power is broken, their revealing power becomes acceptable; the individual is restored to us, not isolated as before we used language, not in a box as when language mastered us, but in 'creation's chorus'.

MOORE'S TECHNIQUE
(*The Philosophy of G. E. Moore*)

In the preface to his *Principia Ethica* Moore wrote 'It appears to me that in Ethics, as in all other philosophical studies, the difficulties and disagreements, of which its history is full, are mainly due to a very simple cause: namely to the attempt to answer questions, without first discovering precisely *what* question it is which you desire to answer'.

I remember with what renewed hope I read these words. I was beginning the study of philosophy and had been reading Johnson's *Logic* and Stout's *Groundwork of Psychology* and there had grown in me an unspoken fear that I should never understand the stuff. Here, in Moore, was someone first-rate suggesting that philosophers themselves do not know very well what they are talking about. And what a pleasure was the simple, direct, child-like quality of what followed in *Principia Ethica*. I was reminded at once of the dialogues of Plato.

And how delighted I was with Moore's lectures. But here I must confess — what I did not at the time own to myself — I was shocked and disappointed when Moore began his lectures on the Soul by saying that he agreed with Ward that the existence of the Soul or Self is an 'inexpugnable assumption'. True he explained that what he meant was that such sentences as 'I see this', 'I feel sick', sometimes express facts and this did seem very unexceptionable. But I felt that though to doubt such things is of course eccentric, nevertheless it is not satisfactory, it is not satisfying, to set aside these doubts without any answering of them, without any attempt to say how we know what we know if we know anything at all. As Mr. J. W. Harvey writes in a paper to the Aristotelian Society

> the attitude of 'common sense' is by no means so brusque and dogmatic and unqualified as Moore would intimate. It is more like this: '*Of course* all these facts are true, and I am quite sure they are; but I suppose that in the strictest sense of all I can't claim to *know* them absolutely. I should be mad to deny them or even to doubt them, and yet — '.[1]

[1] *Proceedings of the Aristotelian Society* for 1940-1, 157.

I have often noticed in people beginning philosophy that when they are confronted with this move of Moore's 'The question isn't "Do we know these things?" but "What is the analysis of what we know in knowing these things?"' then they feel that they came to buy one thing and that the man behind the counter is trying to sell them 'something just as good — better in fact'.

They came for guidance in profound inquiry as to whether what they had always regarded as unquestionable *is* unquestionable. Moore tries to turn them by making their profound questions seem ridiculous and telling them that what they really want is an analysis of what it is they hold unquestionable. In short, Moore's cheerful acceptance of 'we know this, but we don't know how we know it' bothers people.[1] They feel it is *unphilosophical*. Moore is well aware of this. In one of his most recent publications, 'Proof of an External World',[2] he quotes Kant 'It still remains a scandal to philosophy . . . that the existence of things outside of us must be accepted merely on *faith*, and that, if anyone thinks good to doubt their existence, we are unable to counter his doubts by any satisfactory proof'. Moore proceeds to offer a proof that things outside us exist. That they exist follows, he says, from what one knows when, lifting first one hand and then the other, one says 'Here's one hand and here's another'. He then writes (p. 298): 'I am perfectly aware that, in spite of all that I have said, many philosophers will still feel that I have not given any satisfactory proof of the point in question'. And on the last page he explains that he thinks that one reason why people think his proof unsatisfactory is that they think that if he can't *prove* his premiss then he does not *know* it. This he holds to be 'a definite mistake'. That is, he insists that one may know a thing without being able to prove it.

To this, I am sure, people would reply 'Of course *some* things are known without proof. One knows without proof that $1+1$ makes 2, and one knows immediately and without proof that one feels sick or that one sees the appearance of a dagger. But it's different with "There's a real dagger there". That is not known immediately. If it is known, it is known on the basis of

---

[1] It is not that Moore never asks 'How do we know?' but that this never leads him to ask 'Do we know?'

[2] *Proceedings of the British Academy*, Vol. XXV, 1939.

other knowledge which collected together establishes it. But is there anything we know from which we can really establish for certain that there is a real dagger there? If so what is it? This is what we are concerned with. We know well enough what we mean when we say "There's a dagger in the air — a real dagger". The question which interests us is "How do we know that what we mean is so?" '

This brings us to another way in which Moore's practice with its implication as to the proper business of philosophy dissatisfies people. When Moore said that he was going to start from the position that we know that the soul exists in the sense that such a sentence as 'I feel sick' expresses a fact, then I felt 'If you are sure of that why bother about anything more? Who cares about the analysis? What is this analysis you make so much fuss about?' I had expected an inquiry into an age-old doubt into whether we really know that we have souls. Was I to be persuaded to spend my time cutting capers defining these statements which, with more than religious dogmatism, Moore refused to question? It was the same with the existence of matter. I had expected an investigation of the suggestion that all is illusion, that the earth and all that's on it is nothing but the image of a dream, the echo of a thought. Instead I was presented with the double image argument[1] to prove that when, on seeing a brown elliptical sense-datum in my purse, I say 'That's a penny' I am not judging with regard to the sense-datum that it's part of the surface of a penny. I had supposed that we should discuss whether what ordinary men took to be certain and well justified could be passed as such after careful investigation by experts. I had come to ask whether Idealism was true and matter a myth, just as I had come to Moore's lectures on the soul in order to find out whether Materialism was true and minds and souls a fond illusion born of desire that there should be more behind the faces of our friends than there is behind the faces of our clocks, which after all know the time and can't bear a cold bath. And, of course, I wasn't peculiar in this. Many people come to philosophy because they want a basis or a substitute for religion. To adapt the words of the editor of *Contemporary British Philosophy*, they hope to explore with the help of the

---

[1] *Contemporary British Philosophy*, Second Series, 220.

best guides 'the frontier provinces of human experience' and to gain 'authentic tidings of what lies beyond'.

Instead, Moore offers a game of Logic, and a peculiar one at that; for it lacks much that gives satisfaction in ordinary logic and mathematics. In it no architecture of proof is possible, and with that goes too the Q.E.D. with its note of agreement achieved and triumphant discovery.

This brings us to a new source of dissatisfaction with Moore's account of philosophy. It isn't done in the way it should be done, if its questions and conclusions are such as he says. Its logic is not the logic of logic and arithmetic. Consider. Do philosophers (1) prove by chains of demonstrative reasoning what they wish to say or (2), without attempting to support in any way one thing by another, just set out the self-evident or what appears to them self-evident? This question gives one a queer feeling because one wants to answer that they do both and neither. It isn't that they do the one with some of the things they say and the other with other things they say. It is that in the case of their most characteristic claims they seem to rely upon a mixture of self-evidence which isn't quite clear with proof which isn't quite conclusive. And when one of them such as Spinoza or McTaggart, or even Moore in his short demonstrations, attempts a 'geometrical' technique, other philosophers become a little nervous and embarrassed, feeling that somehow this won't do, like hunting people when one of their number, respected because undoubtedly he goes very well, insists on coming out in clothes deplorably reminiscent of the racing stable. It is true that, when we read, for example, Hume's appendix on the analysis of right and good or Broad on theories of the nature of matter, we find that a number of what Mill might call 'considerations capable of influencing the intellect' are advanced. But they are not connected chainwise. They *independently* bear upon the issue.

It is true that, on Moore's account of philosophy as analysis of what is ordinarily meant by ordinary and familiar sentences, we should not expect long chains of reasoning. The question, 'When I say of a picture that it is good, does this amount to a claim about how people feel to it?' doesn't lend itself to long demonstrative argument. After all, if we know what we mean by the one and what we mean by the other, then surely it is easy for us to tell whether what we mean by the one is or is not what we mean by the other? And surely we do know what we mean by these sentences. Moore allows and insists that we know what we mean by everyday sentences in the sense that we understand them, but he also insists that we don't know what we mean in the sense that we don't know the analysis of what we mean.[1]

It is I feel a defect in his essay that he gives no explanation of what it is to know the analysis of what is meant by an expression nor of how this is difficult. Disciples of Moore[2] have said that to know the analysis of the proposition P is to find a sentence 'P₁' which more clearly than the sentence 'P' reveals the structure of P.

To use Moore's example, I know the analysis of the proposition *Alfred is the brother of Bill* when I notice that it is what can also be expressed by 'Alfred and Bill are males and Alfred and Bill have the same parents'. With this account of what analysis is, the difficulty in finding the analysis of a proposition P is the difficulty of finding a sentence 'P₁' which, although it means the same as the sentence 'P', reveals more clearly the structure of the proposition they both express. 'And surely', Moore would say, 'even when we know what two sentences mean, it is sometimes difficult to tell, to see,[3] whether what the one means is the same as what the other means.'

This complaint 'I can't see clearly' is a complaint characteristic of one who does philosophy as if it were analysis, as if it were logic. The complaint 'I can't see clearly' is understandable in a complicated subject-matter (notational game) such as mathematics. But philosophical issues have not this sort of complexity. Have they some other sort of complexity dealt with by philosophical calculation, by advancing considerations? But what, on the logico-analytic account of philosphy, would this other sort of complexity be? We are not told; even the need of it as an explanation of difficulty in philosophy is not recognized. We are left complaining that, though we can see very well the pro-

---

[1] *Contemp. Brit. Phil.*, 198.

[2] A. E. Duncan-Jones, *Aristotelian Society Suppl.* Vol. XVI, 'Does Philosophy Analyse Common Sense?' especially p. 148. John Wisdom, *Aristotelian Society Suppl.* Vol. XIII for 1934.

[3] In this substitution of 'see' for 'tell' lies the ruin of the logico-analytic technique. In the substitution of 'ascertain' for both lies the power of the formal mode which transforms philosophy from a matter of insight into one of industry.

positions expressed by two sentences, we cannot see whether or
no they are identical. At once the impotence of the analytic
technique gives rise to suspicion which finds expression in the
question 'Why can't we see? What mist is it that for ever obscures
the timeless ranges of the abstract?'

This line of inquiry 'What is philosophical analysis? What
makes definition difficult[1] and philosophical definition specially
difficult?' is one way of seeing what is good and what is bad in
Moore's saying that what philosophers ought to concern themselves with is 'What is the analysis of...?' But here I want to
do this in another way, namely by seeing how far he is wrong
(a) in saying that philosophers ought not to have concerned
themselves with the truth of everyday statements but with their
analysis (b) in saying that in fact they have concerned themselves
with the truth of the statements and not with their analysis.

To begin with, notice that not only is it puzzling why philosophy should be so difficult if it is a matter of inspection – there
is the further point that mostly it is not done by inspection but
by 'advancing considerations capable of influencing the intellect'.
Even amongst the purest analysts there lingers still the use of
the words 'plausible', 'unplausible' – shocking survivals of
the scientific theory, i.e. the theory that philosophy is science,
only grander and stricter. For instance Professor C. D. Broad
has, fortunately for the truth, never been properly cured
of this idea. To the horror of his friends he will suddenly
lapse into representing rival philosophical theories as rival hypotheses about what must be the case among the entirely unobservable or obscurely observable in order to account for what
is undoubtedly the case amongst the immediately observable.
The business of philosophers becomes at once that of finding
which is the most probable of these hypotheses in view of the
varied and conflicting evidences we have which bear upon them.
No wonder that, though Broad sometimes speaks, like Moore,
as if philosophy were the job of finding the analysis of what is
naturally indicated by phrases like 'I am seeing a chair', 'I am
hearing a bell', he more often speaks of it as if it were the finding
of the most probable hypothesis explanatory of what we can in

---

[1] A. E. Duncan-Jones, *Aristotelian Society Suppl.* Vol. XVI, 'Does Philosophy Analyse
Common Sense?' 148.

the strictest sense observe – as if it were science, only more so.
What happens is this. When Broad tackles a philosophical
difficulty he finds himself carrying on the dispute in a certain
way; he finds himself considering arguments for and against.
One cannot speak of the logic of a study in one way and of its
conclusions in another. Consequently Broad often speaks of
philosophy as though it were a matter of finding out how much
is probably true of what we ordinarily mean by such statements
as 'The earth has existed for many years past', 'I have half-a-
crown left'. He often speaks as if, although these statements in
so far as they merely record and predict the observable are
unquestionable, they are nevertheless questionable in respect of
a hypothesis tacitly assumed in them. In so far as the statement
that a bucket of water is spinning and the earth stationary merely
records and predicts appearances it is unquestionable. It is only
in so far as it 'involves the hypothesis of absolute motion' that
it is questionable.[1] And isn't the probability of this hypothesis a
scientific matter?

How well this way of putting things suits us! It fits our feeling
that for practical purposes it is mad to doubt such statements as
'I have half-a-crown left' and also our feeling that somehow one
who questions whether we really know them deserves to be
taken seriously. It fits our feeling that philosophy is somehow
about what world we are in and not merely the make up of the
meanings of words. Finally it fits the fact that philosophy is
difficult in the way of estimating the force of different and
opposing reasons, and something that is decided neither by simple
gazing nor by climbing long ladders of proof.

But alas, gently and persuasively as this way of looking at
philosophy is introduced by Broad, the brutal fact remains that
if we follow him we shall be exposed to Moore's too innocent
astonishment. For we shall be talking like Moore's philosopher[2]
who, when asked whether he does or doesn't believe that the
earth has existed for many years past, replies

> It all depends on what you mean by the 'earth' and 'exists'
> and 'years': if you mean so and so, and so and so, and so and

[1] See C. D. Broad on Absolute and Relative Motion in *Scientific Thought*, and *The Mind and Its Place in Nature*, 187.
[2] *Cont. Brit. Phil.*, 198.

so, then I do; but if you mean so and so, and so and so, and so and so, or so and so, and so and so, and so and so, or so and so, and so and so, and so and so, then I don't, or at least I think it is extremely doubtful.

I can't face cutting such a figure as this. Nor can Broad, really. That's why he says '... no one doubts that such phrases as "I see a bell", "I feel a bell", "I hear a bell", indicate states of affairs which actually exist from time to time. People do not begin to quarrel till they try to *analyse* such situations'. Again he says 'I will call such situations as are naturally indicated by phrases like "I am seeing a chair", "I am hearing a bell" by the name of Perceptual Situations. I take it then that everyone agrees that there are such things as Perceptual Situations'.[1]

But though Broad says these things, he also says in the very same paragraphs,

> People do not begin to quarrel till they try to *analyse* such situations, and to ask what must be meant by 'I', by the 'bell', and by 'hearing', if it is to be true that I hear a bell. When they do this they are liable to find that the only senses of 'I', 'bell' and 'hear' which will make the statement true are very different from those which we are wont to attach to these words.[2]

The stresses and strains which have made even such a man as Broad contradict himself here are the very ones I want to bring to light. Let us think how he might try to explain away the contradiction. The things he says elsewhere suggest two ways in which he might try to do this. First he might say, 'When I say that no one doubts that such phrases as "I hear a bell" indicate situations which from time to time exist, I mean nothing incompatible with what is after all a fact; namely that some people raise doubts about the existence of selves or minds and about the existence of physical objects. All I mean when I say that we are all agreed that such situations as are naturally indicated by phrases like "I see a bell", "I hear a bell", exist, is that in so far as

[1] *The Mind and Its Place in Nature*, 140-1.
[2] See also *The Mind and Its Place in Nature*, 184-6, 'I think that it is now abundantly evident that very little can be done for common-sense'. '*Any* theory that can possibly fit the facts is *certain* to shock common-sense somewhere'

these statements merely tell us which pattern of the observable may now be expected they are very often quite right and that no one doubts this. When I say that when we look into the matter of what must be meant by "I", "bell" and "hear", if the statement "I hear a bell" is to be true, then we are liable to find that these must be senses very different from the ordinary, and that some people doubt the existence of selves and bells, what I mean is that in the ordinary use of these expressions *they imply hypotheses* as to what lies beyond the observable, beyond "the frontiers of human experience", and that these hypotheses are entirely doubtful'.[1]

We have seen how this talk suits us; but we have also noticed that it involves saying 'You ask "Do we know that the earth has existed for many years past?" It all depends on what you mean by "the earth" etc.' In fact we have noticed that it involves our being unable to answer the plain question 'Have you a shilling for the gas?' with a 'Yes' or a 'No'.

To avoid this, Broad might reply in another way, and what he says on p. 148 of *The Mind and Its Place in Nature* shows that quite likely he would reply in another way, namely as follows: 'What I mean is that "I hear a bell", in so far as we assume nothing about the analysis of what it expresses, is often undoubtedly true, that is, the situation it describes from time to time exists. But to describe this situation by the phrase "I hear a bell" inevitably suggests a certain mode of analysis for the situation. It suggests that it consists of me and the physical object whose name appears in the phrase, related directly by an asymmetrical two-term relation which is indicated by the verb. And this suggests that the admitted existence of the situation guarantees the existence of me and of the bell, which in their turn guarantees respectively the existence of selves and of physical objects'.

We shall find that this answer takes us back to Moore's account of philosophy and so does not give us the advantages which Broad seemed to promise us. For it is impossible excusably to say that I have sixpence although neither sixpences nor any other material things exist, without turning this apparent negative hypothesis or existential denial into the analytic proposition 'Material things are nothing over and above sensations, i.e.

---

[1] Cf. *The Mind and Its Place in Nature*, 185.

though they are not fictions, they are logical fictions'. How far this is excusable, i.e. how far this is not an entirely unheard-of use of 'Matter exists' is also the question of how far philosophers have been doing what Moore says they should have been doing and of how far they have not been doing what Moore says they have been doing. It is a somewhat intricate investigation.

Notice to begin with that in saying that I may have a sixpence, although there are no sixpences and Matter doesn't exist, Broad is again trying to get the best of both worlds. To avoid shock to common sense, he says that undoubtedly the situations we describe by 'I know the earth has existed for many years past', 'I hear a bell', 'I've got sixpence' exist. To avoid shock to the philosophers, he says that nevertheless the questions 'Does matter exist?' 'Does mind exist?' are serious questions because the existence of the situations does not guarantee the existence of the earth, of the bell, of me, of the sixpence. Undoubtedly I've got sixpence, but maybe there are no sixpences.

Put like this what Broad says sounds just absurd. It is absurd, but of course it isn't just absurd. One can readily feel that Broad says what he does because he knows that once he allows that it is unquestionable that two hands exist, then he will have to allow that it is unquestionable that Matter exists, unless he says that hands aren't material things or else that the existence of material things does not imply the existence of Matter. At the same time he feels that 'Matter exists' is *not* unquestionable in the way that 'I have raised my hands' is.

In this he is in good company and *ipso facto* right. For Berkeley denied that Matter existed but denied that he denied the existence of the gardener's cherry. And when Wittgenstein heard Moore's proof of an external world he said: 'Those philosophers who have denied the existence of Matter have not wished to deny that under my trousers I wear pants'. In fact, Moore's proof is too good to be true — like all good proofs in philosophy its value depends upon its invalidity. I must explain myself. To claim that Moore's proof is valid is to claim that 'Matter exists' is so linked with 'I have two hands' that it cannot be more questionable than 'I have two hands'. And yet, if this is so and 'Matter exists' is as unquestionable as 'I have two hands', then what is the point of the proof?

Someone may protest 'This complaint can be brought against any demonstrative argument. In demonstrative argument the conclusion *at first* seems questionable and *then*, when in the course of proof its connection with an unquestionable proposition is noticed, it itself becomes unquestionable'.

This answer is available in those cases where demonstrative argument feels useful, i.e. in complex cases such as algebraic problems. My point at the moment is that this sort of answer is not available for Moore's proof. For it is quite incredible that the reason why philosophers have found 'Matter exists' questionable whereas they have found 'I have just raised my hands' unquestionable is that they have failed to see a connection between the two.

In the course of a good proof the level of certainty for the conclusion rises to that of the premisses and the level of certainty of the falsity of the premisses rises to the level of certainty of the falsity of the conclusion. When the level of the independent certainty of the premisses is great and there is nothing against the conclusion, as in mathematical calculations, then we speak of proving the truth of the conclusion from the truth of the premisses. When the independent certainty of the falsity of the conclusion is great, whereas the premisses are weak, then we speak of the falsity of the conclusion proving the falsity of the premisses. In the latter case we often speak of the falsity of the conclusion as a premiss and of the falsity of the premisses as a conclusion, and this conceals the reversibility of demonstrative argument. But the reversibility is there. Proof is like putting a pipe between two tubs of water. Now in mathematical argument it is possible to have a conclusion with nothing against it and *apparently* little for it, which is nevertheless connected absolutely with premisses with a high level of certainty, e.g. he has exactly 3068 sheep; for he has thirteen flocks of 236 sheep each. This is because the connection, though flawless and absolute, is in complex cases not apparent. But the simpler the case the more impossible does this become, and always, when a simple demonstrative proof is offered of something which, before the proof was offered, seemed entirely questionable, one is suspicious, especially when the questionableness arises not from absence of forces for or against but from conflict of forces for and against.

This is why Moore's proof is suspect. Such proofs are questioned because they are questionable, however unquestionable are their premisses and the steps involved in them. We can easily begin to see why they are questionable.

Short proofs of the questionable are usually sophistical and their sophisticalness is a play on words. In the simplest and crudest cases the words of the conclusion are ambiguous. This ambiguity in these cases is the explanation of our hesitation as to the conclusion and also of our suspicion of the proof. In one sense the words express something which undoubtedly follows from the premisses and is undoubtedly true and quite unexciting. In another sense the words express something which is exciting but which does not follow from the premisses. These however are the crude cases. They are so crude they hardly confuse us. We are merely amused by a man who argues 'Each day he draws (in black and white) on the bank (of the river) so he must be very rich'. The confusing cases are the subtler ones which rely not upon ambiguity, i.e. an already manifested conflict about the use of a word, but upon a hitherto concealed conflict as to the use of a word. For example, consider the case of Smith who raises Jones's salary on the day he said he would but *only* because he fears Jones's leaving for another job. One philosopher may insist that this is not the keeping of a promise. Another philosopher may *prove* it is a case of promise-keeping. He proceeds somewhat as follows: 'Smith unquestionably has done that which he said he would do. A man who does what he has said he would do keeps his promise. Therefore Smith has kept his promise'. All this proof really does for us is to bring out where and how we are undecided even when fully informed about a case whether to describe it as a promise keeping or not. But, although this is all the proof does, it is to be noticed that it cannot fairly and plainly be called invalid. It neither involves a slip, such as affirming the consequent or taking seven eights to be sixty-four, nor is it a case of ambiguity. This is why even this sample dispute may puzzle us. And in face of it people make the same desperate moves — questioning the unquestionable premiss that Smith has done what he said he would do or turning from that to questioning the unquestionable connection between doing what one has said one will do and keeping one's promises. As in philosophy, unquestionable premisses have led by unquestionable steps to an entirely questionable conclusion. In these cases the difficulty is not removed by doing any of the only three things to be done, namely (1) deny the premiss, (2) protest at a step, (3) accept the conclusion. For, whichever one does, the repressed objectionableness of it leaves a haunting anxiety which in the end leads to rebellion in oneself or others.

We have already seen the same puzzlement and futile attempts at escape produced by Moore's proof of the existence of Matter. This is, I claim, because Moore's proof is sophistical in the subtle way I have been hinting at, though the sources of the sophistry or questionableness are here much more complicated than in the proof that Smith kept his promise. If Moore's proof is sophistical, questionable, that will be no more than was to be expected.

Philosophers who have not questioned that Moore has two hands or have hesitated to deny it have yet questioned and even denied that Matter exists. Now, as we have seen, it is not to be supposed that they did this because, although the latter unquestionably follows from the former, they failed to notice this connection. If this is not the explanation, what is? Moore submits that one reason is that philosophers question his unquestionable premiss. We have noticed Broad's inclination to do this and we can feel an inclination to do the same ourselves. It is indeed part of my contention that the unsatisfactoriness of Moore's proof lies partly in the premiss, because it is my contention that the unsatisfactoriness does not lie wholly in the premiss nor wholly in the connection. But what at the moment I want to do is to question Moore's unquestionable connection or step, and to bring out the inclinations as to the use of 'Matter exists' and 'I put up my hand' which enable Moore to prove in an argument of one step from the unquestionable premiss 'I put up my hand' the so much questioned conclusion 'Matter exists' and enables Broad at the same time to question this step. What I want to do is not to insist that it is questionable whether there is a connection between 'I put up my hand' and 'Matter exists', but to insist that the connection is questionable – like the connection between doing what one has said one will do and keeping a promise.

It is true that some philosophers who deny the existence of

Matter try to be consistent to the bitter end and, when taxed with such a question as 'D'you mean that I am not standing up and talking with you now?' reply: 'Strictly, you are not'. Our inclination to draw this inference and their inclination to accept it makes it not incorrect to say that 'Matter doesn't exist' implies the falsity of statements about hands, sixpences, etc. On the other hand, very many philosophers when taxed with these concrete questions begin to hesitate and to say such things as 'When I said that Matter doesn't exist I meant only that nothing exists over and above or beyond or below our sensations. When a scientist or ordinary man such as the gardener talks about cherries all he says is something about the pattern of sensations which we may expect and these statements are often true enough What I wanted to insist upon was that their truth involves no more than a pattern amongst our sensations, although they are as we say about material things. For material things just are bundles of sensations or, more correctly, they are logical constructions out of sensations. They are not entities whose existence is inferred from sensations. Sensations do not provide a basis for inference to entities other than themselves of which they are shadows on the *tabula rasa* of the mind. Such entities are fictions, and, if by material things you mean such entities, then material things are fictions as gorgons and harpies are fictions. But what I meant was that, though our talk about our sensations and physical things is on the model of a substance acting through the media of our sense-organs and nerves to throw shadows upon a screen in our brains, in fact this is only a figure of speech as when we say that I now can't lift the calf because his weight has so much increased or can't buy diamonds because their value has so much increased. In short, I meant that material things are logical fictions or logical constructions'.

One feels inclined to reply: 'If that's what you meant it's a thousand pities you didn't say so'. Or could one reply: 'It's a thousand pities you didn't say what you meant'? Could one? In view of the fact that on the covers of their books they print the warning 'Philosophy' and that so many of them inside misuse language like this, is it a misuse? For the first thing that strikes me about their sort of talk about Matter, I mean this hedging, modifying, talk about Matter in the course of which 'Matter doesn't exist' is transformed from an iconoclastic denial like 'Fairies, unicorns, dinosaurs don't exist' into the analytic proposition 'Statements about material things can be analysed into statements about sensations', is its familiar ring. I am sure I have heard it before. Now I remember someone saying 'There is really no such thing as beauty', (he covertly looks for shocked faces in his hearers) and a moment later saying 'What we call the beauty of a thing is nothing but our feelings towards it'. The modification which the iconoclast makes is a preparation for defending himself agaist the Moorian attack: 'No such thing as beauty? No difference between Salisbury Cathedral and the Albert Memorial?'

Again I can hear someone say: 'There are no such things as minds or souls, thoughts or feelings'. Again shocked faces. Again a champion sets lance in rest and cries: 'No difference between a dog who greets you and a toy which squeaks, no difference between the words of a friend and the chatter of a talking doll? Don't you believe that I understand what you are saying to me?' The materialist is sure to reply: 'Of course there is a difference, and of course I believe that you understand what I say. What I really meant to say was that personality and mind and understanding are just patterns of bodily movements. When a machine responds in a *very* complicated and mysterious way we say it has a mind'.

In all these cases there is the same oscillation which we found in Broad between saying (*a*) that certain statements which we make in everyday life are never true or at least never justified because we put more into them than we ought, and saying (*b*) that they are all true and that 'Beauty (Mind, Matter) doesn't exist' merely warns us that it is nothing over and above what is undoubtedly involved in the everyday statements, namely feelings of exhilaration, etc. (patterns of bodily movements, patterns of sensations). To put the matter another way: In all these cases people cannot make up their minds between saying that everyday statements involving such and such a category of being, Beauty, Mind, Matter, Necessity, are all false because we put more into them than we ought, and saying on the contrary that they are all true, only we must be careful to remember that they don't involve more than they do.

Those who say the latter explain that when they say that X, the category, does not exist, what they mean is that X's are nothing over and above what is indubitably involved in statements about X. Thus those who say that all the statements we make about Beauty are true explain that what they meant when they said that Beauty does not exist is simply that it is not something over and above our aesthetic feelings. And, to put things the other way round, we can easily imagine that James should not have said that emotions and thoughts just are organic sensations, that love is a heartache, thought a headache, but that he should have said instead that there are no emotions or thoughts; that there is no fear, only a shiver down the back and a feeling of the tensing of the galloping muscles, that there is no anger only a feeling of the clenching of the fist. Indeed, so easily, so nonchalantly, is this transition made from saying that 'X's don't exist' to 'X's are nothing but Y's' that we cannot call eccentric those who say that this is what they mean by 'X's don't exist'. And if we can't call them eccentric we can't call them wrong. For consider: if a man insists on saying that $1 \times 0 = 1$, that $2 \times 0 = 2$, that $3 \times 0 = 3$ and so on and does this consistently, then it is as much as we can do to say he is wrong even if no one goes with him in the matter. If many go with him then to insist that he's wrong is like insisting that those who say that fox hounds are not dogs are wrong. Maybe they have called not only terriers but collies, Alsatians, retrievers and spaniels dogs. Maybe foxhounds have heads and ears and tails and paws and coats extremely like one or other of the sorts of animal which these people have called dogs. We can say if we like that these people use the word 'dog' in a narrow and arbitrary way. But all this does not prove them wrong if enough of them do it. The man who says that $2 \times 0 = 2$ allows very likely that $2 \times 3 = 2 + 2 + 2$ and that $2 \times 2 = 2 + 2$ and that $2 \times 1 = 2$ and the same for 3 and 4 and so on. But all this doesn't prove him wrong. Even if we try to trick him by saying after going through many translations of multiplications into additions '*And in general* where n and m are any two integers $n \times m = n + n + n$ etc. m times', he may still refuse to accept our conclusion. For he may say 'Ah, but 0 is not an integer' or he may say 'Ah, the rule holds for all integers except o – which is different'. And different it is, undeniably it is different.

Likewise Moore may argue '(i) If collies are dogs and terriers are dogs, then if there are two collies sitting in the sun in the yard *or* two terriers chasing each other there *or* one collie sitting there and a terrier trying to make him play then there are dogs in the yard. (ii) If there's a pear and a peach on the wall then there's fruit in the garden. (iii) If there's a Packard and a Pierce Arrow on Fifth Avenue then the automobile still exists in New York. In general, if there's an X and a Y in O and both are Z, then there are Z's in O. Hence, if there's a sixpence in my pocket and a biscuit in the tin there are material things in the world'. Moore may argue like this and, indeed, the argument sets out in words where that difficulty comes from which we feel in saying that though I've got sixpence there are no material things and Matter doesn't exist. The difficulty lies in this, that to speak so goes against all our habits in the use of all genus-species words. But the fact is the most general genus words, i.e. category words, are peculiar and are not related to their species words just as other genus words are related to their species words. In particular, when X is a category word there is an inclination to say: 'When I said "There is no such thing as X" or "Really there are no such things as X's" I did not wish to imply what you might naturally suppose, that all statements about things which are X's are false; I meant only that X's are abstractions, logical fictions, logical constructions, i.e. that statements in which something is said about an X or X's can be analysed into statements which say something, though not the same thing, about Y's'.

This inclination is widespread and obstinate. This in itself makes it impossible to complain to a philosopher who says that by 'Matter doesn't exist' he means 'Statements about matter can be analysed into statements which are not about matter', that he is not saying what he means when he says 'Matter doesn't exist'. Nor is this all. There is no widespread inclination without a widespread cause, and when the cause isn't a slip it's an excuse, a reason. It seems quite natural to express the logical fact that statements about the average man can be analysed, re-formulated, into statements which are about no such thing, in the form of an existential denial, namely, 'The average man doesn't really exist'. It's muddling to express oneself this way and it may temporarily confuse others and even oneself into suspecting those everyday remarks which one makes with the help of the expression 'The average man' such as 'The average man prefers a bitter to a gin and lime'. It's muddling, but it's natural. It's natural because ordinary language suggests that the relation between the average man who somehow represents the taste, etc., of individual men is related to them in the way that a member of Parliament is related to his constituency; and the existential denial very forcibly combats this. 'Matter does not exist' does the same for the relation between material things and sensations, i.e. for the relation between statements about material things and statements about sensations.

We must conclude that often there is good reason for saying of a philosopher who has said that 'Matter doesn't exist' that he means that statements about material things are analysable into statements about sensations and that he is not without precedent and without excuse in doing so.

We have seen with the multiplication by 0 and the foxhounds how, in logic as in ethics and aesthetics, any statement supports itself, especially when made by an expert. So, when Berkeley says that 'Matter doesn't exist' doesn't imply that the gardener is wrong in saying that there are cherries left on the trees, that goes a long way to prove this statement correct. And, when Broad agrees with him, that is further strong support. And we have felt the excuse they have for using 'doesn't exist' in this way. We must notice however that they escape the power of Moore's proof only by making 'Does Matter exist?' an analytic issue and thus claiming that what they have been doing is what Moore says they should have been doing, namely analysis, and thus losing the advantages which Broad seemed to promise us.

On the other hand, we shall find that Moore's claim that philosophers, when saying that Matter does not exist, have been discussing a negative existential hypothesis like 'There are no unicorns' has plenty of excuses. As Moore pointed out to me, McTaggart said: 'So Matter is in the same position as the gorgons and the harpies'.[1] And, undoubtedly, people who say that Beauty and Goodness do not exist expect to shock us. So do

---

[1] McTaggart, *Some Dogmas of Religion*, Second Edition, 95.

those who say 'There's no such thing as logical goodness or
validity, only linguistic habits'. So do those who say 'There's
no such thing as thought or feeling, only patterns of behaviour'.
And they do shock us. They send a fear into our hearts. Wheels
turning other wheels they can see. 'But', they ask, 'what justification have you for claiming that these are the spirit of the
living God?'[1] And for the life of us we can't answer. 'I'll
believe it when I see it', they say, and our hearts sink. For we
know that having seen the wheels there'll be nothing more to
see bar more wheels. 'I'll believe it when I see it', says the
native in the Sudan, when we tell him that water in our country
sometimes gets so hard that a man can stand on it. 'I'll believe
it when I see it', says the sceptical child, when we tell him that
all the movements of animals depend upon the beating of a
little organ hidden in the chest, that the state of the cheese
depends upon the presence of minute creatures breeding at a
frightful pace. And it feels as if it is the same admirable habit
of thought which leads to 'Does the tree still exist when I can't
see it?' which in its turn leads to 'Does a tree exist at all?' True
with these last questions the hard-headed thinker finds himself
hoist with his own petard; like those who, having broken the
images of saints and thrown out the holy water of superstition,
find themselves with nothing in their hands but a manuscript of
uncertain date and the stones of the latest archaeological research.
Here it begins to strike the sceptical philosopher that there is
something queer about his doubts, about his negative hypotheses,
about the shocks he intends for others, about the popular illusions
he aims to correct. For what surprise has he in store for the
gardener with his cherry? But what I want to insist upon is that
this feeling of queerness is still half smothered while he still asks:
'Are there material things, permanent and substantial, behind the
fast-fading shadow shows of sensation? What right have we to
suppose that what lies behind what we observe is of this nature
rather than that or indeed that anything at all lies behind it?'
While philosophers use such words they appear to themselves
and to others to advance a negative hypothesis just as a man
may advance the hypothesis that, though there are lights on the
ship that passes and its sails are well set, there's no one aboard.

[1] Ezekiel.

Pointing out that there is no difference in kind between the cases where we should ordinarily claim to have knowledge that there is a real, physical thing which is responsible for our sensations and cases where we should say that this is doubtful, the sceptical philosopher goes on to say that there is never any real reason to believe that there is anything beyond our sensations. Surely all this makes it impossible to claim that by 'Matter doesn't exist' he means that Matter is a bundle of sensations. His approach to his conclusion and the air with which he brings it out are like those with which a man brings out the conclusion 'There's no one aboard'. If his conclusion is really an analytic proposition he certainly doesn't realize this himself nor do his hearers. I am thus led to say that he is making an analytic claim and not a scientific claim but 'he doesn't realize it'; this is a situation which could also be fairly indicated by saying that he *is* still trying to make a scientific claim, like a man who is trying to run on an endless band which prevents his making any progress. We may even say of the runner that he runs though he makes no progress. So we may say with Moore that the sceptical philosopher is sceptical though his scepticism is inoperative, that he is advancing a negative hypothesis. We may fairly choose this way of describing the small but many differences between one who uses the words 'Matter doesn't exist' and one who says 'Matter doesn't really exist' or 'Matter is nothing over and above sensations' or 'Matter is just sensations'.

The man who says 'Matter doesn't exist', even the man who says 'Matter doesn't really exist', feels very differently as he speaks from one who says 'Statements about material things can be analysed into statements about sensations'. But this is only a small part of the difference between them. When a man brings out a general statement we take it as a guide to what he will say and do in a thousand concrete cases. Now there is something queer and barren about the philosopher's 'I don't believe there's any such thing as Matter' which makes it very different from 'I don't believe there's a tiger in there at all'. The 'concrete consequences' are apt to disappoint the plain man who had half expected to see his ailing body disappear in 'a vortex of pure thought'. On the other hand, the man who says 'Matter does not exist' is very different in his reactions to the implications of what he says from the man who says 'Matter is a logical fiction'. The former doesn't look at you as if you are mad if you infer that he denies that there are cherries on a tree or, more concrete still, that there will be any appearance of cherries when we go to look. It is indeed only at this last stage that the barrenness of his doubt is certain to come out. The man who says that 'Matter is a logical fiction' regards you as mad or as not understanding the technical expression 'logical fiction' if you attempt to deduce anything exciting from what he says. The two are very different and it is not until we trace the concrete consequences of 'Matter doesn't exist' right down into what the man expects to see and what he doesn't that we begin to feel the inclination to say that, though he appears to advance a negative hypothesis, he's doing no such thing. Till then we notice more his differences from one who says merely that Matter is a logical fiction; till then the reactions of one who says 'I don't believe in Matter' are very like one who says 'I don't believe there's anyone aboard'. His reactions are undecided over 'Are there then no cherries on the tree?' Moore's proof forces him to decide, forces him to become unmuddled, to gain a grasp of what he wishes to do with his words 'Matter doesn't exist', what he wishes us to understand by them.

When he begins to do this we find his decisions related to what he says in a way different from what we should expect on the analogy of 'I don't believe there's anyone aboard' and much more like what we should expect from one who said 'Matter is a construction out of sensations' – the queerness of his negative hypothesis and its likeness to an analytic statement then comes out.

The queerness of the negative hypothesis 'Matter does not exist' comes out in this way: both the hypothesis that Matter does not exist and the hypothesis that it does are extremely extensive. Each is so extensive that there does not readily occur to one any simple means of verifying the other. For, like the hypothesis of absolute space, they are hypotheses to account for the observable – quite literally for all that is observable, not merely for all that has been observed. So, of course, whatever you saw on looking over the ship would be accounted for *both* by the hypothesis that Matter exists and by the hypothesis that it does not. So that it can favour neither. And this would be so *whatever you saw wherever you looked*. At once we understand why the doubt, 'Does Matter exist?' seemed queer, why the shock, 'There's no such thing as Matter', came to nothing. Broad is quite right, 'Matter exists' and 'Matter does not exist' are hypotheses about what lies behind the observable; only, let us repeat ourselves, they are hypotheses about what lies behind the observable, *all* of the observable. They are hypotheses, but so are the Copernican and Ptolemaic theories; so is the hypothesis of absolute space.

Nevertheless, although it is partly from bad reasons that the philosopher says 'Matter does not exist' instead of 'Matter is a logical fiction', it is also from good reasons.

For, though he is in many ways unlike a man who corrects a popular illusion, e.g. that all the decisions of the Government are dictated by the King, and in many ways it is wrong to say that he is bringing a shock to the plain man, this is not altogether wrong; and what he does is in many ways like what one who corrects a popular illusion does and unlike the mere translation of one class of sentences, e.g. one involving the word 'brother', into others which are applicable in exactly the same cases. Remember how the translation of sentences about the average man seems to make him vanish.

The hypothesis of the non-existence of Matter is not unique in this way. The hypothesis of the non-existence of Space is like it. And didn't the Copernican theory bring a shock to the man in the street? Because a lance is made of sugar icing and could give no real shock to anyone it doesn't follow that it doesn't give a shock at all to bad men who see it against the sky and hear a trumpet just as loud as one accompanying the use of a real lance.

Did the Copernican theory bring a shock to the man in the street who said the sun is sinking? Shall we say that, until Copernicus, ordinary people who said 'The sun is sinking' spoke falsely? Or shall we say that they spoke truly in so far as they recorded and predicted the pattern of the observable, but that they spoke falsely in so far as their assertions involved the hypothesis that the sun goes round the earth? Or shall we say that they spoke truly, but that their way of describing the situation inevitably suggests a picture, a model, for recalling and predicting the facts about the heavenly bodies which is very cumbersome and inconvenient compared with the picture and model suggested by Copernicus's way of describing the situation? Or shall we say that they spoke truly, but that their way of describing the situation 'inevitably suggests a certain mode of analysis' for the situation which, 'though it seems highly plausible while we confine out attention to certain ordinary cases, becomes very much less plausible when we attempt to apply it in certain more out-of-the-way cases'?[1]

Many people still talk of the sun's sinking in the west. Do they now mean something different by this from what people used to mean? Or do they inconsistently, in their 'unreflective moments', forget their scientific principles and in the press of life say things quite untrue or, if not quite untrue, then at least involving hypotheses false or unsupported?

What I am suggesting by asking these questions which have sometimes been called rhetorical but which I would prefer to call *riddle* questions ('Is a tomato a fruit or a vegetable?') — what I am suggesting is, that in these cases of people saying 'The sun is sinking in the west' there is not all the difference one might expect between the claim that they are speaking falsely and making mistaken assumptions and the claim that they are speaking the truth but using a notation, an analysis, which in certain connections is apt to mislead.[2] But, though I wish to suggest in this way that the question 'Which are they doing?' is not quite what it seems, I do not wish to suggest that there are not some of them who more than others are more appropriately described in one way rather than the other, nor that these differences are not of great philosophical importance. If you are faced with a pre-Copernican and a post-Copernican way of saying that the sun is sinking and forced to say that one is false, you will certainly choose the pre-Copernican, although you know that one who uses the pre-Copernican formulation expects to see and hear nothing relevant to the sinking of the sun in any way different from what

---

[1] C. D. Broad, *The Mind and Its Place in Nature*, 148, 185 and 14, 15.

[2] *The Mind and Its Place in Nature*, 187, '. . . presupposes the doctrine of Absolute Space-Time . . . *starts with rather heavy liabilities . . . has not carried its analysis far enough*'. Also p. 189, '. . . presupposes *Absolute Space-Time, which is probably a sign of inadequate analysis*'. (Italics mine.)

you expect. Here we can see how easily preference for a certain way of formulating facts of the class to which belongs the one we wish to state may well find expression in 'denying a hypothesis involved in' another way of formulating them.

Likewise, though the philosopher who analyses material thing statements into statements about sensations may hesitate to say that one who says 'The sun is sinking' instead of 'Appearances are as of a sinking sun' speaks falsely, he will certainly, if forced to say that one statement is false or involves an unjustified assumption, choose the former or common-sense formulation. So would I, although I know that one who uses the Matter-formulation expects to see and hear nothing relevant to the sinking of the sun in any way different from what I expect. Here again however it is natural (remember the average man) to express a preference for a certain way of formulating facts of the class to which the one we wish to state belongs, by 'denying a hypothesis involved in' another way of formulating them.

'But', it may be said, 'this pre- and post-Copernican case is quite different from the hypothesis of the existence of Matter. This Copernican hypothesis really is a matter of science and of different expectation'.

Now I don't wish to claim that accepting the Copernican theory makes no difference to *any* expectation as to what one will see and hear, although a pre-Copernican and a post-Copernican expect the same from 'The sun is sinking'. But the acceptance of 'Matter exists' or the analysis of it into sensations may also have remote effects on our expectations. Between the plain man and the philosopher who denies the existence of Matter there may be differences in what they would expect to see or hear, although when one of them says 'The sun is sinking' and the other says 'Appearances are as of a sinking sun' there is no difference in what they expect to see and hear *in the way of a verification of this statement*. Consider someone who mistakenly thinks that all the sights we see and sounds we hear from a passing ship are made by a man with a bell and a lantern. Not only will this person have misplaced confidences about what he will see if he goes on board but he will be averse to accepting stories of patterns of sight and sound which cannot be explained on his hypothesis or only with the utmost difficulty. In the same way the man who believes that, who talks as if, the sights and sounds we see and hear are due to material objects may be averse to accepting stories of patterns of sight and sound which cannot be explained on his hypothesis. He may be misled like this, although he is making no mistake comparable to the mistake of expecting to see someone when one goes on board the ship. For example, he may reject your story of how you and your friend saw rings round people's heads although you could feel nothing, not merely on account of the rareness of such a pattern but because your story has for him a sort of impossibility. This impossibility as opposed to improbability arises from the fact that he speaks in terms of sorts of *thing* and *not* of sorts of pattern of sensation. For what sort of thing is a thing which can be seen but not felt or photographed? This question in part reflects the antecedent improbability which your story gets from the rarity of the pattern it records, but it also gives your story unfair unplausibility by assuming that, if your story is true at all, it must be about a *thing*.

Talking of memory as looking back upon the past has the same sort of effect. This way of talking of memory and perception as strings or beams of light running from the eye to objects encourages the question 'How could there be foreknowledge, since this involves seeing what doesn't yet exist?' This question 'How *could* there be foreknowledge?' plays a part in determining whether we 'believe in foreknowledge' and even in whether we accept the stories we are told about the extraordinary powers of Mr. So-and-so.

The fact is, what is being done by one who says 'Matter doesn't exist' is like – and also different from – what is being done by one who says 'Unicorns don't exist', 'Uranium doesn't exist'. It is more like what is being done by one who says 'Gravity doesn't exist', or 'Space doesn't really exist'. These last are more like suggestions for a formulating or analysing of facts than they are like 'There are no cherries left'. At the same time they may prepare one for certain patterns of sensation which would have been more of a surprise if we had stuck to older formulations. And they lead to a special reducing-of-appearances-of-inferred-entities sort of analysis which is very different from, though of course not quite unlike, the analysis of, for example, family relationships into parenthood and sex. And it, instead of 'Matter doesn't exist', one says 'Statements about material things are analysable into statements about sensations', one must remember what sort of analysis this is. In this way we see how near is 'Matter is a fiction' to 'Matter is a logical fiction' and at the same time recognize the difference between one who says the one and one who says the other. The statements 'Matter doesn't exist', 'Matter doesn't really exist', 'Matter isn't anything over and above our sensations', 'Matter is a logical fiction', 'Statements about material things can be analysed into statements about sensations' form a series. As the formulations become more and more logical and analytic and less scientific and like hypotheses, something is gained and something is lost.

For philosophy is not science nor the correcting of popular assumptions; and one way in which this is best brought out is by emphasizing its likeness to logic. At the same time philosophy isn't logic and one way in which it isn't is best brought out by emphasizing its likeness to science and to the correcting of popular assumptions. Philosophy is like other things too, poetry for example; so that we cannot completely rely on any simple and winning formula, such as 'Philosophy begins where science and logic meet'. Nevertheless this formula is useful in considering the dispute as to whether philosophers are and should be concerned with questions about whether certain hypotheses involved in everyday statements are true, or are and should be concerned with the analysis of these everyday statements. Indeed, what I have tried to do is to bring out (1) how philosophy begins where the 'justification' of a 'hypothesis' involved in certain statements, e.g. Freud's about unconscious wishes 'explanatory' of certain facts, e.g. the patients' symptoms, dwindles to an 'analysis' of the statements into the facts, and (2) how the analysis of statements begins to be philosophy as opposed to logic when it is the 'justification' on the basis of certain facts of a 'hypothesis' involved in those statements and 'explanatory' of those facts. I have tried to show how philosophy begins where logic grows into science and science vanishes into logic. I have tried to bring out how far Moore is right when he says that philosophers discuss 'Does Matter exist?' as if it were a negative hypothesis, and how far this is an accusation, that is, how far Moore is wrong in saying that they ought not to inquire into the truth of hypotheses involved in the truth of everyday statements such as 'Here is one hand and here is another' but ought only to inquire into the analysis of these statements.

It is almost impossible to realize now the difficulty of first noticing the peculiarity, the craziness, of the philosopher's doubts and of grasping how near what he is really doing comes to logic. How much Moore has done for philosophy in bringing this out is not yet fully realized. But I have hopes it will be; for we have him with us yet, and while we have we shall not lack the help of an unparalleled combination of sound sense, courage and power.

Summary

1. Moore says that everyday statements such as 'I've got sixpence' are unquestionable, that only their analysis is questionable and that it's not questionable whether we know them, only how we know them.

2. But many of us feel that they are not *absolutely* unquestionable and that their logical analysis is not all we want and that we don't *really* know them till we can say how we know them. We feel too that the method of philosophy is not that of logic.

3. Broad, finding himself doing philosophy by weighing conflicting considerations, represents philosophical inquiry as a matter of estimating the probability of hypotheses about the *absolutely* unobservable in face of the endlessly extensive but chronically insufficient evidences which we have in the observable. He represents everyday statements as unquestionable in so far, but only in so far, as they involve no such hypotheses but merely record and predict the observable.

4. This appeals to us. But it involves questioning the unquestionable premiss 'I've got two hands' or 'I've got sixpence' from which Moore deduces that 'Matter exists'.

5. Consequently Broad wavers and sometimes, instead of questioning Moore's premiss, questions the *validity* of his proof. For Broad suggests that the fact that 'I've got sixpence' expresses a fact does not imply the existence of a sixpence, and thus does not imply the existence of a material thing, and thus does not imply that Matter exists.

6. None of these suggestions are *merely* absurd, especially is it not merely absurd to suggest that, though Moore, as opposed to a penniless tramp, is unquestionably right when he claims to have sixpence, it does not follow that the answer to the old philosophical question 'Does Matter exist?' is unquestionably that it does.

7. It is not, however, that it is questionable whether there is such a connection as Moore claims between his having sixpence and the existence of Matter; it is that the connection is questionable.

8. For many philosophers have used 'Matter does not exist' so that one might almost say that they just mean that Matter is nothing over and above sensations.

9. This has also been expressed by 'Matter is not a fiction, but a logical fiction', i.e. 'Statements about material things can be analysed into statements about sensations'.

10. From this it appears that Broad may accept Moore's premiss without his conclusion that Matter exists, but only by making the philosophical issue 'Does Matter exist?' a purely logical one such as Moore says it should be. Now it was to avoid this that we went to Broad.

11. Though it now begins to look as if Moore was quite wrong about what philosophers have been doing and quite right about what they should have been doing, in fact he is not quite wrong about what they have been doing and not quite right about what they should have been doing.

12. For, though philosophers who have said 'Matter does not exist' have been like the philosophers who have said 'Matter exists but is analysable into sensations', they have also been different. And the difference is important. For those who say 'Matter does not exist' do not realize the difference between what they are doing which amounts to saying 'All is illusion' and the advancing of a genuine hypothesis, e.g. 'That dagger in the air is an illusion'; whereas those who say 'Sentences about material things can be translated into sentences about sensations' do not realize how what they are doing is related as a limit to the advancing of genuine hypotheses, and thus differs from such analysis as the analysis of family relationships or the analysis in logic of one form of proposition, e.g. Propositions of the form *The thing which is S is P*, into other forms.

13. 'A llama is a hairy sort of woolly fleecy goat with an indolent expression and an undulating throat, like an unsuccessful literary man'. Hilaire Belloc.

A goat is an animal in which cow, sheep and antelope vanish into one another. This formula is little use without an explanation of how they vanish into one another. But, given this explanation, the formula comes to have value as a mnemonic line.

A philosopher is an animal in which the scientist vanishes into the logician — not to mention here the poet and the psycho-analyst.

14. For the metaphysical and Copernican discovery of how nearly philosophy is really logic Moore did as much as, and perhaps more than, any other man.

CHAPTER X

GODS

By John Wisdom

1. *The existence of God is not an experimental issue in the way it was.* An atheist or agnostic might say to a theist 'You still think there are spirits in the trees, nymphs in the streams, a God of the world.' He might say this because he noticed the theist in time of drought pray for rain and make a sacrifice and in the morning look for rain. But disagreement about whether there are gods is now less of this experimental or betting sort than it used to be. This is due in part, if not wholly, to our better knowledge of why things happen as they do.

It is true that even in these days it is seldom that one who believes in God has no hopes or fears which an atheist has not. Few believers now expect prayer to still the waves, but some think it makes a difference to people and not merely in ways the atheist would admit. Of course with people, as opposed to waves and machines, one never knows what they won't do next, so that expecting prayer to make a difference to them is not so definite a thing as believing in its mechanical efficacy. Still, just as primitive people pray in a business-like way for rain so some people still pray for others with a real feeling of doing something to help. However, in spite of this persistence of an experimental element in some theistic belief, it remains true that Elijah's method on Mount Carmel of settling the matter of what god or gods exist would be far less appropriate to-day than it was then.

2. *Belief in gods is not merely a matter of expectation of a world to come.* Someone may say 'The fact that a theist no more than an atheist expects prayer to bring down fire from heaven or cure the sick does not mean that there is no difference between them as to the facts, it does not mean that the theist has no expectations different from the atheist's. For very often those who believe in God believe in another world and believe that God is there and that we shall go to that world when we die.'

This is true, but I do not want to consider here expectations as to what one will see and feel after death nor what sort of reasons these logically unique expectations could have. So I want to consider those theists who do not believe in a future life, or rather, I want to consider the differences between atheists and theists in so far as these differences are not a matter of belief in a future life.

3. *What are these differences? And is it that theists are superstitious or that atheists are blind?* A child may wish to sit a while with his father and he may, when he has done what his father dislikes, fear punishment and feel distress at causing vexation, and while his father is alive he may feel sure of help when danger threatens and feel that there is sympathy for him when disaster has come. When his father is dead he will no longer expect punishment or help. Maybe for a moment an old fear will come or a cry for help escape him, but he will at once remember that this is no good now. He may feel that his father is no more until perhaps someone says to him that his father is still alive though he lives now in another world and one so far away that there is no hope of seeing him or hearing his voice again. The child may be told that nevertheless his father can see him and hear all he says. When he has been told this the child will still fear no punishment nor expect any sign of his father, but now, even more than he did when his father was alive, he will feel that his father sees him all the time and will dread distressing him and when he has done something wrong he will feel separated from his father until he has felt sorry for what he has done. Maybe when he himself comes to die he will be like a man who expects to find a friend in the strange country where he is going, but even when this is so, it is by no means all of what makes the difference between a child who believes that his father lives still in another world and one who does not.

Likewise one who believes in God may face death differently from one who does not, but there is another difference between them besides this. This other difference may still be described as belief in another world, only this belief is not a matter of expecting one thing rather than another here or hereafter, it is not a matter of a world to come but of a world that now is, though beyond our senses.

We are at once reminded of those other unseen worlds which some philosophers 'believe in' and others 'deny', while non-philosophers unconsciously 'accept' them by using them as models with which to 'get the hang of' the patterns in the flux of experience. We recall the timeless entities whose changeless connections we seek to represent in symbols, and the values which stand firm[1] amidst our flickering satisfaction and remorse, and the physical things which, though not beyond the corruption of moth and rust, are yet more permanent than the shadows they throw upon the screen before our minds. We recall, too, our talk of souls and of what lies in their depths and is manifested to us partially and intermittently in our own feelings and the behaviour of others. The hypothesis of mind, of other human minds and of animal minds, is reasonable because it explains for each of us why certain things behave so cunningly all by themselves unlike even the most ingenious machines. Is the hypothesis of minds in flowers and trees reasonable for like reasons? Is the hypothesis of a world mind reasonable for like reasons—someone who adjusts the blossom to the bees, someone whose presence may at times be felt—in a garden in high summer, in the hills when clouds are gathering, but not, perhaps, in a cholera epidemic?

4. *The question 'Is belief in gods reasonable?' has more than one source.* It is clear now that in order to grasp fully the logic of belief in divine minds we need to examine the logic of belief in animal and human minds. But we cannot do that here and so for the purposes of this discussion about divine minds let us acknowledge the reasonableness of our belief in human minds without troubling ourselves about its logic. The question of the reasonableness of belief in divine minds then becomes a matter of whether there are facts in nature which support claims about divine minds in the way facts in nature support our claims about human minds.

In this way we resolve the force behind the problem of the existence of gods into two components, one metaphysical and the same which prompts the question 'Is there *ever any* behaviour which gives reason to believe in *any* sort of mind?' and one which finds expression in 'Are there other mind-patterns in

[1] In another world, Dr. Joad says in the *New Statesman* recently.

nature beside the human and animal patterns which we can all easily detect, and are these other mind-patterns super-human?'

Such over-determination of a question syndrome is common. Thus, the puzzling questions 'Do dogs think?', 'Do animals feel?' are partly metaphysical puzzles and partly scientific questions. They are not purely metaphysical; for the reports of scientists about the poor performances of cats in cages and old ladies' stories about the remarkable performances of their pets are not irrelevant. But nor are these questions purely scientific; for the stories never settle them and therefore they have other sources. One other source is the metaphysical source we have already noticed, namely, the difficulty about getting behind an animal's behaviour to its mind, whether it is a non-human animal or a human one.

But there's a third component in the force behind these questions, these disputes have a third source, and it is one which is important in the dispute which finds expression in the words 'I believe in God', 'I do not'. This source comes out well if we consider the question 'Do flowers feel?' Like the questions about dogs and animals this question about flowers comes partly from the difficulty we sometimes feel over inference from *any* behaviour to thought or feeling and partly from ignorance as to what behaviour is to be found. But these questions, as opposed to a like question about human beings, come also from hesitation as to whether the behaviour in question is *enough* mind-like, that is, is it enough similar to or superior to human behaviour to be called 'mind-proving'? Likewise, even when we are satisfied that human behaviour shows mind and even when we have learned whatever mind-suggesting things there are in nature which are not explained by human and animal minds, we may still ask 'But are these things sufficiently striking to be called a mind-pattern? Can we fairly call them manifestations of a divine being?'

'The question', someone may say, 'has then become merely a matter of the application of a name. And "What's in a name?"'

5. *But the line between a question of fact and a question or decision as to the application of a name is not so simple as this way of putting things suggests.* The question 'What's in a name?' is engaging because we are inclined to answer both 'Nothing' and 'Very much'. And this 'Very much' has more than one source. We might have tried to comfort Heloise by saying 'It isn't that

Abelard no longer loves you, for this man isn't Abelard'; we might have said to poor Mr. Tebrick in Mr. Garnett's *Lady into Fox* 'But this is no longer Silvia'. But if Mr. Tebrick replied 'Ah, but it is!' this might come not at all from observing facts about the fox which we have not observed, but from noticing facts about the fox which we had missed, although we had in a sense observed all that Mr. Tebrick had observed. It is possible to have before one's eyes all the items of a pattern and still to miss the pattern. Consider the following conversation:

' "And I think Kay and I are pretty happy. We've always been happy."

'Bill lifted up his glass and put it down without drinking.

' "Would you mind saying that again?" he asked.

' "I don't see what's so queer about it. Taken all in all, Kay and I have really been happy."

' "All right," Bill said gently, "Just tell me how you and Kay have been happy."

'Bill had a way of being amused by things which I could not understand.

' "It's a little hard to explain," I said. "It's like taking a lot of numbers that don't look alike and that don't mean anything until you add them all together."

'I stopped, because I hadn't meant to talk to him about Kay and me.

' "Go ahead," Bill said. "What about the numbers." And he began to smile.

' "I don't know why you think it's so funny," I said. "All the things that two people do together, two people like Kay and me, add up to something. There are the kids and the house and the dog and all the people we have known and all the times we've been out to dinner. Of course, Kay and I do quarrel sometimes but when you add it all together, all of it isn't as bad as the parts of it seem. I mean, maybe that's all there is to anybody's life."

'Bill poured himself another drink. He seemed about to say something and checked himself. He kept looking at me.'[1]

Or again, suppose two people are speaking of two characters in a story which both have read[2] or of two friends which both

---

[1] *H. M. Pulham, Esq.*, p. 320, by John P. Marquand.
[2] e.g. Havelock Ellis's autobiography.

have known, and one says 'Really she hated him', and the other says 'She didn't, she loved him'. Then the first may have noticed what the other has not although he knows no incident in the lives of the people they are talking about which the other doesn't know too, and the second speaker may say 'She didn't, she loved him' because he hasn't noticed what the first noticed, although he can remember every incident the first can remember. But then again he may say 'She didn't, she loved him' not because he hasn't noticed the patterns in time which the first has noticed but because though he has noticed them he doesn't feel he still needs to emphasize them with 'Really she hated him'. The line between using a name because of how we feel and because of what we have noticed isn't sharp. 'A difference as to the facts', 'a discovery', 'a revelation', these phrases cover many things. Discoveries have been made not only by Christopher Columbus and Pasteur, but also by Tolstoy and Dostoievsky and Freud. Things are revealed to us not only by the scientists with microscopes, but also by the poets, the prophets, and the painters. What is so isn't merely a matter of 'the facts'. For sometimes when there is agreement as to the facts there is still argument as to whether defendant did or did not 'exercise reasonable care', was or was not 'negligent'.

And though we shall need to emphasize how much 'There is a God' evinces an attitude to the familiar[1] we shall find in the end that it also evinces some recognition of patterns in time easily missed and that, therefore, difference as to there being any gods is in part a difference as to what is so and therefore as to the facts, though not in the simple ways which first occurred to us.

6. *Let us now approach these same points by a different road.*

6.1. *How it is that an explanatory hypothesis, such as the existence of God, may start by being experimental and gradually become something quite different can be seen from the following story:*

Two people return to their long neglected garden and find among the weeds a few of the old plants surprisingly vigorous. One says to the other 'It must be that a gardener has been coming and doing something about these plants'. Upon inquiry they find that no neighbour has ever seen anyone at work in their garden.

---

[1] 'Persuasive Definitions', *Mind*, July, 1938, by Charles Leslie Stevenson, should be read here. It is very good. [Also in his *Ethics and Language*, Yale, 1945.—EDITOR.]

The first man says to the other 'He must have worked while people slept'. The other says 'No, someone would have heard him and besides, anybody who cared about the plants would have kept down these weeds'. The first man says 'Look at the way these are arranged. There is purpose and a feeling for beauty here. I believe that someone comes, someone invisible to mortal eyes. I believe that the more carefully we look the more we shall find confirmation of this.' They examine the garden ever so carefully and sometimes they come on new things suggesting that a gardener comes and sometimes they come on new things suggesting the contrary and even that a malicious person has been at work. Besides examining the garden carefully they also study what happens to gardens left without attention. Each learns all the other learns about this and about the garden. Consequently, when after all this, one says 'I still believe a gardener comes' while the other says 'I don't' their different words now reflect no difference as to what they have found in the garden, no difference as to what they would find in the garden if they looked further and no difference about how fast untended gardens fall into disorder. At this stage, in this context, the gardener hypothesis has ceased to be experimental, the difference between one who accepts and one who rejects it is now not a matter of the one expecting something the other does not expect. What is the difference between them? The one says 'A gardener comes unseen and unheard. He is manifested only in his works with which we are all familiar', the other says 'There is no gardener' and with this difference in what they say about the gardener goes a difference in how they feel towards the garden, in spite of the fact that neither expects anything of it which the other does not expect.

But is this the whole difference between them—that the one calls the garden by one name and feels one way towards it, while the other calls it by another name and feels in another way towards it? And if this is what the difference has become then is it any longer appropriate to ask 'Which is right?' or 'Which is reasonable?'

And yet surely such questions *are* appropriate when one person says to another 'You still think the world's a garden and not a wilderness, and that the gardener has not forsaken it' or 'You still think there are nymphs of the streams, a presence in the hills, a spirit of the world'. Perhaps when a man sings 'God's in His heaven' we need not take this as more than an expression of how he feels. But when Bishop Gore or Dr. Joad write about belief in God and young men read them in order to settle their religious doubts the impression is not simply that of persons choosing exclamations with which to face nature and the 'changes and chances of this mortal life'. The disputants speak as if they are concerned with a matter of scientific fact, or of trans-sensual, trans-scientific and metaphysical fact, but still of fact and still a matter about which reasons for and against may be offered, although no scientific reasons in the sense of field surveys for fossils or experiments on delinquents are to the point.

6.2. *Now can an interjection have a logic?* Can the manifestation of an attitude in the utterance of a word, in the application of a name, have a logic? When all the facts are known how can there still be a question of fact? How can there still be a question? Surely as Hume says '. . . after every circumstance, every relation is known, the understanding has no further room to operate'?[1]

6.3. When the madness of these questions leaves us for a moment *we can all easily recollect disputes which though they cannot be settled by experiment are yet disputes in which one party may be right and the other wrong* and in which both parties may offer reasons and the one better reasons than the other. *This may happen in pure and applied mathematics and logic.* Two accountants or two engineers provided with the same data may reach different results and this difference is resolved not by collecting further data but by going over the calculations again. Such differences indeed share with differences as to what will win a race, the honour of being among the most 'settlable' disputes in the language.

6.4. *But it won't do to describe the theistic issue as one settlable by such calculation,* or as one about what can be deduced in this *vertical* fashion from the facts we know. No doubt dispute about God has sometimes, perhaps especially in mediaeval times, been carried on in this fashion. But nowadays it is not and we must look for some other analogy, some other case in which a dispute is settled but not by experiment.

[1] Hume, *An Enquiry concerning the Principles of Morals.* Appendix I.

6.5. *In courts of law* it sometimes happens that opposing counsel
are agreed as to the facts and are not trying to settle a question
of further fact, are not trying to settle whether the man who
admittedly had quarrelled with the deceased did or did not
murder him, but are concerned with whether Mr. A who
admittedly handed his long-trusted clerk signed blank cheques
did or did not exercise reasonable care, whether a ledger is or is
not a document,[1] whether a certain body was or was not a public
authority.

In such cases we notice that the process of argument is not a
chain of demonstrative reasoning. It is a presenting and representing of those features of the case which *severally co-operate*
in favour of the conclusion, in favour of saying what the reasoner
wishes said, in favour of calling the situation by the name by
which he wishes to call it. The reasons are like the legs of a chair,
not the links of a chain. Consequently although the discussion
is *a priori* and the steps are not a matter of experience, the procedure resembles scientific argument in that the reasoning is not
vertically extensive but *horizontally* extensive—it is a matter of the
cumulative effect of several independent premises, not of the
repeated transformation of one or two. And because the premises
are severally inconclusive the process of deciding the issue becomes a matter of weighing the cumulative effect of one group
of severally inconclusive items against the cumulative effect of
another group of severally inconclusive items, and thus lends
itself to description in terms of conflicting 'probabilities'. This
encourages the feeling that the issue is one of fact—that it is a
matter of guessing from the premises at a further fact, at what is
to come. But this is a muddle. *The dispute does not cease to be a*
priori *because it is a matter of the cumulative effect of severally inconclusive premises.* The logic of the dispute is not that of a chain of
deductive reasoning as in a mathematic calculation. But nor is
it a matter of collecting from several inconclusive items of

[1] *The Times*, March 2nd, 1945. Also in *The Times* of June 13th, 1945, contrast the case
of Hannah v. Peel with that of the cruiser cut in two by a liner. In the latter case there
is not agreement as to the facts. See also the excellent articles by Dr. Glanville L. Williams
in the *Law Quarterly Review*, 'Language and the Law', January, and April 1945, and
'The Doctrine of Repugnancy', October, 1943, January, 1944, and April, 1944. The
author, having set out how arbitrary are many legal decisions, needs now to set out
how far from arbitrary they are—if his readers are ready for the next phase in the dialectic
process.

information an expectation as to something further, as when a doctor from a patient's symptoms guesses at what is wrong, or a detective from many clues guesses the criminal. It has its own sort of logic and its own sort of end—the solution of the question at issue is a decision, a ruling by the judge. But it is not an arbitrary decision though the rational connections are neither quite like those in vertical deductions nor like those in inductions in which from many signs we guess at what is to come; and though the decision manifests itself in the application of a name it is no more merely the application of a name than is the pinning on of a medal merely the pinning on of a bit of metal. Whether a lion with stripes is a tiger or a lion is, if you like, merely a matter of the application of a name. Whether Mr. So-and-So of whose conduct we have so complete a record did or did not exercise reasonable care is not merely a matter of the application of a name or, if we choose to say it is, then we must remember that with this name a game is lost and won and a game with very heavy stakes. With the judges' choice of a name for the facts goes an attitude, and the declaration, the ruling, is an exclamation evincing that attitude. But *it is an exclamation which not only has a purpose but also has a logic*, a logic surprisingly like that of 'futile', 'deplorable', 'graceful', 'grand', 'divine'.

6.6. *Suppose two people are looking at a picture or natural scene.* One says 'Excellent' or 'Beautiful' or 'Divine'; the other says 'I don't see it'. He means he doesn't see the beauty. And this reminds us of how we felt the theist accuse the atheist of blindness and the atheist accuse the theist of seeing what isn't there. And yet surely each sees what the other sees. It isn't that one can see part of the picture which the other can't see. So the difference is in a sense not one as to the facts. And so it cannot be removed by the one disputant discovering to the other what so far he hasn't seen. It isn't that the one sees the picture in a different light and so, as we might say, sees a different picture. Consequently the difference between them cannot be resolved by putting the picture in a different light. And yet surely this is just what can be done in such a case—not by moving the picture but by talk perhaps. To settle a dispute as to whether a piece of music is good or better than another we listen again, with a picture we look again. Someone perhaps points to emphasize certain features and we see it in a different light. Shall we call this 'field work' and 'the last of observation' or shall we call it 'reviewing the premises' and 'the beginning of deduction (horizontal)'?

If in spite of all this we choose to say that a difference as to whether a thing is beautiful is not a factual difference we must be careful to remember that there is a procedure for settling these differences and that this consists not only in reasoning and redescription as in the legal case, but also in a more literal re-setting-before with re-looking or re-listening.

6.7. *And if we say as we did at the beginning that when a difference as to the existence of a God is not one as to future happenings then it is not experimental and therefore not as to the facts, we must not forthwith assume that there is no right and wrong about it,* no rationality or irrationality, no appropriateness or inappropriateness, no proce-dure which tends to settle it, *nor even that this procedure is in no sense a discovery of new facts.* After all even in science this is not so. Our two gardeners even when they had reached the stage when neither expected any experimental result which the other did not, might yet have continued the dispute, each presenting and re-presenting the features of the garden favouring his hypothesis, that is, fitting his model for describing the accepted fact; each emphasizing the pattern he wishes to emphasize. True, in science, there is seldom or never a pure instance of this sort of dispute, for nearly always with difference of hypothesis goes some difference of expectation as to the facts. But scientists argue about rival hypotheses with a vigour which is not exactly proportioned to difference in expectations of experimental results.

The difference as to whether a God exists involves our feelings more than most scientific disputes and in this respect is more like a difference as to whether there is beauty in a thing.

7. *The Connecting Technique.* Let us consider again the tech-nique used in revealing or proving beauty, in removing a blindness, in inducing an attitude which is lacking, in reducing a reaction that is inappropriate. Besides running over in a special way the features of the picture, tracing the rhythms, making sure that this and that are not only seen but noticed, and their relation to each other—besides all this—there are other things we can do

to justify our attitude and alter that of the man who cannot see.
For features of the picture may be brought out by setting beside
it other pictures; just as the merits of an argument may be
brought out, proved, by setting beside it other arguments, in
which striking but irrelevant features of the original are changed
and relevant features emphasized; just as the merits and demerits
of a line of action may be brought out by setting beside it other
actions. To use Susan Stebbing's example: Nathan brought out
for David certain features of what David had done in the matter
of Uriah the Hittite by telling him a story about two sheep-
owners. This is the kind of thing we very often do when someone
is 'inconsistent' or 'unreasonable'. This is what we do in referring
to other cases in law. The paths we need to trace from other
cases to the case in question are often numerous and difficult to
detect and the person with whom we are discussing the matter
may well draw attention to connections which, while not
incompatible with those we have tried to emphasize, are of an
opposite inclination. A may have noticed in B subtle and hidden
likenesses to an angel and reveal these to C, while C has noticed
in B subtle and hidden likenesses to a devil which he reveals to A.

Imagine that a man picks up some flowers that lie half withered
on a table and gently puts them in water. Another man says to
him 'You believe flowers feel'. He says this although he know,
that the man who helps the flowers doesn't expect anything of
them which he himself doesn't expect; for he himself expects the
flowers to be 'refreshed' and to be easily hurt, injured, I mean,
by rough handling, while the man who puts them in water does
not expect them to whisper 'Thank you'. The Sceptic says 'You
believe flowers feel' because something about the way the other
man lifts the flowers and puts them in water suggests an attitude
to the flowers which he feels inappropriate although perhaps he
would not feel it inappropriate to butterflies. He feels that this
attitude to flowers is somewhat crazy *just as it is sometimes felt that
a lover's attitude is somewhat crazy even when this is not a matter of
his having false hopes about how the person he is in love with will
act.* It is often said in such cases that reasoning is useless. But the
very person who says this feels that the lover's attitude is crazy, is
inappropriate like some dreads and hatreds, such as some horrors

of enclosed places. And often one who says 'It is useless to reason proceeds at once to reason with the lover, nor is this reasoning always quite without effect. We may draw the lover's attention to certain things done by her he is in love with and trace for him a path to these from things done by others at other times[1] which have disgusted and infuriated him. And by this means we may weaken his admiration and confidence, make him feel it un-justified and arouse his suspicion and contempt and make him feel our suspicion and contempt reasonable. It is possible, of course, that he has already noticed the analogies, the connections, we point out and that he has accepted them—that is, he has not denied them nor passed them off. He has recognized them and they have altered his attitude, altered his love, but he still loves. We then feel that perhaps it is we who are blind and cannot see what he can see.

8. *Connecting and Disconnecting*. But before we confess our-selves thus inadequate there are other fires his admiration must pass through. For when a man has an attitude which it seems to us he should not have or lacks one which it seems to us he should have then, not only do we suspect that he is not influenced by connections which we feel should influence him and draw his attention to these, but also we suspect he is influenced by connec-tions which should not influence him and draw his attention to these. It may, for a moment, seem strange that we should draw his attention to connections which we feel should not influence him, and which, since they do influence him, he has in a sense already noticed. But we do—such is our confidence in 'the light of reason'.

Sometimes the power of these connections comes mainly from a man's mismanagement of the language he is using. This is what happens in the Monte Carlo fallacy, where by mismanaging the laws of chance a man passes from noticing that a certain colour or number has not turned up for a long while to an improper confidence that now it soon will turn up. In such cases our showing up of the false connections is a process we call 'explaining a fallacy in reasoning'. To remove fallacies in reasoning we urge a man to call a spade a spade, ask him what he means by 'the

---

[1] Thus, like the scientist, the critic is concerned to show up the irrelevance of time and space.

State' and having pointed out ambiguities and vaguenesses ask him to reconsider the steps in his argument.

9. *Unspoken Connections.* *Usually, however, wrongheadedness or wrongheartedness in a situation, blindness to what is there or seeing what is not, does not arise merely from mismanagement of language but is more due to connections which are not mishandled in language, for the reason that they are not put into language at all.* And often these misconnections too, weaken in the light of reason, if only we can guess where they lie and turn it on them. In so far as these connections are not presented in language the process of removing their power is not a process of correcting the mismanagement of language. But it is still akin to such a process; for though it is not a process of setting out fairly what has been set out unfairly, it is a process of setting out fairly what has not been set out at all. And we must remember that the line between connections ill-presented or half-presented in language and connections operative but not presented in language, or only hinted at, is not a sharp one.

Whether or not we call the process of showing up these connections 'reasoning to remove bad unconscious reasoning' or not, it is certain that in order to settle in ourselves what weight we shall attach to someone's confidence or attitude we not only ask him for his reasons but also look for unconscious reasons both good and bad; that is, for reasons which he can't put into words, isn't explicitly aware of, is hardly aware of, isn't aware of at all— perhaps it's long experience which he *doesn't* recall which lets him know a squall is coming, perhaps it's old experience which he *can't* recall which makes the cake in the tea mean so much and makes Odette so fascinating.[1]

I am well aware of the distinction between the question 'What reasons are there for the belief that S is P?' and the question 'What are the sources of beliefs that S is P?' There are cases where investigation of the rationality of a claim which certain persons make is done with very little inquiry into why they say what they do, into the causes of their beliefs. This is so when we have very definite ideas about what is really logically relevant to their claim and what is not. Offered a mathematical theorem we ask for the proof; offered the generalization that parental

[1] Proust: *Swann's Way*, Vol. I, p. 58, Vol. II. Phoenix Edition.

discord causes crime we ask for the correlation co-efficients. But even in this last case, if we fancy that only the figures are reasons we underestimate the complexity of the logic of our conclusion; and yet it is difficult to describe the other features of the evidence which have weight and there is apt to be disagreement about the weight they should have. In criticizing other conclusions and especially conclusions which are largely the expression of an attitude, we have not only to ascertain what reasons there are for them but also to decide what things are reasons and how much. This latter process of sifting reasons from causes is part of the critical process for every belief, but in some spheres it has been done pretty fully already. In these spheres we don't need to examine the actual processes to belief and distil from them a logic. But in other spheres this remains to be done. Even in science or on the stock exchange or in ordinary life we sometimes hesitate to condemn a belief or a hunch[1] merely because those who believe it cannot offer the sort of reasons we had hoped for. And now suppose Miss Gertrude Stein finds excellent the work of a new artist while we see nothing in it. We nervously recall, perhaps, how pictures by Picasso, which Miss Stein admired and others rejected, later came to be admired by many who gave attention to them, and we wonder whether the case is not a new instance of her perspicacity and our blindness. But if, upon giving all our attention to the work in question, we still do not respond to it, and we notice that the subject matter of the new pictures is perhaps birds in wild places and learn that Miss Stein is a bird-watcher, then we begin to trouble ourselves less about her admiration.

It must not be forgotten that our attempt to show up mis-connections in Miss Stein may have an opposite result and reveal to us connections we had missed. Thinking to remove the spell exercised upon his patient by the old stories of the Greeks, the psycho-analyst may himself fall under that spell and find in them what his patient has found and, incidentally, what made the Greeks tell those tales.

10. *Now what happens, what should happen, when we inquire in this way into the reasonableness, the propriety of belief in gods?* The

[1] Here I think of Mr. Stace's interesting reflections in *Mind*, January, 1945, 'The Problem of Unreasoned Beliefs'.

answer is: A double and opposite-phased change. Wordsworth writes:

'. . . And I have felt
A presence that disturbs me with the joy
Of elevated thoughts; a sense sublime
Of something far more deeply interfused,
Whose dwelling is the light of setting suns,
And the round ocean and the living air,
And the blue sky, and in the mind of man:
A motion and a spirit, that impels
All thinking things, all objects of all thought,
And rolls through all things . . .'[1]

We most of us know this feeling. But is it well placed like the feeling that here is first-rate work, which we sometimes rightly have even before we have fully grasped the picture we are looking at or the book we are reading? Or is it misplaced like the feeling in a house that has long been empty that someone secretly lives there still. Wordsworth's feeling *is* the feeling that the world is haunted, that something watches in the hills and manages the stars. The child feels that the stone tripped him when he stumbled, that the bough struck him when it flew back in his face. He has to learn that the wind isn't buffeting him, that there is not a devil in it, that he was wrong, that his attitude was inappropriate. And as he learns that the wind wasn't hindering him so he also learns it wasn't helping him. But we know how, though he learns, his attitude lingers. It is plain that Wordsworth's feeling is of this family.

Belief in gods, it is true, is often very different from belief that stones are spiteful, the sun kindly. For the gods appear in human form and from the waves and control these things and by so doing reward and punish us. But varied as are the stories of the gods they have a family likeness and we have only to recall them to feel sure of the other main sources which co-operate with animism to produce them.

What are the stories of the gods? What are our feelings when we believe in God? They are feelings of awe before power, dread of the thunderbolts of Zeus, confidence in the everlasting

[1] *Tintern Abbey.*

arms, unease beneath the all-seeing eye. They are feelings of guilt
and inescapable vengeance, of smothered hate and of a security
we can hardly do without. We have only to remind ourselves of
these feelings and the stories of the gods and goddesses and heroes
in which these feelings find expression, to be reminded of how
we felt as children to our parents and the big people of our
childhood. Writing of a first telephone call from his grandmother, Proust says: '... it was rather that this isolation of the
voice was like a symbol, a presentation, a direct consequence of
another isolation, that of my grandmother, separated for the first
time in my life, from myself. The orders or prohibitions which
she addressed to me at every moment in the ordinary course of
my life, the tedium of obedience or the fire of rebellion which
neutralized the affection that I felt for her were at this moment
eliminated. . . . "Granny!" I cried to her . . . but I had beside me
only that voice, a phantom, as unpalpable as that which would
come to revisit me when my grandmother was dead. "Speak to
me!" but then it happened that, left more solitary still, I ceased
to catch the sound of her voice. My grandmother could no
longer hear me . . . I continued to call her, sounding the empty
night, in which I felt that her appeals also must be straying. I was
shaken by the same anguish which, in the distant past, I had felt
once before, one day when, a little child, in a crowd, I had lost
her.'

Giorgio de Chirico, writing of Courbet, says: 'The word
yesterday envelops us with its yearning echo, just as, on waking,
when the sense of time and the logic of things remain a while
confused, the memory of a happy hour we spent the day before
may sometimes linger reverberating within us. At times we think
of Courbet and his work as we do of our own father's youth.'

When a man's father fails him by death or weakness how much
he needs another father, one in the heavens with whom is 'no
variableness nor shadow of turning'.

We understood Mr. Kenneth Graham when he wrote of the
Golden Age we feel we have lived in under the Olympians.
Freud says: 'The ordinary man cannot imagine this Providence
in any other form but that of a greatly exalted father, for only
such a one could understand the needs of the sons of men, or be
softened by their prayers and be placated by the signs of their

remorse.. The whole thing is so patently infantile, so incongruous with reality. . . .' 'So incongruous with reality'! It cannot be denied.

But here a new aspect of the matter may strike us.[1] For the very facts which make us feel that now we can recognize systems of superhuman, sub-human, elusive, beings for what they are—the persistent projections of infantile phantasies—include facts which make these systems less fantastic. What are these facts? They are patterns in human reactions which are well described by saying that we are as if there were hidden within us powers, persons, not ourselves and stronger than ourselves. That this is so may perhaps be said to have been common knowledge yielded by ordinary observation of people,[2] but we did not know the degree in which this is so until recent study of extraordinary cases in extraordinary conditions had revealed it. I refer, of course, to the study of multiple personalities and the wider studies of psycho-analysts. Even when the results of this work are reported to us that is not the same as tracing the patterns in the details of the cases on which the results are based; and even that is not the same as taking part in the studies oneself. One thing not sufficiently realized is that some of the things shut within us are not bad but good.

Now the gods, good and evil and mixed, have always been mysterious powers outside us rather than within. But they have also been within. It is not a modern theory but an old saying that in each of us a devil sleeps. Eve said: 'The serpent beguiled me.' Helen says to Menelaus:

> '. . . And yet how strange it is !
> I ask not thee; I ask my own sad thought,
> What was there in my heart, that I forgot
> My home and land and all I loved, to fly
> With a strange man? Surely it was not I,
> But Cypris there !'[3]

---

[1] I owe to the late Dr. Susan Isaacs the thought of this different aspect of the matter, of this connection between the heavenly Father and 'the good father' spoken of in psycho-analysis.

[2] Consider Tolstoy and Dostoievsky—I do not mean, of course, that their observation was ordinary.

[3] Euripides: *The Trojan Women*, Gilbert Murray's Translation. Roger Hinks in *Myth and Allegory in Ancient Art* writes (p. 108): 'Personifications made their appearance very

Elijah found that God was not in the wind, nor in the thunder, but in a still small voice. The kingdom of Heaven is within us, Christ insisted, though usually about the size of a grain of mustard seed, and he prayed that we should become one with the Father in Heaven.

New knowledge made it necessary either to give up saying 'The sun is sinking' or to give the words a new meaning. In many contexts we preferred to stick to the old words and give them a new meaning which was not entirely new but, on the contrary, *practically* the same as the old. The Greeks did not speak of the dangers of repressing instincts but they did speak of the dangers of thwarting Dionysos, of neglecting Cypris for Diana, of forgetting Poseidon for Athena. We have eaten of the fruit of a garden we can't forget though we were never there, a garden we still look for though we can never find it. Maybe we look for too simple a likeness to what we dreamed. Maybe we are not as free as we fancy from the old idea that Heaven is a happy hunting ground, or a city with streets of gold. Lately Mr. Aldous Huxley has recommended our seeking not somewhere beyond the sky or late in time but a timeless state not made of the stuff of this world, which he rejects, picking it into worthless pieces. But this sounds to me still too much a looking for another place, not indeed one filled with sweets but instead so empty that some of us would rather remain in the Lamb or the Elephant, where, as we know, they stop whimpering with another bitter and so far from sneering at all things, hang pictures of winners at Kempton and stars of the 'nineties. Something good we have for each other is freed there, and in some degree and for a while the miasma of time is rolled back without obliging us to deny the present.

The artists who do most for us don't tell us only of fairylands.

early in Greek poetry. . . . It is out of the question to call these terrible beings "abstractions". . . . They are real daemons to be worshipped and propitiated. . . . These beings we observe correspond to states of mind. The experience of man teaches him that from time to time his composure is invaded and overturned by some power from outside, panic, intoxication, sexual desire.'

> 'What use to shoot off guns at unicorns?
> Where one horn's hit another fierce horn grows.
> These beasts are fabulous, and none were born
> Of woman who could lay a fable low.'—

The Glass Tower, Nicholas Moore, p. 100.

Proust, Manet, Breughel, even Botticelli and Vermeer show us reality. And yet they give us for a moment exhilaration without anxiety, peace without boredom. And those who, like Freud, work in a different way against that which too often comes over us and forces us into deadness or despair,[1] also deserve critical, patient and courageous attention. For they, too, work to release us from human bondage into human freedom.

Many have tried to find ways of salvation. The reports they bring back are always incomplete and apt to mislead even when they are not in words but in music or paint. But they are by no means useless; and not the worst of them are those which speak of oneness with God. But in so far as we become one with Him He becomes one with us. St. John says he is in us as we love one another.

This love, I suppose, is not benevolence but something that comes of the oneness with one another of which Christ spoke.[2] Sometimes it momentarily gains strength.[3] Hate and the Devil do too. And what is oneness without otherness?

[1] Matthew Arnold: *Summer Night.*
[2] St. John xvi, 21.
[3] 'The Harvesters' in *The Golden Age*, Kenneth Grahame.

PHILOSOPHY AND PSYCHO-ANALYSIS
(*Polemic No. 4*)

I. PHILOSOPHICAL CONFLICT

WITTGENSTEIN once said that he '*holds no opinions in philosophy*' and, again that he tries to remove '*a feeling of puzzlement, to cure a sort of mental cramp*'. This emphasizes much more what evil philosophy removes than what good it brings. Nevertheless, all who have felt the old philosophical puzzles know the cramp Wittgenstein refers to. Indeed if one thinks of a philosopher one thinks of a man who talks like this, for example: '*We fancy we sometimes know what other creatures are thinking and how they are feeling. But all we really know is how they nod and smile at this, bark and frown at that. No reasoning from such information will justify a conclusion about how they think and feel; it won't even tell us that they think and feel at all, much less will it tell us what goes on in the souls behind their faces. True we can infer from the faces of clocks what goes on within. But that is different. For some of us have sometimes noted a clock's face and quickly looked within. None of us has ever noted a friend's face and then quickly looked within. Maybe we have looked within his body and found a decayed tooth or other sand in the transmission. But not in the happiest days have we ever viewed the landscapes he alone can view. And yet though it seems we can't know how others think and feel surely we often do know*'.

The trouble spreads. The philosopher soon finds himself saying: '*Not only do I not know how or whether anything else thinks or feels but also I cannot really know what is happening in any place hidden from me, in the inside of a clock, for example, or beyond the horizon. I can open some clocks quickly but none quickly enough. On Tuesday at 2 p.m., I know only what is happening near me, within the walls of my room, in my own little ark. For what is happening far away on the waste of waters or in the roaring Strand, I am obliged to rely on doves and telephones. However fast I hurry to the place I'm always late. The dove brings a leaf perhaps, but by the time I reach the distant Spring the leaves are turning or it's full Summer. For, if not, it wasn't Spring but still Winter when I started. Finding fallen leaves in November I may say I was right when in April, in Germany, I thought it was*

Spring in England. But the fallen leaves are not the Spring of which I dreamed in April. That is now for ever in the past. Even that I don't really know, obliged as I am to rely for all knowledge of the past upon dead leaves, bones, stones, documents and the faded photos in the family album and my memory. Nor do I know the future. For even if I knew what had happened this wouldn't guarantee what will happen.

'And now if I know nothing of the past and nothing of the future then all I seem to see and hear may have no more substance than a dream. For just as a phoenix is not a phoenix unless it renews itself in its own ashes so bread that comes down from Heaven isn't bread but manna, and a dagger that vanishes is not a dagger but an image.

'Further, even if I knew the future and could with perfect propriety predict to all eternity the pattern of my sensations, would this give substance to the shadows in a mirror that mirrors nothing?

'And yet, surely, I do know these things it seems I can't know? I do know that where there's smoke there's fire, that the stone I kick is real, that the friend who speaks with me is not a talking doll.'

So spreads and swings the philosophic hesitation. Driven by a caricature of curiosity which is kept for ever hungry by an inexorable desire to be logically perfect and factually infallible the philosopher diminishes his claims to knowledge; agnosticism about the minds of others· becomes agnosticism about all things but his own thought as he thinks it – in other words Solipsism. And Solipsism soon becomes Scepticism, the 'claim' that we know nothing. For when the philosopher become Solipsist fancies himself about to reap the reward of his logical purity in perfect knowledge, limited indeed but invulnerable, just then the statement he had hoped to make dwindles to the senseless whimper of an elderly infant in the mansions of the dead.[1] I don't mean, of course, that all philosophers in the end become Sceptics and find peace in death. On the contrary, no philosopher becomes really a Sceptic; because if a man really feels what the Sceptic says he feels then he is said to have 'a sense of unreality' and is removed to a home. In fact the sceptical philosopher never succeeds in killing his primitive credulities which, as Hume says, reassert themselves the moment he takes up the affairs of life and ceases to murmur the incantations which generate his philosophic doubt.

[1] With apologies to Paul Nash. For fuller treatment see *Other Minds*, VII, John Wisdom.

More than that, most philosophers refuse to be Sceptics even in their philosophic moments; these travellers on the road to Nothing mostly look back and would return whence they have come, but cannot. In this sad case, some talk of trans-sensual spheres glimpsed by a trans-sensual awareness, an apprehension of Reality mediated by, but not limited to, the sights and sounds, the headaches and the heartaches to which we seem confined; others, the Realists, pretend that nothing's happened, that everything's all right, that fine-spun argument can never shake the common sense they had and hold; others, the Phenomenalists, say that everything's all right because the ideal of knowledge of reality beyond appearance is only unattainable because it's unintelligible; others hurry agitatedly from one cult to another; others stand poised 'betwixt a world destroyed and world restored', paralysed in the cramp of conflict.

We have come upon these people before – in other difficulties; indeed they are ourselves. And none of them is at ease. This comes out plainly in those who say they are not. But even those who have erected a temple for tranquillity have often a hidden fear of its falling about their ears. The Transcendentalist must constantly defend himself against the Sceptic and even against the Realist, who are the more menacing because they are not only outside him but also within. The realist must keep forgetting the philosophic qualms which though crammed down into Tartarus are not dead – the confidence he professes is never what it was before he ate of the forbidden tree. The phenomenalist protests too much that there was no baby in the bath water he threw away. None of them is easy – or if he is, he shouldn't be. This last qualification reminds us of the incompleteness in the description of the proper philosopher as one who tries to cure uneasiness. He may set himself to disturb complacency. So may a psycho-analyst. We may recognize this without forgetting how much philosophy and analytic work by patient and analyst is conflict and the cure of it.

II. PHILOSOPHICAL AND OBSESSIONAL DOUBT

I have used words with a clinical flavour in the sketch of philosophers which I have just given because I want to bring out likenesses, connections, between states of philosophical stress and

other states of stress arising from internal sources as opposed to
states of stress arising from external sources. A general or a
business man who has to decide what to do in a complicated
situation may go over the many relevant considerations carefully
and may do so many times. A judge considers carefully, even
anxiously, the arguments of contending counsel. But the general,
the business man and the judge may consider their problems very
patiently and still be very different from the neurotic. The
neurotic may discuss his problems – he may indeed – but he
never means business; the discussion is not a means to action, to
something other than itself; on the contrary, after a while we get
the impression that in spite of his evident unhappiness and desire
to come from hesitation to decision he also desires the discussion
never to end and dreads its ending. Have you not quite often
had this impression with philosophers? – philosophers other
than ourselves, for we, of course, are never neurotic. I once
discussed with a man in a mental hospital whether he should
continue to starve himself and study the Scriptures or take more
nourishment and lend a hand at home. He put the matter well
and with an admirable impartiality, but some months later I
learned that he had died in the hospital, still, I believe, unable to
settle the issue. And we have all read of the man who cannot be
sure that he has turned off the tap or the light. He must go again
to make sure, and then perhaps he must go again because though
he knows the light's turned off he yet can't *feel* sure. He is
obsessed by a chronic doubt. Has he done what he ought about
the light or the tap? Perhaps his doubt is less limited, perhaps he
is constantly questioning himself as to whether he has done what
he ought. Such a man will often want rules of life to save him
from continual conflict. Or again, his doubt may be less a matter
of whether he has done this or that, or what he ought, and more a
doubt as to what is happening where he can't see. He has slammed
his front door, he hasn't much time to catch his train, but still
he turns back because he wants to feel perfectly sure that things
are all right behind the door – to which fortunately he has a key.
At least he has a key until, like a philosopher, he wishes to see
behind the door without opening it. Instantly it becomes 'a veil
past which I cannot see' and in the darkness of the cave one cannot
tell whether She smiles or frowns. If we are watching shadows

on a wall and want to know whether the shadows are telling the truth about what is going on behind our backs we can turn our heads and look; we aren't like an infant who, helpless in his cradle, cannot turn his head and cries when his mother goes out of sight; nor like philosophers who perpetually feel they don't know what's going on behind their backs, and who, still like the child, dread to know, cling to their ignorance. God or the gods know what really is so, what goes on among 'objective realities', but we know only what goes on among our own toys, copies of real things. The gods know but they never tell us anything, as James Forsyte continually complained when age now instead of youth confined him to his bed. The gods know but they tell us nothing — a conspiracy of silence among the arch-deceivers.

Yesterday a man just beginning philosophy told me that he had said to a friend: '*Some philosophers don't believe in material things and I am now not sure that I do.*' His friend said, taking hold of the table, '*You don't believe there's a table here? You're mad.*'

I said '*Your friend's right. There is something very odd about the situation when a philosopher says* "I don't believe there's a table here" *or* "I doubt whether there's a table here." *It's not that his question is odd, I mean it's not simply his uttering these words* "I'm not sure whether there's a table here" *which strikes us as odd. If when you are seeking water in the desert someone gazes at what looks like water in the distance and says* "I doubt whether there's really water there", *you don't think him absurd. But the philosopher says* "I am not sure" *while he's drinking the water; he says it when no one would, or when no one but a madman would, or when no one but a madman or a philosopher would. And then also he is queer in that he doesn't act, doesn't feel, doesn't anticipate the future in the way his words suggest. In this he is at once more and less queer than a madman. The madman says, perhaps,* "I shouldn't open that door" *and his eyes widen in almost furious terror. You say* "Why not?" *and continue to walk towards the door. He clutches your arm and says, softly,* "There's a tiger in there." *You say* "Nonsense, I've only just been in the room. You don't suppose a furniture firm has just driven up outside, erected a ladder, and slipped a tiger in through the window, do you?" "Ah!" the madman says, "He hides" or "You can't see him".'

This is the psychotic and he is different from the neurotic who says that he must make sure that he hasn't left the lights on but that, of course, it's all nonsense and that he really knows he has turned them off, or that he must make quite sure that his hands are quite clean although it is true he has only just washed them. The neurotic, we might say, doesn't believe what he says. Still he does go back at the risk of losing his train to make sure that the lights are off. The philosopher doesn't. His acts and feelings are even less in accordance with his words than are the acts and feelings of the neurotic. He, even more than the neurotic and much more than the psychotic, doesn't believe what he says, doesn't doubt when he says he's not sure. (Compare wishes when he says he doesn't, i.e. unconsciously wishes.) But if we say that the philosopher doesn't believe what he says, that he's only pretending to doubt, then we must remember that he's very different from someone who, wishing to deceive us, pretends. The philosopher isn't one who merely makes it seem to others that he is in doubt; he also seems to himself to doubt. In other words, although many of his acts and feelings are unsuitable to his words, some are suitable and, in particular, as he speaks he has much of the feeling characteristic of doubt. When he says *'Perhaps it's all in my mind'*, he feels something of the relief or disappointment of one who fearing this, hoping that, says *'Maybe it's all a dream'*.

But now what is it that makes philosophers go on in the way they do?

III. The Philosopher is Different

There is a big difference between the philosopher and both the psychotic and the obsessional neurotic. It lies in the flow of justificatory talk, of rationalization, which the philosopher produces when asked why he takes the extraordinary line he does. It is true that both the psychotic and neurotic listen to reason and defend themselves. The philosopher defends himself more elaborately. But this is not the point. The point is, aren't his rationalizations reasons?

When we call justifying talk 'rationalization' we hint that we are not impressed by it and do not expect others to be. But we are impressed by the philosopher's talk, it has a universal effect, reluctantly we are impressed by it. The trouble is that it doesn't impress us quite enough to make us satisfied with his conclusions while yet it impresses us; the reasons seem not quite good enough and not quite bad enough and — connected fact — it seems the same with the reasons for opposing conclusions. At the same time the position is not what it is in science or crime where some evidence lends probability to one hypothesis and other evidence lends probability to another and we may contentedly wait for more evidence to tip the scales. For the philosopher's proofs profess to be *proofs* or nothing. And yet, too, we cannot, as in mathematics or logic, bring the conflict to an end by finding the slip in one of the calculations which purport to demonstrate the conflicting conclusions. There's something queer about philosophical reasons and the reasoning goes on too long.

IV. First as to the Queerness of Philosophical Reasons and Conflict

Contrast a logical conflict. Lately it was reported in the Press that a railway official upon being asked the cause of a recent run of accidents replied, '*Well, the men are tired, the rolling stock a little the worse for wear, but it's not so much that as the working out of the law of averages*'. This explanation is based on the logical doctrine that the longer a die has been thrown without a six the more probable is a six on the next throw, and we may imagine someone who argues for this as follows: when a die is about to be thrown 100 times the probability of at least one six being thrown is very great, namely .999999988 approximately. It may happen, however, that no six has appeared in the first 25 throws. In such a case unless a six appears in the next 75 throws there will have been 100 throws without a six and this, as we have seen, is improbable to the degree .000000012. Therefore it is improbable to the degree .000000012 that no six will appear in the next 75 throws. Again, if it should happen that no six appears in the first 99 throws then unless a six appears in the next throw there will have been 100 throws without a six and this is improbable to the degree .000000012. Therefore it is then improbable to the degree .000000012 that there will not be a six on the next throw while before the throws started this was not improbable but probable to the degree 5/6.

This reasoning may temporarily impress us but we soon reply: The probability of a six after a long run of anything but sixes is still one in six if we assume that the die is not loaded, while if we do not assume this the probability of a six, so far from having increased as you suggest, has decreased, for the long run of throws without a six suggests that there is something about the die which prevents its falling six uppermost. Your reasoning in favour of the increasing probability of a six is tempting but it's fallacious. When you say '*It may happen that no six has appeared in the first 25 throws — in such a case, unless a six appears in the next 75 throws there will have been 100 throws without a six and this, as we have seen, is improbable to the degree* .000000012' — do you mean that we have seen that given only that a die is about to be thrown 100 times then it is improbable to a degree .000000012 that there will be no sixes? or do you mean that we have seen that given that a die has been thrown 25 times without a six and that it will be thrown another 75 times, then it is improbable to a degree .000000012 that at the end there will have been no six thrown? The former is true, the latter is false. For given that a die has been thrown 25 times without a six and that it will be thrown another 75 times, the improbability that at the end of the 100 throws no six will have been thrown is the improbability of throwing a six in the next 75 throws, that is $1-\left(\frac{5}{6}\right)^{75}$.[1]   And when 99 throws have been made and another is about to be made, the improbability of this series of 100 throws not including a six, is the improbability of not throwing a six in the next throw, that is 5/6.

Here the difficulty is cleared up; one proof is definitely mistaken and the mistake is found; the other proof is sound and the matter is settled. So much for the Monte Carlo fallacy.

It may seem a pity that philosophy cannot be conducted on these lines. But it cannot. A philosophical conflict is like a logical or arithmetical conflict. But it's different too. The peculiarity of philosophical conflicts has only lately been grasped. Philosophical theories such as '*Matter (or Mind) does not exist*' are neither

[1] Neglecting the fact that the 25 throws without a six suggest slightly that the die is loaded. This, negligible in a small number of throws, is not negligible in a large number of throws. It is this, I think, and not the explanation offered in Keynes's *Probability*, p. 316, which is the main source of the Petersbourg Paradox.

theories nor theorems; they are what they sound like — paradoxes; and philosophical questions are not questions (scientific) nor problems (logic) — but are more like riddles such as 'Can one man do what another does? Surely he can. And yet surely it can't be that he can. For suppose A scratches his head. Then if B scratches his head he doesn't do what A does since it's not B's head but A's that A scratches. But if B scratches A's head then again he doesn't do what A does since A scratches his own head and B scratches someone else's'. But here drinks are served all round. For now nobody cares whether we say 'No man can do what another man does', or say 'If a man, A, scratches his head and a man, B, also scratches his, B's, head then each does what the other does', or say 'If a man, A, scratches his head and a man, B, also scratches A's head then each does what the other does'. And now that nobody cares, the original paradox 'No man can do what another does' cannot be mistaken for a theory about human powers like 'No man can play billiards like Lindrum'. And, what is more, now that everybody understands, now that everybody has explained his reasons, the doctrine 'No man can do what another does' can no longer be mistaken for a theorem like 'No man can draw isosceles triangles with the angles at the base unequal'. In fact the paradox now appears as a paradox though in doing so it ceases to be one. For it now appears that one who says 'No man can do what another does' cuts a caper and encourages us to do likewise, not pointlessly but in order to reveal a concealed curiosity, namely that one man does what another does only when he does something different. One who says 'No man can do what another does' introduces a new logic to show up a hidden feature of the old, uses language oddly in order to show up an oddity in our usual use. And one who says 'No man can know the mind of another as he does his own' or 'No one can really know the mind of another' does the same sort of thing. His statement doesn't come out of experience in the way 'No one can know what a Red man feels' comes out of experience; and it doesn't come out of ordinary language in the way 'No one can know what a good poker player is thinking' or 'No one can marry his widow's sister' does. It is not a statement of fact nor of logic. It comes out of language and out of experience — but in its own way — like 'Tyger, tyger! burning bright'. It comes from extraordinary experience of the ordinary calling for extraordinary use of ordinary language. And to burst this way the bonds of habitual modes of projection is no more extraordinary than a caricature, or a picture that is not a photograph.

The consequence is that paradoxes are not established by experiment and statistics and cannot be proved by conclusive-deductive reasoning. They can be supported by inconclusive-deductive reasoning. The reasoning cannot be conclusive for, if it were, then the opposite of the paradox could not also be supported, and if its opposite could not be supported it would not be a paradox. And the reasoning will not be effective unless it leads to or comes from a new apprehension of the familiar – without that it will be dead words, for after all tigers don't burn even in forests at night.

A paradox is a flag which declares a discovery – not a new continent nor a cure for pneumonia but a discovery in the familiar – but often it is also the Blue Peter of a new voyage. For often we don't properly understand a paradox until, beginning by regarding it literally, we have noted objections to it and held to it because of the reasons for it, and again noted objections and again held to it, and have come by this route to a state where we are no longer driven to assert it or to deny it. There's no short cut to this; for if *before* treating a paradox and its denial as incompatible and arguing for a win we say '*No doubt there's much in both*' this leaves us entirely vague as to what is in either. No – the journey to the new freedom is mostly long and arduous, the work of bringing to light and setting in order with respect to one another what drives us to accept, and what forces us to deny, a paradox, what makes it so fascinating, so attractive and so repugnant, may fairly take a long time. But it can take too long.

V. Philosophical Dispute Can Go on Too Long

It may fairly take a woman a long time to decide which of two men is the right one for her to marry and it may take a man a long time to decide which of two professions is the right one for him to take up. But again in each case it may take too long. At first as we review with our friend the many considerations that bear on the issue we accompany him with interest, later with patience, but at last with irritation. For in time we feel that the difficulty is no longer a matter of coming to know his own mind, but of making up his mind. He still represents himself as ignorant of what would suit him and in this way conceals his incapacity to choose. *'Win or a place, win or a place'* shout those who quote the possible investments, but still he hesitates. And why can't he decide? Not merely because the considerations are so balanced. There's often nothing to choose on looks, form, breeding and price between one horse and another, but this doesn't prevent people deciding before the flags go down which one to back. No, his chronic indecision, whether it takes the form of enthusiastic oscillation or melancholy inactivity, is due to the fact that besides the reasons revealed in the course of talking the matter over there are others which remain hidden. Family disputes are often very interminable and often have an unpleasant sweetness because they are conducted wholly in terms of what is 'right' or 'reasonable' while each disputant knows that forces quite other than those mentioned are at work and often knows the other knows. It is not that the things mentioned, the things brought up in the discussion, are not at work but that other things unmentioned and unmentionable are also at work and being unmentioned do not work themselves out, so the disputes get their character — unpleasantly sweet and interminable.

The man I mentioned earlier who died in hospital discussing with himself an issue between altruism and the development of the true self, analysed himself in vain. Had he overweighted this? Had he neglected that? We struggle to pass from conflict into harmony, to find, as Aristotle said, the proper point between opposites. But unlike Aristotle we cannot face the prospect of choices without end and feel we must have rules to live by. To represent a difficult choice as ignorance of our duty in the situation we are in enables us to escape from facing the hidden sources of our hesitation. How much more can we escape into the wider inquiries of what acts, in general, are right and what, in general, makes good things good. Here we may wander for ever and when darkness begins to fall still build an altar to an unknown god.

When earlier I introduced the Monte Carlo fallacy I did so because I thought of it as one which arises purely from linguistic sources, as one which can be removed by turning the light on to linguistic confusion. And it is true that this trouble is more completely curable by linguistic treatment than are more philosophical troubles where the relevant facts of language form such a labyrinth that pressed in one quarter one may always take cover in another. But now it strikes me how very persistent and how very prevalent is even the simple Monte Carlo fallacy. One constantly hears people say '*Ah! that was too good to last*' or '*When we were having all the fine weather I thought we should have to pay for it*' or again, after a run of misadventures, '*Something will turn up. The luck must turn.*' Of course, to expect specially bad weather after specially good is not irrational if records show that regularly soon after specially good weather specially bad weather comes. But so far as I know there are no such records and so far as the people who use this argument know there are no such records. What they rely upon is '*the laws of chance working themselves out*'; what they rely upon is their feeling that though they don't know what card Fate will next deal them they do know what pack she holds so that if till now there have been no aces there'll be a lot of them soon to make up. True, there are people who when all has gone well for a long time feel more confident than ever; *they* feel that this just shows that Fate is with them. But there are others who begin to feel that they've had more than they deserve and that Fate will soon remind them that they are mortals, Polycrates and Amasis. And this last feeling finds expression, 'justification', rationalization, in talk about the laws of chance – confused talk because without the confusion it wouldn't express the way they feel. It's the same when things go badly; some fall into despair, others feel that they have been punished enough and that even the most implacable Fate will now be prepared to 'give them a break'. So it appears how even this very purely logical paradox is not purely logical. It is true that the reasoning which leads to it, though fallacious, is plausible, it impresses us, and it does so partly because we have not a very firm and adequate understanding of the use of our linguistic tools in many discussions about probabilities; *but it does so also because the resulting paradox suits many people and suits something in most of us.* Gambling has a peculiar and half-secret fascination for many people; so also for many has the most theoretical talk about probability and chance. I submit that though the logical or linguistic explanation of the Monte Carlo fallacy is very adequate we would have a still more adequate explanation were we able to bring out not only the features of language that make for the committing of that fallacy but also other causes hidden beneath the flow of talk. And *if this is true of the Monte Carlo fallacy it is much more true of the philosophical paradoxes.*

Chance and Necessity, Freedom and Deity, Mind and Matter, Space and Time – these words have in them the detachment of the intellect but also echoes from the heart, and the fascination of them is not confined to professional philosophers. I remember how years ago one night in the 'Elephant' a gentleman who, it was plain, had already been there some time took me aside in order to explain to me something of the connection between Mind and Matter. The big words of metaphysics have an appeal which is wide and deep and old and we cannot fully understand and resolve the riddles they present without understanding that appeal. In this sketch of philosophers I have been hinting at this. I have been hinting at connections with what psycho-analysts try to bring into the light. True, philosophy has never been merely a psychogenic disorder nor is the new philosophical technique merely a therapy. There's a difference. Philosophers reason for and against their doctrines and in doing so show us not new things but old things anew. Nevertheless, having recognized how different is philosophy from therapy it is worth noticing the connections: (*a*) how philosophical discussion is the bringing out of latent opposing forces like arriving at a decision and not like learning what is behind a closed door or whether $235 \times 6 = 1420$; (*b*) how, often, when the reasoning is done we find that besides the latent linguistic sources there are others non-linguistic and much more hidden which subtly co-operate with the features of language to produce philosophies; (*c*) how, in consequence, a purely linguistic treatment of philosophical conflicts is often inadequate; (*d*) how the non-linguistic sources are the same as those that trouble us elsewhere in our lives so that the riddles written on the veil of appearance are indeed riddles of the Sphinx.

Howe's *Invisible Anatomy*, Glover's *Psycho-analysis*, Layard's *The Lady of the Hare* and Sears' *Survey of Objective Studies of Psychoanalytic Concepts*

(*Mind Vol. LV*)

1. PART I of *Invisible Anatomy* discusses, the author says, 'the simplified patterns of the nervous system with special reference to that most widespread disorder which we know as "nerves" '. Part II 'includes ten doctored case-histories, to illustrate the sort of experience that we suffer in our nervous and emotional disorders'. Part III gives 'my own idea as to the metaphysical background out of which all problems emerge, as variants of what I regard as our "normality" '. Part IV is 'a more detailed study of the nature, cause, prevention and cure of that common emotional disease known as Hysteria'. Part V 'suggests some clues as to the meaning and mystery of sex, and how our lives can be conducted so as to avoid some of the more common pitfalls of ill health, unbalance and unhappiness'.

'*Invisible Anatomy: A study of Nerves, Hysteria and Sex.*' How well the title and the sub-title of this book hint at what is within! 'Anatomy' — science we trust; 'invisible' — mystery we hope, 'nerves and sex' — familiar words for what we know and wish someone would speak of. We are reminded of D. H. Lawrence's physiological mythology for psychological description. But this book has not the consistency of Lawrence. In it triangles and the central and autonomic nervous systems, snakes, chalices, some of the concepts of Freud and Jung, and stories of men, women and children contented and distressed, are inextricably mixed in an attempt to describe, to order, the psychological ills of humanity. Is it more than the hocus-pocus of a medicine man using scientific terms with the fearful facility of the inmates of mental hospitals? And yet, how simply and vividly Dr. Graham Howe tells the stories which illustrate his 'theories'. Certainly he knows the creatures he writes of and I feel that what he writes can give us more wisdom in dealing with ourselves and others. And yet, what is it that I deplore about this book even while I admire its courageous, kindly flow? The answer is that there is in it too much wallowing in mystery. I love mystery and Heaven forbid that we should become nervously shy of admitting metaphors and models to our scientific descriptions – lines of force and planetary atoms, censors and super-egos, all are welcome, and we know the crudities of misplaced simplicity which result when we are too determined to work only one explanatory apparatus. But we may be economical without being parsimonious. And we must be. We have good science when every model is a hard-worked machine for connecting observations. *Invisible Anatomy* is too lush for science, and it doesn't pretend to be literature – perhaps persons less academic than myself will accept it as neither. Certainly many laymen will get more from it than from Dr. Glover's *Psycho-analysis*.

2. *Psycho-analysis*. This book is not written for laymen, but for practitioners. Even to them I fear it will not mean much unless they have already read other books on psycho-analysis. Nevertheless it may do what the author hopes, namely, give some idea of the existing scope and future possibilities of the science. It is an outline, and, as Dr. Glover says, the task of condensing the theory and practice of psycho-analysis within about 140 pages is by no means easy.

The book is in three sections. The first has chapters on the Embryology, the Dynamic Aspects, the Structure, and the Economics of Mind and on Phases of Mental Development, Dreams and Symptomatic Acts, and Symptom Formation.

In Section II there are chapters sketching types of psycho-neurosis, psychosis, psycho-sexual disorder and other social disorders, and a chapter on the psycho-analysis of children.

Section III is on practical applications of psycho-analytic theory. It contains notes for the physician on the examination of a patient with a view to diagnosis, prognosis and recommendation of treatment, on the duration and cost of treatment, and on the various sorts of treatment. The three pages on this last point, which is treated under the heading *The Nature of Psycho-analysis*, are interesting and one wishes that there were more of them.

I think that the three 'approaches' – the structural, the dynamic and the economic, which Dr. Glover says are essential to the full understanding of every mental event, should have been more fully explained because of the part they play in his presentation of the facts.

In the first place, it is not easy to see at once how these metaphors are to be worked in the description of human behaviour. However, a little care reduces this difficulty.

One may (a) describe the structure of a machine, say a hydraulic system, and then (b) tell where the water is in it at a given time, and then (c) state the laws in accordance with which the water flows from part to part of the system. One may (a) describe the structure of a society, for example, the king and queen, the priests, the barons, the pedlars, the butchers and bakers and the serfs, and then (b) say where the wealth now is in a given society, or say where it is liable to be in any society of a given age, and then (c) state the laws in accordance with which it moves or does not move from class to class. One may describe (a) the structure of a simpler society — the family — the father and the mother, the elder brothers and sisters, the children, the wicked uncle, the step-mother. Here again we may describe (b) where the power and influence at a given time lies and also (c) the laws of how from time to time it shifts.

It may then strike one that the structure and dynamics of societies, *and especially of the family*, are to an unsuspected degree mirrored in individual minds — mirrored profoundly but in appalling, ridiculous and sublime caricature — a Moloch of blood and flames and the Madonna of the Eucharist.

Sometimes a society acts as if all power lay in the hands of the most babyish and animal members, and sometimes as if all power lay in the hands of strict old men, and sometimes it acts more as a whole — mostly when there's a war on. Sometimes a man is not himself and acts as if a babyish man or cunning animal had gained control — that's the id — sometimes as if an exacting parent, a sarcastic schoolmaster, or an implacable deity possessed him — that's the super-ego. Sometimes a man is more himself and acts more as a whole, a new whole which is not a combination but a synthesis of the id and the super-ego. Some are constantly at the mercy of the id, some are slaves to the super-ego, in some first one and then the other gains an unhappy victory in a continual struggle, and in some conflict and control have vanished into co-operation as with a man hunting hounds on a horse that knows the work and likes it.

So far so good. But if we now try to divide the description of the structure of mind from its dynamics and its economics, we are at once in difficulties. It is comparatively easy to describe the structure of a machine without describing its functioning, for example, a water mill without telling where the water lies or the way it flows. It is far harder to describe the classes of society without describing where the wealth lies and how it flows. And it is impossible, as Stout remarked, to describe a mind without reference to what it minds, what it wants and how it reacts; that is, to describe a mind *is* to describe where its energy lies and how it flows. Consequently, if one is to divide the description of the structure of mind from the description of where the water of life in it lies and the laws of its flow, one must divide (*a*) the description of the things a mind *might* be interested in, or the things *minds* are in fact *from time to time* interested in, from (*b*) the description of what they are interested in *at a given age* or what *a particular mind* is or was interested in at a particular time, and from (*c*) the description of the laws in accordance with which interest is re-distributed. One might expect that an attempt to separate these three descriptions so very closely connected would break down — interfere with exposition and result in repetition.

So it does, I think. Nevertheless, Dr. Glover is to be congratulated upon getting so much that is valuable into so small a book.

3. *The Lady of the Hare* by John Layard is in three parts. The first is a very interesting account of how an unhappy situation involving a woman, her sister, her daughter and her husband was successfully treated on Jungian lines in twelve interviews. A dream about a hare played an important part in this, and the second part of the book (pp. 100-229) is concerned with the significance of the hare in the world's mythological systems. The third part (pp. 230-48) is called 'More Dreams about Hares and Rabbits — showing the mythological motives on which they are based and their relation to everyday life'.

I cannot even summarize here the story of the treatment. The mother, Mrs. Wright, told her dreams, and the analyst, Mr. Layard, gently and carefully offered interpretations in such a way as to encourage her to use her own powers of interpretation. In the section on the subsequent development of the daughter (p. 96) we read that Mrs. Wright reports that Margaret is 'bright and happy and not the Margaret we used to know'. Before the treatment of Mrs. Wright, Margaret would hardly speak to anyone, wrapped herself up in her reading (Edgar Wallace, for preference) and always went out of any room her aunt came into. The husband also disliked the presence of the aunt but agreed with the mother that she could not be turned out, because she had nowhere to go to. The first indication of a big change in Margaret was when she started to have daylight visions which Mr. Layard says were continuations and extensions of Mrs. Wright's night-time dreams. 'These visions' he says, 'quickly developed into what can only be termed "second sight" combined with knowledge of certain aspects of her mother's past history obtained through visionary and auditory contact with her mother's father, who had died when Margaret herself was only three years old. This visionary perception of her maternal grandfather soon became merged with the traditional figure of Bonnie Prince Charlie . . . and this concept in turn was replaced by a higher concept still, that of the Heavenly Father, under whose direct guidance she now believes herself to be' (p. 98).

What happened in the twelve interviews with Mrs. Wright? The first answer we want is the one a cine-camera and a dictaphone would provide. But even if we had such a complete account of what happened in the interviews we might still ask 'What happened?' in the way we might ask this of a chemist who had done something astonishing, even though we had had a clear view of all he did and were confident he had no rabbits up his sleeve. The chemist would tell us a story of molecules and atoms hurrying, clinging, and separating and he would tell it to us with the air of an engineer who tells us what happens inside the machine which so cleverly prints and pushes towards us for 2d. a ticket to the Marble Arch. But really, the chemist is quite different from the engineer. He has never seen anything different from the sort of incident we now observe with him. It's only that he has seen more of them. Nevertheless, fantastic as is his story, it serves its purpose, for, like the engineer's, it connects the incident before us with thousands of others with which we should never have connected it but for his myth of the molecules.

Well, what happened in the twelve interviews? Mr. Layard does not in this book do much towards answering this. He writes a section called 'Brief Theoretical Discussion' (pp. 86–96) but it is so very brief and it is not all explanation. However, he writes enough to make me at least very confident that Dr. Graham Howe would write 'a very like account and Dr. Glover a very different one. Two questions arise: (1) How far are the different accounts incompatible? (2) Which is the better? or which is the better for this purpose and which for that? I can't deal with these questions because I don't know enough about Freud and Jung nor about Mrs. Wright to guess what the accounts would be. But even if the accounts were written out for me I should, I believe, still find difficulty in describing the differences and the likenesses between them. However, I venture the following remarks. Margaret's attitudes to her mother, her aunt, and her father, were connected on the one hand with her feelings to her mother's father and, on the other hand, with her feelings to Bonnie Prince Charlie and to her Heavenly Father.[1] Neither Dr. Graham Howe nor Mr. Layard nor Jung nor Dr. Glover nor Freud would deny the importance of either of these connections. But a Jungian would stress, I believe, the connections with the Heavenly Father and the Freudians would stress the connection with the maternal grandfather. (And what about her own, earthly father? Is it to be supposed that he had nothing to do with the case?)

Eckerman in his report of conversations of Goethe says (Jan. 10th, 1830) 'This afternoon Goethe afforded me great pleasure by reading the scene in which Faust visits the Mothers . . . Although I had heard and felt the whole, yet so much remained an enigma to me that I asked Goethe for some explanation. But he, as usual, wrapped himself up in mystery, as he looked on me with wide open eyes and repeated the words "Die Mütter! 'Mutter' klingt so wunderlich." "I can reveal to you no more," said he, "except that in ancient Greece mention was made of the mothers as divinities . . ." ' Eckerman goes on to offer what he calls his view of why the passage has so powerful an effect. He says . . . 'Could we imagine that that huge sphere our earth had an empty space

[1] 'Duncker (1938) reported a reversal of children's food preferences following the reading of an animal story in which the mouse hero indicated a decided preference for the food previously unpreferred by the children'. *Survey of Objective Studies of Psychoanalytic Concepts*, p. 56.

in its centre . . . this would be the abode of these unknown goddesses . . . beyond all place . . . beyond all time . . . all souls and
forms of what has been, or will be, hover about like clouds in the
vast space of their abode. So are the Mothers surrounded; and
the magician must enter their dominion, if he would obtain
power over the form of a being and call back former existences
in seeming life'.

This reminds me both of Jung and of Freud, of Dr. Graham
Howe and of Dr. Glover. It manages to bring out at the same
time both a man's feelings as a child, as an infant animal, to his
earthly mother, and his feelings as a religious adult to the All-
mother, who came out of chaos and gave birth to the Gods. And
we need both these connections if we are to understand a man's
attitude to his mother or to the woman with whom he has just
fallen in love. But though we need them both we must note that
the one explains in a way for which the other only prepares us.

Suppose a man tells us of a horse that its back tendons are
sprained. Then he not only tells us what symptoms we may
expect, he also gives us in this description of the present an outline
of the history which he guesses led to it. Suppose another man
tells us of a horse that it is now in a peculiar condition since,
though the Evil Eye has fallen upon it, gradually the Life Force
is triumphing in it. This is descriptively useful if we know the sort
of patterns of unfortunate symptoms of mysterious origin associated with the Evil Eye, and the sort of recovery processes,
equally mysterious, which are attributed to the Life Force rather
than to Harvey's Condition Powders. But this 'explanation'
though it describes the horse's condition tells nothing of its
cause although it pretends to do so.

Likewise – to say that there is in a man's attitude to the woman
with whom he is in love something of his attitude to his mother
and something of his attitude to his father or the cat he used to
cuddle in his cot, is not merely to analyse his attitude; it also hints
at its aetiology. On the other hand, to say of a man who has never
heard of the Virgin Mother nor of the Venusberg that in his
attitude to the woman with whom he is in love, struggles his
attitude to the Madonna and his attitude to the Venus of the
Venusberg, is to describe his attitude but not to say whence it
comes. Such a description analyses his attitude, places it with

reference to psychological fixed stars and so connects it with other attitudes and so prepares the way for a causal guess about it. But it does not itself make a causal guess. It does not even lead to one unless and until we venture not a description merely but a causal story for the power of the Venus and the Virgin.

Of course a hypothesis may be both descriptive or connective and also explanatory. In fact most hypotheses are thus mixed. We may know that a man has been brought up to love and reverence the Virgin, and then by saying that *in* his attitude to the woman with whom he is in love is his attitude to the Virgin we are not merely describing his attitude, we are also saying something of where it comes from, just as when we say that *in* his attitude to the woman with whom he is in love is his attitude to his mother. But the fact that in a hypothesis may be combined the functions of connecting description and of explanation, though it makes it less easy to apply the distinction between success at the one job and success at the other, does not make it less important — not if we are to arrive at a just estimate of what a given hypothesis accomplishes and what it does not and of how hypotheses conflict and of how they are to be supported and how refuted.

If we are told that a woman's eccentric act is due to her implacable super-ego then this hypothesis not only classifies her act but also outlines its aetiology. But if we are told that it comes from her neglect of her faculty of introverted intuition (compare Mr. Layard p. 235) this connects her act with others,[1] but does not outline an aetiology until we are provided with an account of the sort of past which produces such neglect. In short, we don't 'resolve the present into the past' if we don't. Mr. Layard, quoting Mr. Johan Jacobi, says (p. 22) that Freud succeeds (or would he say 'tries to succeed?') in doing so.

He also says that Jung builds up 'out of the actual situation towards the future'. And that may well be so. For the fact that a psychologist does not provide a causal account of the disorders he treats by no means shows that 'his therapeutic notions are . . .

---

[1] Of course, a hypothesis does this only if the meanings of terms involved in it, such as 'introverted intuition', have been taught, and that not by connecting them with other mysterious words (compare Mr. Layard's quotations from Jung) but by connecting them with familiar words. When and in so far as the meanings aren't thus taught, either by synonyms or by samples, then we had better call mumbo-jumbo by its name and have done with it.

inept', as Mr. Philip Toynbee says Jung's are.[1] On the contrary, his notions of what to do for a patient may be just the thing. Perhaps he can't tell us *what happened* when the cure worked, perhaps he can't tell us what past events made effective the words of the interviews any more than he can tell us what past events made the symptoms appear. But the curative power of talk *in* a cure is not necessarily connected with the truth of that talk, still less with the adequacy and correctness of talk *about* the cure when the magician tries to say why it worked. Revivalist preachers have cured people quicker than any analyst, but this does not in itself establish the truth of the doctrines they taught.

One might indeed suspect that often a cure may be more quickly effected by connecting present reactions with other present reactions than by explaining them in connecting them with past reactions. It is not only that the past ones occurred so long ago that it is hard to remember what they were; it is also that the patient may be averse to remembering them and that his arrangements for avoiding doing so are more firmly established than his arrangements for keeping present reactions separate from each other. One might suspect also that cure by connecting contemporary patterns would give a less stable psychical equilibrium and one of a different quality and that it might in certain cases fail. Even so, speed is a serious consideration. Surely what treatment it is wise to try depends upon the case (see Glover, p. 126).

No one must suppose from all this that Jungian psychologists never refer to the past and no one must forget that Freudian psychologists consider most carefully contemporary connections. What, for example, is insistence upon the transference connection if it is not insistence upon a connection as present as possible?

In Part II of his book Mr. Layard collects a vast amount of material about the mythology of the hare. I have not read it all. What I have read shows that though the hare stands for like things in different times and places, it also stands in different contexts for very different things. Consequently one cannot be confident about what it stands for in a given instance, for example, in a dream, without additional information about the context of the dream. It seems to me that in Part III, Mr. Layard interprets

[1] *Polemic*, May, 1946, pp. 54, 55.

certain features of a number of dreams as if such interpretation were a much simpler process than it is and as if symbols were much more regular in their significance than they are. I had better confess that I get the feeling that in some degree he spins the interpretations out of his 'inner consciousness'. There is, I know, no harm in that if there's a check-up process — but is there?

4. Mr. Robert R. Sears aims — thank heaven — at having a check-up process for every question. *Survey of Objective Studies of Psychoanalytic Concepts* is 'a summary and appraisal of published investigations, both experimental and observational, that relate to problems and concepts deriving from Freudian theory'.

Chapter I is on oral, anal and genital eroticism. Figures are given for the frequency of thumb-sucking, nail-biting, and oral gestures in various groups; figures for the frequency of thumb-sucking among 122 children with various degrees of opportunity for sucking during the regular feeding process; and figures for — but I cannot summarize the data. Mr. Sears says in conclusion to this chapter (p. 21) 'Freud first applied the properties of adult sexuality to infantile activities centred around the oral and anal-urethral body zones and then assumed that there was a specific quantum of pleasure-seeking that could be channelized through the various zones, making one a substitute for another. The evidence cited here supports the general correctness of the first point, but throws less light on the latter'.

Chapter II is on the erotic behaviour of children. Here, for example, is a table giving the rank order of frequencies with which different types of sex questions were asked by the 1797 children of 981 Minneapolis mothers. Mr. Sears concludes that the data (1) support Freud's claim that the commonest questions of young children concern the origin of babies, but (2) provide no evidence (a) that boys think that it is from injury that girls lack a penis, (b) that girls envy the penis, and (3) flatly disprove the universality of such reactions as (a) and (b) (p. 30).

It seems to me that the data do indeed make one regard with suspicion these claims of Freud's but that a much less crude method of verification would be required to disprove them. A boy's suspicion that a girl lacked a penis from injury might well not appear in his mother's answers to questions about what sex questions he asked, and a girl's penis-envy might also be very much hidden. I am all for getting clear about what technique would settle a question, and no one is more eager than I to ask an analyst what sort of discovery would make for his statement and especially what sort of discovery would make against it. But I do feel that, here and in other places, Mr. Sears in his desire to make the technique clear makes it over simple. No doubt the unconscious is irritatingly like ectoplasm — gone whenever the light is strong enough to see it. But still, provided a psychologist's prescription for settling his claim is clear, we must continue to be patient however complicated it is.

Chapter III is on Object Choice—the self as object, the Oedipus situation, the latency period, homosexuality. Mr. Sears says (p. 57) 'One conclusion stands out above all others: emotional development, as couched in terms of successive object choices, is far more variable than Freud supposed, but there are certain points at which Freud's skilled clinical observation provided generalizations that are largely supported by later and more objective observations'.

Chapter V shows how the results of certain experiments with animals are connected in a most interesting way with Freud's theories of regression.

In other chapters, objective data are brought to bear also on some of Freud's theories about Distortions of Sexuality, Repression, Projection and Dreams. By the way, why is there 'no aid to the interpretation of any particular dream in knowing that dreams are efforts at wish-fulfilment'? (p. 132).

In the concluding chapter Mr. Sears says something about whether psycho-analysis is or can become a *good* science and concludes that when the psycho-analytic 'method is used for uncovering psychological facts that have objective validity it simply fails' and that 'other methods must be sought for ... the validation of scientific findings' (p. 133) although 'social and psychological sciences must gain as many hypotheses and intuitions as possible from psycho-analysis' (p. 143).

I should like to write at length upon this matter, but I must confine myself to saying that it seems to me that Mr. Sears, like most of us academic persons, is unduly dominated by a desire for cut-and-dried, very verbally manageable, evidence such as is to be had from crucial experiments or data from which correlation coefficients can be extracted. But the fact is that most convictions come from evidence the excellence of which cannot be so conveniently described, and surely convictions based on such evidence can yet be thoroughly rational. I should *like* to walk with Mr. Sears swiftly down the main street counting heads upon the side-walk, for I'm soon sick of playing games with no rules in the adjoining swamps and woods with Dr. Graham Howe and Mr. Layard. But I have an uneasy fear we'll be missing something and even that people may laugh at us in spite of our slide-rules and statistical propriety. I am aware that the inclination to do science *a priori* and out of the 'inner consciousness' is still not dead and that we still need to attack every pretence of knowing about things or animals without watching them. A statement is a statement, I agree, only in so far as we all know what makes for it and what against it (tautology) and a statement provides new information in the way the engineer's, the chemist's, or the doctor's does, only if, like their statements, it better prepares us for aches and pains and sights and sounds. 'The incidence of nail-biting is a function of age' does thus prepare us. But so does 'Jealousy is cruel as the grave',[1] though here no questionnaire will prove, much less disprove it, and we cannot present the evidence for it in a correlation coefficient with its standard deviation. It is not that the ideas of questionnaire, experiment and correlation coefficient are entirely out of place in connection with it. They are not. But they cannot be applied to it in the simple way they can to 'Nail-biting is a function of Age' – though even here, as Mr. Sears remarks (p. 10, second paragraph), their application requires care.

Reading Mr. Sears I recall Dr. Graham Howe saying 'Some still seem to think that there is no other truth but Science' (p. 6). I don't know what this means, but I happen to read now in a book before me 'The remarkable thing about Mr. Flood is that he has bred hundreds of lion cubs and never lost one.

'He will tell you that the secret is understanding lions, which does not carry you far. How do you understand a lion? No two lions are alike, he will tell you . . .'[2] At once we know that Mr.

---

[1] So does Dr. Graham Howe's profound 'Life exacts death as the price of its own renewal' (p. 241).

[2] *In Search of Ireland*, H. V. Morton, p. 34.

Flood does not think that 'there is no other truth but Science', and yet if a basis in years of careful observation makes opinions scientific Mr. Flood's were scientific, though not many of them were generalizations about all lions and the evidence for them was neither crucial experiment nor correlation coefficients.

'No two lions are alike', he said. But doesn't this make science impossible? It's the opposite to 'All lions are alike really, though of course some are bigger than others like motor cars'. These two principles do not as they appear to do, make incompatible statements about lions, about Nature. They express two opposite attitudes in the investigation of Nature. But though the attitudes are opposite they are both needed in the scientist. The principles express two opposite calls for endless patience, to both of which the scientist must respond. For if when two things, apparently without reason, react differently he gives up looking for the reason why and says 'They're just different', that is to fall into magic, to give up science and no longer look for the unity in Nature. But also he must be prepared to find that he never comes to the end of the relevant differences, never gets in his list all the reasons — for otherwise he will be apt to call unscientific and un-logical those who still seek unity even in infinite variety and where the pattern of things cannot be presented in black and white on the forms provided by the logicians.

BERTRAND RUSSELL AND MODERN PHILOSOPHY

History of Western Philosophy and its connexion with Political and Social Circumstances from the earliest times to the Present Day.

'THE circumstances of men's lives do much to determine their philosophy, but conversely, their philosophy does much to determine their circumstances' (p. 11). This interaction, Russell says is his topic. But his topic is more than this. For centuries men have asked big questions about the world and their place in it, about mind and matter, space and time, and about the connections between what might be, what should be and what is. Here is the story of their efforts from 500 years before Christ to the present day, from Miletus to Chicago. True, the story is told so as to set their thinking in the context of their lives but the book is the story, not an investigation of the social causes and effects of philosophical theories.

Book I, Ancient Philosophy, covers the Pre-Socratics (pp. 21-94), Socrates, Plato and Artistotle (pp. 102-231), the Cynics, the Sceptics, the Epicureans and the Stoics. It tells of the Roman Empire in relation to culture and of Plotinus (pp. 252-308).

In Book II, Catholic Philosophy, there is more general history than in Books I and III. This is because Catholic Philosophy is 'essentially the philosophy of an institution, namely the Catholic Church'. During this period thought is especially closely bound up with religion and religion with politics. Part I (pp. 328-95) of Book II tells of the rise of Christianity, the life and times of the Fathers of the Church, the fall of the Western Empire, the conversion of the invaders, the growth of monasticism and the controversies within the Church. Part II (pp. 408-99) continues the story of the Church and the State and of philosophy now become Scholasticism. The Church, Russell says 'achieved power and wealth by means of its creed. The lay rulers who were in frequent conflict with it, were defeated because the great majority of the population, including most of the lay rulers themselves were profoundly convinced of the truth of the Catholic faith' (p. 322). 'Until the fourteenth century . . . philosophy . . . is written from the standpoint of the Church.'

In Book III, the Modern Period, Part I (pp. 511–700) is headed 'From the Renaissance to Hume', Part II (pp. 701-864) 'From Rousseau to the Present Day'. That Rousseau appears in the heading is an important clue for anyone wishing to guess at Russell's main interests in writing this history of philosophy.

In Chapter I, on the general characteristics of the 'modern' period, Russell says that it has 'a mental outlook which differs from that of the medieval period in many ways. Of these, two are the most important: the diminishing authority of the Church, and the increasing authority of science ... States increasingly replace the Church as the governmental authority that controls culture. The government of nations is, at first, mainly in the hands of Kings; then, as in ancient Greece, the Kings are gradually replaced by democracies or tyrants ...' (p. 511). 'The ancient world found an end to anarchy in the Roman Empire but the Roman Empire was a brute fact, not an idea. The Catholic world sought an end to anarchy in the Church, which was an idea, but was never adequately embodied in fact. The problem of a durable and satisfactory social order can only be solved by combining the solidity of the Roman Empire with the idealism of St. Augustine's City of God. To achieve this a new philosophy will be needed.' (p. 515). Does he mean here by 'philosophy', a recipe for a way of life individual and political, what I think he would call (see p. 815) 'an organic whole of extra-rational decisions on practical matters' or does he mean also new answers to the old questions about how we know mind and matter, necessity, goodness and beauty – the meta-psychological, metaphysical, meta-ethical questions?

Book III includes chapters on The Italian Renaissance, the Reformation, the Rise of Science, Bacon, Hobbes, Descartes, Spinoza, Leibniz, Locke, Berkeley, Hume, Rousseau, Kant, Hegel, Byron, Schopenhauer, Nietzsche, the Utilitarians, Marx, Bergson, James, Dewey, and the Philosophy of Logical Analysis.

The last chapter is about seven and a half pages in length. It does not mention G. E. Moore or Ludwig Wittgenstein and it hardly mentions Russell. This seems to me a pity. The reader having read so much of what philosophers have thought will wish to know something of what they now think. And to have told him would have been to show him the last scenes of the drama.

For isn't philosophy in its prime and *ipso facto* dying, consuming itself in its own fire? If philosophers unable to bear the heat, or others bent on their own business, extinguish the flames, then there will remain only blackened confusion. But if the fire burns itself out then from the ashes will be born something like but different.

Even if Russell could not present things this way because he doesn't believe they are this way it is still true that a fuller account of recent developments would have been a fit ending to the story he has told and told so well that a reader cannot but feel an interest in how things now stand with philosophers. As I have said Russell makes some attempt to tell us but in seven and half pages he cannot manage it. I now venture a few remarks intended to supplement a little these last pages.

(1) No doubt it is true that 'from Frege's work it followed that arithmetic, and pure mathematics generally, is nothing but a prolongation of deductive logic' (p. 858) and also that this prolongation 'was set forth in detail in *Principia Mathematica*' but to put the matter this way does much less than justice, I feel sure, to Russell and Whitehead's work. If we describe *Principia Mathematica* as nothing but the setting out of corollaries from Frege's results we must remember that, even if deductive consequences are in a sense always contained in their premises, it is not everyone who can detect them there.

(2) On the other hand, I do not think that one ought to say that proof that mathematics is nothing but a prolongation of logic disproves the theory that arithmetical propositions are 'synthetic' without remarking that it does so only with the help of the premise that no logical propositions are synthetic, i.e. that all are analytic, i.e. that every deductive conclusion is contained in its premise, i.e. that every valid argument is circular.[1] We do not, of course, owe our knowledge of this premiss to Wittgenstein but it is generally accepted that his work upon it was extremely valuable. (See Russell, *Introduction to Mathematical Philosophy* p. 205, Lewis and Langford, *Symbolic Logic*, p. 24, Wittgenstein *Tractatus Logico – Philosophicus* 61.)

---

[1] Kant is commonly said to deny this proposition. I am very ignorant of Kant, but I must report that upon reading some words of his own on this matter it did not appear to me that he did deny it in the sense in which it is true. Indeed I have the temerity to wonder whether the usual account of Kant's theory of necessary propositions is not very unfair to him.

(3) With reference to the work of Cantor upon the puzzle about the number of even numbers being the same as the number of whole numbers Russell says: 'Consider the **two rows**:

$$1, 2, 3, 4, 5, 6, \ldots$$
$$2, 4, 6, 8, 10, 12, \ldots$$

There is one entry in the lower row for every one in the top row; therefore the number of terms in the two rows must be the same, although the lower row consists of only half the terms in the top row. Leibniz, who noticed this, thought it a contradiction, and concluded that, though there are infinite collections, there are no infinite numbers. Georg Cantor, on the contrary, boldly denied that it is a contradiction. He was right, it is only an oddity.' (p. 858).

But this provocative dogmatism is misleading and blocks an opportunity to explain what sort of thing is done in the philosophy of mathematics. Surely the position is this. In almost all cases in which we speak of sets of things we also speak of the number of things in the sets and also say truly (1) that if one set contains all the things in another set and other things besides then the number of things in the one set is greater than the number of things in the other, (2) that if for every member of one set of things there is just one member in another set of things and vice versa then the number of things in the one set is equal to the number of things in the other. This holds even when the sets are for example the number of numbers up to 1000 and the number of numbers from 1000 to 2000. Likewise for 1,000,000, and so on.

If now, with a little qualm but only a little one, we speak of the number of numbers and the number of even numbers we shall expect to find that the questions we ask about the number of teaspoons, whether it's as great as it was and whether it is equal to the number of people coming to tea, will still make sense when asked about the number of numbers. And we are disappointed. The fact is it is not even true that all questions which make sense about the number of teaspoons still make sense when asked about the number of numbers up to 10. For it makes no sense to ask 'Is the number of numbers up to 10 as great as it was in 1900 A.D.' though we may conceal this by answering 'Yes, of course, for numbers are eternal' – which we may say without noticing that this sentence expresses a truth only in the sense that it's contradictory is meaningless. And there are great advantages in speaking of the numbers up to 10 or up to 100 as having a number in spite of the fact that the technique for deciding how many there are and how many there were is peculiar. For if we don't speak so we may well not notice that though some of the questions we ask about the number of teaspoons become silly when asked about the numbers up to 10 or up to 1000, *others do not*. We shall not notice that though all the statements we make about the numbers applicable to teaspoons and mice have to be modified in sense when applied to the numbers of numbers up to 10 or 1000, these modified senses will in most instances very naturally occur to everyone and, further, that in these modified senses a whole set of the old true theorems will remain true and the false ones false. And, when we come to questions and statements about all numbers we find natural interpretations for the sentence, S_1, 'to every even number there corresponds just one number and vice versa' and also for sentence S_2, 'besides all even numbers there are odd ones'. But unfortunately these new but natural interpretations are both true and consequently if we are to preserve the old connections between S_1 and S_2 and S_1', 'The number of items in these two sets are equal,' and S_2', 'the number of items in these two sets are not equal', we shall have to say that these last two sentences, namely S_1' and S_2', also both express truths. We could do this and say that in the world of infinite numbers contradictions of this kind do occur. But it would be very confusing. Or we could, like Leibniz say that though both S_1 and S_2 express truths neither S_1' nor S_2' do, because there is no sense in talking about the number of numbers or the number of even numbers. Or we could say that there is no sense in talking about the number of numbers being equal or not equal to the number of even numbers. Or we could break the connection between S_1 and S_1', without breaking the connection between S_2 and S_2'. that is we might say that though there is a one-one correspondence between numbers and even numbers that doesn't prove in our language that the number of numbers and the number of even numbers is equal. Or we could break the connection between S_2 and S_2' and say that though there are odd numbers as well as even numbers that doesn't prove that there are more numbers than even numbers. None of these alternatives is right or wrong. They are all among the things we may choose to say in face of the difficulties of interpretation arising in fitting an old notation to a new situation. But though none of these alternatives is wrong or right it may make a great difference which we choose. For if we say there is no sense in talking about the number of numbers or the number of even numbers this doesn't encourage us to give it sense. On the other hand if we say that there are infinite numbers and that there is sense in such talk this encourages us to give it a sense. And in fact it has turned out to be fruitful to say that though the sets are equal in number the one set contains members which the other does not i.e. the set of numbers contains a set which has as many members as itself. And we say that when we use 'number' so that this may be said we are talking of infinite numbers, that is we define infinite numbers as those of which this may be truly said. No wonder we prove Leibniz wrong.

(4) Now set beside this controversy as to whether infinite numbers are really numbers the controversy as to whether 'existence' is really a 'predicate'. We see the same things happening upside down. For while existence was spoken of as a predicate the likeness between the logical character of such statements as 'Lions do not exist' and 'Lions do not sing' was emphasized and the repressed unlikenesses made themselves felt in the form of puzzled hesitations arising from the attempt to ignore them and treat 'Lions do not exist' like 'Lions do not sing'. Kant said, I am told, that existence is not a predicate. Since then what is at the back of this statement has been explained, that is the relevant oddities of this predicate have been set out. (Russell, Moore, *Aristotelian Society* Supplementary Vol. 15, 1936.) And now that this has been done we may if we like go back to saying that existence is a predicate, provided we don't forget its peculiarities just as we may go back to saying that statements of relation such as 'Alfred hates George' are statements in which a predicate is attributed to a subject, provided we don't forget those differences between such statements and non-relational statements such as 'George is unwell' which modern logicians have emphasized by refusing to call relational predicates 'predicates'.

I would like to say more about the difficulties connected with statements asserting and denying existence. For these difficulties are members of a group of muddles which have been wiped out by that battery of definitions which is called the Theory of Descriptions and no history of philosophy down to the present time is adequate without an account of this engagement. Russell, it seems to me, describes it incompletely, inaccurately, confusedly and without a *full* appreciation of its full importance. He doesn't tell us who built the battery. Russell built it. And we must not allow him to escape the grateful and delighted applause which is his right.

I cannot in short space reproduce fully all or any of the unsatisfactory arguments the definitions in the theory of descriptions demolish. But: (a) Imagine that a child hears his father discussing with his uncle whether the golden ram which carried Phrixus from Greece to Colchis flew or swam.[1] The child says 'Does uncle really think the ram flew? Rams can't fly. And there aren't any golden rams.' His mother replies 'Uncle knows rams can't fly and that there aren't any golden ones. What he means is: when the people of long ago told a story of a man, Phrixus, and a golden ram, did they always say the ram flew or did they say he swam?' This receipt for definitions: When uncle says 'S is P' he often means 'The ancients said "S is P" ' makes clear to the child that often the treatment appropriate to his uncle's questions and statements is not what the child's experience to date with like utterances would suggest.[2]

It may seem incredible that philosophers should have confused themselves in answering the child's question and they might never have done so had it not been connected with more unmanageable questions.

(b) Suppose someone says ' "Lions roar" means "If a thing is a lion it roars" or else it means "There are lions and they all roar", and "Lions do not roar" means "If a thing is a lion it does not roar" or else it means "There are lions and none of them roar". So either (1) "Lions exist" means "If a thing is a lion it exists" and "Lions don't exist" means "If a thing is a lion it doesn't exist" or (2) "Lions exist" means "There are lions and all of them

[1] *The Flight of Phrixus* by Professor D. S. Robertson in the 'Classical Review', March, 1940.
[2] See W. E. Johnson's *Logic*, Vol. I, Chap. X.

exist" and "Lions don't exist" means "There are lions and none of them exist". Now (1) and (2) are both absurd.'[1]

The answer again is simple. 'Lions do not exist' has neither of the absurd interpretations which it must have if it is interpreted by the rules which hold for what it looks so like namely 'Lions do not roar', 'Lions do not sing', 'Lions do not breathe', 'Lions do not smoke', etc. What does it mean? How do we check a man's statement that lions exist? By looking for a lion. And 'Lions do not exist' means of course 'There are no lions' which means 'It is not the case that there is a lion'. It is instantly apparent that 'That is a lion' is related to 'Lions exist' like 'That is Alfred's wife' is related to 'Alfred is married'.

'Lions do not exist' can also be put 'The description *is a lion* applies to nothing'. (Russell says what implies that 'Lions exist' means 'The description *is a lion* exists'. But this absurdity is an unfortunate, persistent slip.) This awkward translation of 'Lions do not exist' would not be necessary if it were not that statements about existence are liable to be affected by another source of trouble, a source which affects also 'Lions are what Mr. Jones thinks about all day and dreams about all night'. This source of trouble, also affects in a different way even the most ordinary statements about lions such as 'Lions roar', 'Some lions roar', 'The oldest lion in the Zoo roars'. It even affects 'A lion is an animal'. The trouble is this. In all these cases if someone asks 'What is the speaker speaking about?' the answer is 'Lions'. It appears then that no one could say or think anything about lions without there being lions for him to speak or think about. As for 'Mr. Jones dreams of lions all night' not only is it true that no one could think that lions are so constantly in the dreams of Mr. Jones without there being lions for him, the thinker, to think of, but also what he thinks of Mr. Jones couldn't be true unless Mr. Jones often dreams of something and that something is often a lion.

This of course is all nonsense. Mr. Jones' dreams of lions and our thoughts of lions no more by their existence imply the existence of lions than do Mr. Chirico's pictures of horses

---

[1] See Broad *Journal of Theological Studies* for this and its connection with the ontological argument for the existence of God.

imply there are such horses. What is wrong with this silly argument is best shown up by rewriting the statements from which it starts in such a way as to remove the inclination to take the absurd steps involved in it. This may be done with the help of the following definitions: (i) 'Lions exist' means 'The description *is a lion* applies to something'; (ii) 'Some lions roar' means 'The description *is a lion* applies to something to which the description *roars* applies'; (iii) 'The lion roars' means 'The description *is a lion* applies to something and not to another thing and it applies to something to which *roars* applies'; (iv) 'All lions roar' means 'The description *is a lion* applies to something to which *roars* applies and it does not apply to something to which *roars* does not apply'; (v) 'Someone is thinking of lions' means 'The description *a person thinking in terms of the description (is a lion)* applies to something'; (vi) 'Lions must be animals' means 'The description *is a lion* includes the description *is an animal*'; (vii) 'The horses of the gods could fly' means 'People used to think that there were gods who owned horses who could fly'. This battery of definitions generalized is the Theory of Descriptions.

It is easy to see how it blows up the silly nagging arguments it is designed to deal with. Instead of speaking of a man as thinking of lions, or whether they exist or roar, we speak of him as wondering whether the description *is a lion* applies to something, whether the complex description *is a lion and roars* applies to something and so on. Not even a philosopher can infer from this that there are lions. A tailor may make a coat which would fit a giant without creating giants. And instead of speaking of the horses of the gods we speak of men having thought there were gods who owned horses, that is men who supposed the description *horses of the gods* to apply to something.

It is to be noted that if someone now asks 'What is a description?' or 'What is something?' the theory of descriptions does not provide an answer. It does not in itself solve the problem of 'universals' nor the problem of the 'variable'.

Also although the theory of descriptions deals with what you and I are talking about when we are talking about what writers of fiction have talked about, it does not deal with what the writer of fiction were talking about. It does not deal with the puzzle that what Lewis Carroll wrote about did not exist although h

wasn't speaking falsely. For Lewis Carroll when he first spoke
about Alice was not talking about stories told by others or by
himself. And he was not wondering whether a certain description
applied or not. He didn't care. And therein is the answer to the
puzzle question 'How is it that though he said that a white rabbit
dropped a glove, and no rabbit ever did such a thing, he wasn't
speaking falsely?' This puzzle cannot be dealt with by translating
the puzzling sentences into others about descriptions. It can be
met only by noticing that not all sentences which appear to be in
the indicative really are indicative, and that this is so not only
where they are concealed questions or commands, so that
grammar provides a name for the mood they are in, but also
where this is not so.

(5) Although the theory of descriptions will not do everything
it opened a new era in metaphysics. Once it had been seen how
the inmates of the universe of legend and of dream, imagination,
and thought were *logical constructions* out of ordinary things so
that statements about them could be checked with our eyes and
ears as well as any statements about spades and lions it quickly
occurred to Russell and Whitehead[1] that the same might be true
of other things including spades and lions. Philosophers had often
represented us seated sadly guessing from the images in the
mirrors of our minds at what was happening in reality. Berkeley
indeed sometimes said that such talk was senseless but he wavered
and sometimes talked very differently saying that there is a reality
behind our perceptions and that it consists in the perceptions of an
all-seeing God. Hume too was never quite decided whether to
say that our beliefs in permanent things are unfounded though
they have a correspondence with practical equivalents about the
order of our impressions or to say that our beliefs are reasonable
and often right because they *are* the beliefs about the order of our
impressions.

Russell in his books *Our Knowledge of the External World, The
Analysis of Mind* and *History of Western Philosophy* oscillates in
the same way between these two inconsistent positions. However

---

[1] (a) I think it is fair to say that Jeremy Bentham first introduced logical constructions.
The relevant passages from Bentham's work are collected in *Bentham's Theory of Fictions*
by C. K. Ogden.

(b) For Russell on construction *v.* inferences see *Our Knowledge of the External World* and
Analysis of Mind.

when he said that the realities we speak of are not guessed at from appearances but are logical constructions out of them and there-fore follow deductively from them he substituted for an old and muddling model of the connection between realities and appear-ances a new model.

For to say that a chair is a logical construction out of appear-ances of a chair is to say that a chair is related to its appearances *not* as a thing is related to the images of it in a mirror, *not* as a member of parliament to his constituents, but as the average plumber to plumbers, as a family to its members, as energy to its manifesta-tions, as electrons to the evidence for electrons.

It is easy to forget the great value of this connecting move of Russell's and Whitehead's. True, Berkeley had compared the relation between a thing and its appearances to that between a faggot and the sticks that make it up. But he didn't finish bringing out this analogy. Whitehead and Russell gave it new life with new analogies. Mounted on logical constructions philosophers of the 'twenties were able to cut exhilarating but confusing capers round about their less up to date contemporaries. Logical constructions enabled philosophers to ride down the dragons of mythology, to come up with the elusive 'beings for thought'. No wonder they asked 'What price now they'll catch the creatures of the noumenal, super-sensual worlds of matter, mind, value and necessity?'

But logical constructions are hard to handle and even those who understand them best easily get into trouble with them. For example, I said above that the inmates of the universe of legend and of thought are logical constructions. This statement may easily lead to error. It is true (1) that when a man speaks of unicorns or dragons he is in these days, usually speaking of inmates of the universe of mythology or of heraldry. And these are logical constructions. But it does not follow that unicorns are logical constructions, it follows only that the legendary unicorns of which he is speaking are, and even this follows only in the sense that his statements about unicorns can be turned into other statements about other things, namely statements about what peo-ple used to say long ago. Again (2) when a man says 'Unicorns are what Jones is thinking of' he speaks *in a sense* of unicorns and what he speaks of is Jones' objects of thought and these are logical constructions. But it does not follow that unicorns are logical constructions. Further, ordinary matter of fact statements about unicorns and lions can be translated as we have seen into statements from which the expressions 'unicorn' and 'lion' and synonyms have vanished in Russell's phrase. But this does not imply that lions and unicorns are logical constructions though this mistaken inference may have encouraged this fruitful idea. The fruitful idea is correct however only if ordinary statements about lions such as 'Lions sleep by day' can be turned into other statements about other things in the way in which extraordinary statements about unicorns such as 'Unicorns are sometimes rampant sometimes passant' can be turned into statements about coats of arms that is, in the way in which ordinary statements about the average plumber can be turned into other statements about individual plumbers.

Clearly if statements about a spade can be turned into statements about our sensations then the question 'Confined as we are to our sensations how do we know of the existence of spades?' becomes absurd. But *can* statements about real, physical, material things be turned into statements about sensations? *Are* physical things logical constructions out of the immediate objects of sense? — that was the question that then arose.

It was here that the pedigree of logical constructions misled us. What I mean is this. When it was asked 'Have infinite collections numbers' we fancied there was no point in answering 'Yes' unless that was true in exactly the old sense of number; i.e. unless infinite numbers had *all* the essential features of numbers. But it may be useful to call a locomotive an iron horse, it is useful to speak of an electrically charged wire as carrying a current, provided we keep on remembering that *not all* inferences legitimate in the older, narrower application of the words in question will still be legitimate.

In the original simple contexts when we spoke of logical constructions and of turning sentences about Xs into sentences about Ys the rule for the turning provided exact or nearly exact translations. But we need not insist on this exactitude. Indeed while the statement 'The average plumber is 5 ft. 6 in.' has an exact equivalent in terms of individual plumbers this is not true of 'The average plumber does not arrive on the day you expect him'. Nevertheless the average plumber is still a logical construction out of plumbers in the sense that statements about him have no meaning over and above their verification in terms of individual plumbers, so that it's silly to say 'Confined as we are to individual plumbers how can we claim knowledge of the average plumber?' In the case of spades and sensations there are other difficulties beside the impossibility of providing for statements in terms of spades *exact* translations in terms of sensations of spades. But like the impossibility of exact translations these other confusing features leave it appropriate to say that the lament 'Confined as we are to our own sensations how can we claim knowledge of spades?' is a senseless lament. Or rather these confusing features will leave it appropriate to say that the lament's sense is simply to reveal these confusing features. These confusing features upon patient examination cease to be difficulties and are seen as no more than the differences which make the connection between statements about chairs, tables, etc., on the one hand, and statements about sensations on the other hand, what it is and not something else.

Every different puzzle requires different treatment, perhaps very different, perhaps negligibly different. How like two treatments must be for us to say that the same method is employed in each I will leave to the reader to decide. What I do want to do is to draw attention to the fact that in all the puzzles we have glanced at the trouble arose from deducing how a sentence *must* work from a rule which fitted like cases to date, while the trouble was removed by reminding ourselves of how the sentence does work. We do this by running over how we decide whether one who utters it is right or wrong; noticing whether these methods give a definite result, as with 'He has a spade', 'Twice sixty four is one hundred and twenty eight', or can give only an indefinite result as with 'Infinite collections have numbers', noticing whether there are no such methods appropriate to the utterance, as with a story-teller's 'Once upon a time there lived a miller who had three sons...', noticing what sort of work the utterance then does, noticing how an utterance may work in several ways at once and how innumerably different are the ways utterances work, how like are the very different ways and so on till the cows come home.

As we all know it's not that rules are wrong but that they easily grow too powerful. Without them there is no order, no connecting one thing with another. But it is only too easy to substitute the manipulation of rules for looking carefully at the individuals they cover. There have always been a few people who, while able to detect connections which others have missed, have never lost the child-like power of seeing each thing for what it is. We owe much to them and Russell is one of them. Russell says on his last page that it is now true that in philosophy we have a method 'in which each new stage results from an improvement, not a rejection of what has gone before'. Perhaps this has always been true. Perhaps it isn't true now. But it is true now in a way it never was before.

If you like history done backwards this book of Russell's is not your cup of tea. For it is not written to make the present philosophical work throw light upon the past nor vice versa. Russell mentions (p. 352) the controversies about the Trinity and the Incarnation[1] but he does not connect them with controversies about the nature of what lies behind appearance, as to whether our friends dumb and not dumb have any thoughts or feelings, as to whether they have or could have unconscious thoughts and feelings and so on.

Again, I can imagine somebody saying 'Philosophy in 1000 pages. English Literature in 2000 pages. Save time and at the Criterion see the Himalayas in forty-five minutes'. If you feel like this don't read this history of western philosophy. Don't read any history of western philosophy. You don't have to. Personally I am sure I would like to see photographs of the Himalayas at the cinema though only threats would make me call this seeing the Himalayas. And reading Russell on say Spinoza or Berkeley isn't reading Spinoza or Berkeley. By no means. Of course not. This leaves it true that Russell has presented us not with photographs but with sketches which for all their multiplicity are united into a moving picture of successive generations of men trying to make an outline map of where they are and trying to gain such a grasp of their own methods of projection that these

---

[1] Controversies which 'have shaken the pillars of the church and state'. Gibbon *The Decline and Fall of the Roman Empire*, chap. XLVIII. Compare Broad *Scientific Thought*, pp. 156, 215.

will not muddle or fossilize their apprehension of the world. Their endeavours, their energy, ability, integrity and dishonesty in these endeavours have not been unconnected with their hopes and fears, their sense of sin and desire of salvation. Here is the story told by an old explorer still full of the life and courage that did not fail him or his companions whether in the icy regions of logical space or in the equatorial tangles that lie between us and the conquest of happiness.

A NOTE ON PROBABILITY

Philosophical Analysis. A Collection of Essays. Cornell
University Press

WHAT is probability? In other words how are disputes about probability settled? Some one way, some another. But we want to know what these ways are, how they are connected with each other and with ways of settling disputes which are not about probability but, for example, about entailment.

Some disputes about the probability of q given p are a priori, that is, settleable provided only that one knows the language; others involve claims of fact. For example 'Given that he is to be married in the next fortnight from today, Monday, and not on a day next a Sunday, what is the probability that he will be married on a Tuesday?' is an a priori question; but 'What expectation of life has a butcher of 50?' is a question of fact. And the question 'Given that he is to be married in the next fortnight from today, Monday, and not on a day next a Sunday, what is the probability that he will be married on a Tuesday?' is a question of fact whenever the answer is taken to depend on the frequency of marriages on the several days of the week.

Amongst these questions about probability which are questions of fact, some make a *definite* factual claim which if satisfied enables one to reach by a definite calculation a figure for the probability of q given p; others are concerned with a claim which is enormous and hazy and such that, though if it is satisfied a figure may be reached, this figure is not reached by arithmetical calculation. For example, a definite, limited claim is made by the statement 'The expectation of life of a butcher of 50 is 10 years'. For it says that there are facts of a certain sort which together with the fact that a man is a butcher of 50 give a probability of $\frac{1}{2}$ to his reaching the age of 60. The facts in question are records of the ages at death of butchers for the last n years and the probability is obtained by counting how many of them in these years, having reached 50, later reached 60 and how many did not. The question what, *given* the fact that a man is a butcher of 50 and these records, is the probability of his reaching 60 is an a priori question – it is settled by arithmetic.

A large, hazy, factual claim is made by 'Liberty Light is a 66-to-1 chance for the Cambridgeshire'. This means 'There are ascertained facts which together with the fact that Liberty Light is running in the Cambridgeshire give a probability of 1 in 67 of his winning'. Here the facts are anything that's relevant – form, pedigree, weight, conformation, whispers, physiology, biochemistry – nothing barred. The figure for the probability is not arrived at by arithmetic. (Of course a bookmaker may arrive at a figure by a calculation based on the bets that are coming in, like the totalisator does, but we are not considering that case.) Here we cannot complete the *statement* of the relevant facts; but the more nearly we do so, the more nearly a priori is a claim that, in view of these facts and the fact that Liberty Light is a runner, the proper odds to offer against him are 66-to-1.

It is this fact that we cannot state all the evidence and not the fact that the figure for the odds is not reached by calculation which prevents such assertions about probability being perfectly a priori. Given that all Englishmen are perfidious and that Jack is an Englishman the probability that Jack is perfidious is 100 per cent. This is an a priori truth, but the figure is not arrived at by calculation. In this case not only does p entail that the probability of q is what it is; it also entails q. With argument from past experience and present observation to the future, p does not entail q; indeed their connection is of course contingent. But this leaves necessary the connection between p, the incompletely stateable past experience plus the incompletely stateable present experience, and the statement 'probably q', e.g. '66-to-1 against Liberty Light'.

Amongst a priori questions of probability there are those cases where q entails p and the probability depends upon the nature of this entailment and those where it does not. Where q is the proposition that a certain man will reach the age of 60 and p the proposition that he is a butcher of 50 plus the actuarial records for the past ten years, q does not entail p, although p entails that q has the probability it has. Again where q is the proposition 'A six *will* be uppermost *in a moment*' and p is the proposition that a die *is* falling plus records of, say, all past throws, q does not entail *p*. But where *q* is the proposition 'A six will be uppermost in a moment' and *p* is the proposition 'A die will have fallen in a moment' then *q* entails *p*. In such cases questions as to what probability *p* gives *q* are settled by considering how much *q* *overentails p*. *q* overentails *p* if *q* entails *p*, but *p* does not entail *q*. 'This is red and hard' overentails 'This is red'. *r more* overentails *p* than does *q* if *r* overentails *q* and *q* overentails *r*. Thus 'A six' more overentails 'Either a six or a five or a four or a three or a two or a one' than does 'Either a six or a five' and 'Either a six or a five' more overentails 'Either a six or a five or a four or a three or a two or a one' than does 'Either a six or a five or a four', and so on; 'He will be married next Sunday' overentails 7 to 1 'He will be married next week'. 'He will be married next Sunday or Monday' overentails 7 to 2 'He will be married next week'. If we have an understanding as to how we count the alternatives in two propositions such as 'A die has fallen' and 'A number less than four is uppermost', we can have a rule for calculating a number measuring overentailment. We shall say *q* overentails *p* by *m* to *n* provided *p* is, or is equivalent to, an alternative proposition with *m* alternatives and *q* is or is equivalent to an alternative proposition made up of *n* of these same alternatives. '*q* overentails *p* by *m* to *n*' means the same as 'the probability of *q* given *p* is $\frac{n}{m}$.' Just as the peculiar logic of '*p* entails *q*' is brought out by explaining how its truth arises from the way *q* repeats *p*, i.e. by the equation '*p* entails *q*'='*p* and *q*=*p*', so the peculiar logic of this class of statements of the form '*p* lends probability to *q*' is brought out by saying that in them '*p* lends probability to *q*' means '*p* or *q*=*p*'.

It will be noticed that the examples chosen by mathematicians to teach the mode of settling probability claims of the last kind — I mean the examples of dice, balls in bags, etc. — have two features: (1) They incline us to confuse different sorts of probability claim, question, or dispute. (2) Because of this they explain why the mathematicians choose to use the words of their calculus as they do and to count alternatives as they do.

If one says 'With a die the probability of a six is 1 in 6', one is right whether one intends this as (a) the tautology 'A die has fallen' is overentailed 6 to 1 by 'A six is up' and is comparable to 'He will be married next week' gives a possibility of 1 in 7 to 'He will be married next Tuesday'; or as (b) the statement of fact 'In throws with dice to date the proportion of sixes has been 1 in 6'; or as (c) the statement of fact 'All facts of nature observed to date give us no reason to expect one side of a die rather than another; that is, combined with the information that a die has fallen one side uppermost, all facts of nature give a probability of 1 in 6 to a six and, given the information that a die is in the air, they give a probability to a six negligibly less than 1 in 6, since though they give us no reason to expect one side of a die rather than another they give the best of reasons for expecting a die now in the air to fall and to fall one side uppermost and not poised on one corner.'

Only when we set 'With a die the probability of a six is 1 in 6' beside 'With a man who is to be married next week the probability of his being married on a Tuesday is 1 in 7' do we realize how 'With a die the probability of a six is 1 in 6' may be a tautology but also a summary of experience like 'With a goat you can bet your life it'll get out however you fence it in'. That there are two interpretations is obvious with 'Given that a man is to be married next week the probability of his being married on Sunday is 1 in 7'. We can easily see why the figure 1 in 7 is given; we can also easily realize that someone might insist on saying that the statement is false because records show that people seldom marry on Sunday. We can easily see how absurd would be a dispute between such a person and one who read off the probability from the number of days which a week is defined as having.

It is now possible to correct and explain the confused sentence I wrote in *Mind*: 'A probability claim about the future cannot be a transformation of premisses about the present and the past'.[1] The statement 'The probability of a butcher of 50 living another ten years is $\frac{1}{2}$' is a transformation from the actuarial records; and one who says 'This man is a butcher of 50, the records run thus and thus so the probability that this man will live another ten years is $\frac{1}{2}$' is making a purely deductive move. It follows that what I said was false.

What I ought to have said was this. 'The idea that a claim of the form "It is probable that such and such will happen" can be a transformation of data about the present and the past *in the way*

[1] LVII (1948), 419.

that "It is probable that *q*" is a transformation of "*p*" when *q* overentails *p*, is absurd.' It is a corollary that the idea that a claim of the form 'It is probable that such and such will happen' can be a transformation of premisses about the present and the past in the way that 'A six will be uppermost is probable to the degree 1 in 6' is a transformation of 'A die will be lying with one side upper-most' is absurd. 'A die is about to be thrown' or 'A die is falling' does not *in this way* give the faintest probability to a six. This is obscured by the fact that the step from 'A die is falling' to 'A die will be lying with one side uppermost' is so very reasonable in the light of experience. The consequence is that, told that a die will be thrown a thousand times and asked what I will bet against a run of 6 sixes, I pass without noticing that I do so from the given premiss to a new one 'A die will fall a thousand times with one or other side uppermost and not come down poised on one corner or remain in the air'. From the new premiss I arrive at proper odds for a bet by considering the ratio among those things, one or other of which it says will happen, which will give me a win to those that will make me lose — as I might consider whether it is advisable to play with a man who explains that he is about to throw a penny and that if it comes down heads he wins while if it comes down tails I lose.

Another, a different, fact conceals the absurdity of the idea that premisses about the present and the past can give probability to a conclusion about the future in the way that has demonstration as a limit, i.e. as 'A die will fall' gives probability to 'A six will be uppermost'. It is the fact that statements which appear to be about the present contain claims about the future. Thus suppose we stand before a house of three storeys and notice three bell buttons. We know that the top-storey bell is connected either with the top button, the middle button, or the lowest button. It seems a deduction in accordance with the ratio formulas that the probability of the top button being the right one, being the one connected with the top storey, is 1 in 3. We press the top button and a bell rings but not on the top storey, so we infer that the bell for the top storey is connected either with the middle button or with the bottom button; and it seems a deduction in accord-ance with the ratio formulas that the probability that it is con-nected with the bottom bell is now increased to 1 in 2. We press

the middle button and still the bell on the top storey doesn't ring
so it is not connected with the middle button. We now have
premisses which seem to demonstrate that the bell on the top
storey is connected with the bottom button.

But the expression 'x is connected with y' may mean 'a wire
links x with y' and may mean 'whenever x is pushed y rings'.
This ambiguity is of no practical importance because experience
makes it so safe a step from the one to the other. But, if we are
concerned to describe the nature of the argument above, it is of
great importance. For if (1) in that argument expressions of the
form 'x is connected with y' are employed in the same sense
throughout, then our deductions as to probability are conducted
in accordance with the ratio formulas. But then also either (a)
the conclusion means merely that a wire links the bottom bell
with the top storey and says nothing about what will happen; or
(b) the first premiss claims not merely that the bell on the top
storey is linked by a wire to either the top, the middle, or the
bottom button but that it is connected with one of these buttons
in the sense that whenever that button is pressed the bell rings,
and thus makes a concealed claim about the future.

And if (2) in the argument above expressions of the form 'x is
connected with y' are not used in the same sense throughout but
are first used to mean 'A wire links x with y', so as to have premisses which make no claim about the future, and then used to
mean 'Whenever x is pushed y will ring', so as to have a conclusion which predicts the future, then at that point in the argument where the sense is changed a step is taken, which, though
experience in this instance makes it safe, is not in accordance with
the ratio formulas.

There remain other sorts of probability claim, and one of these
I would like to mention. When we say 'The expectation of life
of a butcher of 50 is such and such', we may, as we have said, be
making a claim only about past records, but also we *may* be
making a claim not only about past records but also about future
records. In other words we *may* so use this statement about the
butcher that the mortality among butchers *subsequent* to the
statement we make is relevant to it. If we do we may then say
'It *seemed* that the probability was such and such but in fact it
was so-and-so'. Thus in spite of Keynes, the Times Racing

Correspondent writes, May 28th, 1936, 'It seemed then all Lombard Street to a China orange than Thankerton would win. For he is by Manna,a Derby winner, out of Verdict, the dam of Quashed. Suddenly when all seemed over Thankerton began to stop'.

Here the fatal word 'seemed' speaks of the old model for expressing hopes and fears – one of the Fates holds high the balances in which the chances for us and against us lie; but what is in those balances we can never quite see.

THINGS AND PERSONS

(*The Arist. Soc. Suppl. Vol. XXII*)

1. PROFESSOR MACKINNON is right it seems to me and on a matter of importance – those who write books on ethics seldom take ethical problems seriously. In his paper he gives hints as to what he means by this. He says that writers like Kierkegaard, Buber and Marcel are significant because they do take ethical problems seriously, while it is plain from what he says elsewhere that he would say that the utilitarians, for example, do not. It is plain too that he thinks that there is a connection between not taking ethical problems seriously and, to use his own words, 'trying resolutely to eliminate from the discussion any appeal whatsoever to that which transcends observation'.

2. There seems to me confusion over this last point. Sidgwick and Moore are utilitarians and don't take ethical problems seriously in MacKinnon's sense, yet both are transcendentalists who say that 'good' is neither a word like 'irritable' which tells us what a man is like nor a word like 'irritating' which tells us how people feel to him. They say that goodness is a special kind of quality apprehended in a special way.

I would like to make two points here: –

(1) I am not saying that an anti-transcendental account of the role of ethical utterances doesn't make against 'taking ethics seriously'. On the contrary such a meta-ethic when subjective may seem to make it impossible to take ethics seriously. And this can cause distress. About a year ago I was talking to a man who had been reading that ethical statements really express our feelings. Some philosophers have spoken as if we cannot show an ethical statement to be correct or find it incorrect. This sort of thing had led to or increased in this man a feeling of despair, a feeling that nothing really matters, a feeling that the world is water, without form and void. And this was not a man with a 'half-baked' acquaintance with the meta-ethics that affected him. I said to him, 'Suppose the goodness of a person were as objective as the goodness of an argument'. 'Ah', he said, 'but is it?'

A few weeks ago someone complained to me that so many people feel at a loss about values and asked whether there wasn't someone who gave help in that matter. Here again we come on ethical uneasiness, ethical distress, and upon the wish, the need, to make ethical effort.

To understand the despair which finds confirmation in subjectivism imagine a child who has been struggling to do what his mother and father want and suddenly notices that they are laughing at him.

One may say indeed that a subjective meta-ethics though it may temporarily smother the need for ethical effort may also by refusing to meet that need bring it into the open. One may say too that the idea that there are experts on living as there are experts on cooking is an illusion, and an illusion which cannot be cured without going through the feeling which subjectivism expresses, the feeling that there is no land and that therefore the sooner one stops swimming the better. Subjectivism makes one realize one must choose.

At the same time one may feel that the idea that there are experts on living as there are on cooking or the management of sheep is not an illusion — there are after all people with extra experience and insight into life.

(2) But I submit that it is not only subjective meta-ethics which in some ways makes it difficult to 'do ethics seriously'. A transcendental meta-ethics may also have this effect. A subjective meta-ethics over-emphasizes and in crude forms over-simplifies the place of the sentiments in ethical effort. A transcendental meta-ethics, on the other hand, over-intellectualizes the process and sterilizes it. Professor Stebbing wrote a book called *Ideals and Illusions*. It is true that no one can say that this book encouraged one to take ethics easily. In it a great deal is said about getting clear about ideals and this is not represented as easy. But when I read the book I had the feeling that little or nothing was done in it to help one to get clear about ideals *except by indirection*. (By indirection something was done, indeed it was. For the honesty and courage which appears between the lines even in so dry a work as Sidgwick's *Methods of Ethics* was also between the lines of *Ideals and Illusions*.) The very phrase 'getting clear' takes one out of ethical distress into intellectual

effort and *ipso facto* away from doing ethics seriously, since for that the intellect *by itself* is helpless.

When we wish to present the meaning, the function, the role of a class of sentences which perform a role complicated and peculiar compared with others, we tend to do so by presenting them as being about an object or objects obscure to observation like a man behind the scenes or blocks of very transparent ice. We guess at the nature, condition and movements of an arch criminal by putting together the small but observable manœuvres of his satellites. Only occasionally do we catch a glimpse of him slipping by in a dark limousine. When we wish to make a statement to which our observations of many individual things are relevant we put that statement in a form which suggests this model of the man in the shadows and speak of, for example, the average man, the plain man, the dog, and so on. When we wish to make statements to which many observations of two sorts of event going together are relevant we speak of there probably being a *connection* between events of these sorts. When in logic we make a statement to which many observations as to the usage of words are relevant and in a peculiar manner, we again put the statements in a form which suggests illusive objects, though the objects are now said to be abstract and the connections between them timeless. No wonder that when we are asked to describe the role of such classes of statements and their relation to what we mention in supporting or refuting them we are apt to say that the relation is that which holds in the model which their form and so much of our practice with them suggests.

In certain situations the inappropriateness of the model is forced on our attention; we throw it aside and in an effort to present the closeness of the connection between the class of statements with which we are concerned and the observations on which we in fact rely in making them, we identify the statements with descriptions of the observations, that is represent them as related to the observations like statements about the average man to observations of individual men. In thus representing the statements as descriptions of the observations we over-simplify their mode of connection with the observations and usually we over-simplify our account of the relevant observations. Should it seem that in our efforts to get down to earth we have caricatured the statements we started with, then this is explained away by saying that the caricature only represents their meaning in so far as they are susceptible of rational justification. They may have in addition an exclamatory, hortatory, emotive, imaginative function, but this is represented as irrelevant to their logical position. Thus is the oneness of logic preserved regardless of expense.

How a narrow idea about justification leads to a metaphysical drive towards scepticism or transcendentalism or positivism, how these doctrines correct each other and are all both wrong and right, I shall not attempt to set out here. But I would like to offer two examples of the practical, non-metaphysical growth of a positivistic doctrine, of its non-metaphysical usefulness and of the way it over-simplifies.

Suppose a man notices a tendency amongst others to make claims about causal connection from an armchair and to carry on disputes about such claims without that vigorous and laborious field observation they really demand. Suppose he then becomes a positivist and says 'Whether one thing is causally connected with another is a matter of whether when one happens the other does'. This is an over-simplification but it does put our effort in the right place. A transcendentalist will continue to deplore the over-simplification. The complexity and difficulty of causal investigation will appear in his account. It will appear in the distorted form of the transparency and illusiveness of the object, the relation, which he insists the claim is about. Still it will appear. And it will do no harm provided he doesn't really take any notice of his own talk about the possibility of a shorter way to knowledge of causal connection.

The transcendentalist who says that logical and philosophical questions are questions about the inter-relations of timeless objects so obscures by an inappropriate model the procedure that settles them that only where they are easy can they be settled, and where they are hard we are paralysed. The positivist who says that they are questions about words so misrepresents the procedure proper to them by an over-simple model that however serious and difficult they are we can't take them seriously and carefully. Meta-metaphysics has had a powerful influence on metaphysics, i.e. description of the role of metaphysical sentences has had a powerful influence on the way we proceed with them. In contrast description of the role of sentences about material things has practically no effect on our firmly established procedure – metaphysics cuts no ice with train-starters. Meta-ethics has some influence on ethics. It is easy to exaggerate that influence and easy to underestimate it.

3. To return. MacKinnon wants ethical problems taken seriously, and perhaps we ought to say that he wants them taken seriously not merely by people who have a particular problem to deal with, but also by people who are dealing with a problem of some generality even though, as in a problem play, the problem is presented through a particular case.

Connected with this which is, I believe, his main concern are two other points: (1) He thinks that many ethical problems are better put in terms of people than in terms of acts. Thus he says that writers like Kierkegaard, Buber and Marcel raise the problem of the individual. He also says that Butler, as opposed to a utilitarian, argues that the proper subject of the moralist is the individual or person in his nature and in his relation with his fellows, and that he refuses consequently to allow that we can so to speak 'absorb ethical reflection in discussion of the means of promoting good'.

(2) MacKinnon insists that the results of ethical reflection are not something that can be presented in a principle or set of principles. He says that Butler and Kant are wrong if they suppose that ethical ideas can be conceived in terms of a general formula. 'The use of any such formula', he says, 'can only have the effect of drawing an artificial boundary to contain that which in its nature cannot be contained. The responsiveness of man to man, the 'disponability' of a man in the presence of his fellows, the diversity of human love – these are not things that can be mapped. You cannot set out even in the most rarified formula what is that which through the intimacies of personal exchange a man is called to become'.

4. But to consider these points. And first someone may ask 'What is it to take ethical problems seriously? Don't we all want to take them seriously? Don't many of us take them too seriously? Who doesn't take them seriously? Hume, Bentham, Mill, Sidgwick, Moore or Ross?' MacKinnon says: 'In utili-

tarianism one encounters a clear example, clear to the point of a caricature, of the approach to ethics which refuses altogether to take personal existence seriously. You see this in the insistence that the notion of happiness is fundamentally simple, that in effect happiness can be so defined as to constitute the twin of the whole analysis. It is insisted that in human satisfaction there is nothing mysterious'.

4.1. One may pick up a book on art and it may be dull. It is dull when it tries to give rules, canons, which will enable us to deduce whether a picture or a poem is good. It is dull when it tries to set out in general terms what makes a good picture good, like a logician sets out what makes a good demonstration good. It happens that this can be done for demonstrations[1] with a very high degree of success. A short statement of the necessary and sufficient conditions of formal perfection is presented in axioms and just what the axioms cover can be set out more and more specifically for anyone who wishes this done. Even here there is danger of the explanation being taken to be more adequate than it is. It can lead to shallowness and to blunting of the sense of the soundness of arguments in a ridiculous submission to the rules which should serve and co-operate with that sense.

When it comes to what makes a good picture good or a good poem good the whole plan is a failure and is apt to lead not to understanding and discriminating feeling for what is good, but to that rigid and dead reaction to recognized points sometimes found in dog fanciers and characteristic of the Pharisees.

It is the same with a book on ethics which tries to set out what makes right acts right and good men good. Even if the author has given up as futile the idea of setting out conditions necessary and sufficient for goodness or rightness and merely tries to set out a list of the circumstances which are always, if present, considerations for or against an act, the game is a bore and a menace.

---

[1] And also for the statements of the form 'p gives probability to q' where q is a specification of p, i.e. where q entails p. This is a very different class of statements from those of the same form of which it is true merely that p entails *It is probable that* q. The former are simply entailment statements about p and q reversed and in their case degrees of probability are obtained in so far as there are conventions about degrees of *specification* or *over-entailment*. Thus 'A die lies with a six up' over-entails 1 to 6 'A die lies with either a one or a two or a three or a four or a five or a six up'. When p is about the past or present and q is not, but e.g. about the future the conditions for the goodness of argument from p to q cannot be satisfactorily set out in formulae.

For in this game he confines himself to the evident and thus to the obvious.

The only ethical principles worth attention are ones which are false like 'Dishonesty to oneself is the only crime'. They do represent serious ethical effort when they are first hand.

(I think no one now pretends to give formulae adequate for the moral life. To quote a few platitudes *as examples in order to illustrate the conflict of duties* – here I think of Ross – is quite a different matter though I am not sure that Ross said enough to make clear that he neither regarded the platitudes he quoted as interesting in themselves nor thought them capable of covering ethics.)

4.2. One may pick up a book on art and it may not be dull.

To some people it will not be dull if it contains a lot of stories about painters, writers and musicians – how one was very poor and kept a little dog and so on. But that's not aesthetics.

To some people it will not be dull if it is about what beauty is, what sort of difference there is between two people when one praises a poem and the other says it's very poor. But that's meta-aesthetics.

There is however a third and proper way in which a book on art may not be dull. Mr. Lionello Venturi who writes the Introduction to the Phaidon Botticelli helps one to see Botticelli. Mr. Edmund Wilson, the author of *Axel's Castle*, helps one to a juster apprehension of the works he writes about. In general a good critic by his art brings out features of the art he writes about, or better, brings home the character of what he writes about, in such a way that one can feel and see, see and feel that character much better than one did before. Such a critic tackles aesthetic problems, with his head and with his heart, with his heart and with his head and so tackles them seriously.

It is worth noticing how such revealing, moving talk, such rhetoric, as his, need not be directed towards showing that a work is good or bad. It may be directed simply towards showing it to us for what it is. It may be directed for example to showing us that though Mr. Thornton Wilder's *Heaven's my Destination* and much of the work of Mr. Thurber at first seem comic, they are really tragic. Chekhov called *The Cherry Orchard* a comedy. But obviously anyone perfectly content with this description has not, as we say, understood *The Cherry Orchard*. Mr. Venturi writes, p. 13 of the Introduction to the Phaidon Botticelli, 'In the episodes from the life of St. Zenobius we find a new chromatic tendency. Not only do all the individual colours assume a new intensity but their relationship with one another is based entirely on contrasts and oppositions. This does not result in a bursting forth of light for the contrast is not one of complementary colours functioning as light and shadow. It is a contrast of tints, expressing dramatic despair with its own means'.

The art of giving us a fuller apprehension of a work of art is a wider aesthetics, a wider activity than that of showing that it is beautiful or ugly.

Primary art itself, very often, reveals the familiar, shows us what we have looked at but not seen. A poem may show us swans as birds which survive from a world of calm and light before the sad, dim morning of the Fall or again as swans on a river, as it might be three ducks on a pond. Our eyesight may be all right or at least good enough to enable us to see a bandstand in a park. And yet a picture of the bandstand in the park may make us say 'I never noticed how here the bizarre meets the banal and dread hunts gaiety up spiral pillars to the sky'. In short an artist may enable us to see what we have looked at so often and never seen, or even to see again what we had lost the power to see. After writing this I opened Oscar Wilde's *The Decay of Lying* and read 'To look at a thing is very different from seeing a thing. One does not see anything until one sees its beauty . . . At present, people see fogs, not because there are fogs, but because poets and painters have taught them the mysterious loveliness of such effects'. He might have added that one does not see a thing until one sees its ugliness, its charm, its grace, its banality, and so on. Mr. Rylands in his introduction to his Shakespeare anthology, *The Ages of Man*, says that Samuel Johnson decided that Shakespeare's plays are not tragedies or comedies but 'compositions of a distinct kind exhibiting the real state of sublunary nature which partakes of good and evil, joy and sorrow, mingled with endless variety of proportion and innumerable modes of combination'.

5. And of course it is possible to do ethics seriously. Novelists do often. *Crime and Punishment*, *Anna Karenina*, *The Brothers*

Karamazov, Mr. Marquand's *H. M. Pulham Esq.*, Mr. Greene's *The Heart of the Matter*, Mr. de la Mare's *The Almond Tree*, are all novels in which this is done. Something particular is presented, but so presented that in it something universal is seen, though without any attempt to net in a formula the infinite idiosyncracy of the stuff of Time. A critic speaks perhaps of a particular picture and just that picture is his subject. But somehow he so speaks that we can the better see not only that picture but others also. When Rembrandt paints an old woman's head just that old woman's head is what he paints. At the same time we want to say that it is by no means just that old woman's head that he has painted.

It is possible to make in ethics and aesthetics remarks which are general and still not worthless. This happens when some value is for a time undervalued or perhaps has always been undervalued. Clive Bell emphasized the importance of the formal features of a work of art by saying that beauty depends entirely upon these. Nietzsche re-emphasized certain values apt to be underestimated in Christian ethics. And Christ emphasized certain values which perhaps had never been adequately emphasized. The phrase 'to emphasize a neglected value' stands for a process which can be small and can be big enough to demand a very big man.

The novels which I have mentioned could be called studies of acts, but clearly they are better called studies of persons. A person is an exceedingly complex pattern in time. Anything which helps us to see the pattern in the apparently largely chaotic procession of incidents which make up a person's life-story helps us to 'see him for what he is', just as remarks which order the incidents of a novel for us help us to see that novel for what it is, and remarks which order the parts of a visual or auditory pattern help us to see or hear that pattern for what it is. There are general psychological remarks which can very much help us in making sense out of nonsense just as other scientific hypotheses have made sense out of a chaos of facts.

I would like to add that I am aware that the novels I spoke of are not primarily ethical studies in the ordinary sense of studies with a view to a verdict 'Good' or 'Bad'. In a court of law, even when the facts are agreed upon, the situation is studied with a view to a verdict, but the verdict is expressed not in critical words like 'good' and 'bad' but in words like 'murder in the first degree', 'manslaughter', 'negligence', and so on. The novels I mentioned are special efforts to see people for what they are. This is not an exotic process but one which in some degree goes on in us all the time we are concerned with others.

How understanding of people is connected with ethics I shall not here try to say. But this much may be said: before we pay much attention to a man's judgment of others, whether ethical or not, we must have confidence that he understands them and that we understand him so that we may understand his judgment of them.

6. Wider aesthetics and wider ethics are, I realize, not metaphysics or philosophy in the sense in which I have been using these words, but they are, I submit, connected with metaphysics in two ways worth mentioning. First it is part of the business of metaphysics to correct misleading accounts of what they are in the same way that it corrects misleading accounts of any other procedure for discovery, such as mathematics and metaphysics. And this is necessary although we have been familiar with the aesthetic and ethical procedures for centuries.

Secondly there is a likeness between the techniques used in art criticism, ethics, and art on the one hand and metaphysics on the other. Selection of the typical, caricature, metaphor, paradox, all are used to discover the familiar.

Suppose we call all such attempts to see things for what they are, to find the reality in appearance, philosophy or metaphysics. Then we begin to understand why people who are not philosophers obstinately expect something of philosophy of which they feel cheated if we tell them that philosophy is the curing of mental cramp which has been induced by the fascination of certain analogies suggested by our language, by too narrow an idea of the logic of our language. They still feel cheated when we offer the more positive description that philosophy is the attempt to gain a better grasp of the roles of types of statements.

There are in people two feelings here: (1) that philosophy is wider than the study of how we know the categories matter, mind, time, space, necessity, value (2) that even this study of the categories is not adequately described as a certain sort of study of words.

I believe there is a good deal of illusion and confusion here. Light is thrown on our desire to bring philosophy nearer to life in J. O. Wisdom's study 'Three Dreams of Descartes' in *The International Journal of Psychoanalysis*, Vol. XXVII, Part I, and less directly in his study of Schopenhauer. At the same time metaphysics can come into literature. For example there are one or two places in Proust where it can be seen how metaphysics can grow out of life and how metaphysics can help us to show ourselves life. After I had written this sentence I happened to open a collection of essays by the Greek poet Demetrios Capetanakis and there read 'There are moments in Proust's work when the need to find a solution in philosophy of the most urgent problems of existence is so painful that we begin to feel that we cannot go on. We summon our intelligence to our aid, to give us a moment of rest, of respite; but only a moment, because philosophic anxiety can never cease . . . Proust's affirmation, for instance, that love is only a kind of madness and that the individuality of the person we love is an illusion, has nothing definitive about it. We turn the page, and we find Proust fighting with all his strength to find another solution to this problem that in reality has no solution'.

Those who think that philosophy can help are apt to think that philosophers have some special knowledge which enables them to answer the questions that trouble the inquirer, or that they have a technique which the enquirer himself has not which if applied to the questions of life might solve them. What the philosopher in the narrower sense of one who studies the procedures suitable to various categories of question can do is to make clearer what procedure is suitable to these questions about what this and that really is. It then appears that the suitable procedure is like the philosopher's when he asks what value, necessity, mind and matter really are.

We may now recall that such statements as 'There are no acts which are really unselfish', 'There are no acts which are really free' and even such typical metaphysical paradoxes as 'No one really knows what goes on in the mind of another', 'There is really no such thing as matter', 'Nothing is really good or bad, it is only that we regret some things and not others', are not themselves meta-statements, that is they are not statements about statements. They are statements which in the ordinary usage of language are false; they are statements in a new language which is a distortion of ordinary language. One way of answering 'What point have these paradoxes?' is to reply 'They show up the roles, the inter-relations between the roles, of categories of statements (or sentences)', but another way of answering is to reply 'They show up the nature of, the inter-relations between, categories of rational procedure, of thought', and another way of answering is to reply 'They show up the nature of the inter-relations between categories of fact, of being'. And with this we return to the starting-point of our circular tour through 'Philosophy is about words'.

When someone, Proust perhaps, says 'Individuality is an illusion' or 'Love is madness' it is something about the world which he has grasped and felt which forces him to make these outrageous statements. 'Altruism is an illusion', 'Value is an illusion', 'Mind is an illusion', 'The rationality of scientific reasoning is an illusion' arise in a way which though it is different and more a matter of confusion about words is yet not altogether different.[1]

I have represented all these paradoxes as coming wholly from reflection on things already experienced, but 'Individuality is an illusion', 'Love is an illusion', 'Altruism is an illusion', may, as we know, come in part from new experience — surprises, disappointments. 'The table isn't solid', 'The sun we see is the sun which existed 8 minutes ago', 'Every sound is everywhere', 'People have thoughts and feelings they don't know of', come largely or in part from discovery of new facts. Scientists, as we know, are not all or only concerned with collecting new facts. What is more they are not concerned only with predicting the future. Copernicus gave us a new picture of the world. Freud makes sense out of nonsense. Science of this kind, philosophy, and certain art, are akin in that they reveal what lies not behind or beyond but in the obvious.

[1] John Wisdom, *Other Minds*, pp. 192ff.

NOTE ON THE NEW EDITION OF PROFESSOR AYER'S
LANGUAGE, TRUTH AND LOGIC
(*Mind Vol. LVII*)

1. CHAPTER 1 of *Language, Truth and Logic* is called 'The Elimination of Metaphysics' and is concerned with 'verifiability as a criterion for testing the significance of putative statements of fact' (p. 35). On page 41 a metaphysical statement is defined as one 'which purports to express a genuine proposition but does, in fact, express neither a tautology nor an empirical hypothesis'. In Chapter II it is claimed that the function of philosophy is analysis, not the '*a priori* justification of our scientific or common sense assumptions', although 'the task of defining rationality is precisely the sort of task which it is the business of philosophy to undertake' (p. 50). This last remark is, in my opinion, excellent though (1) the word 'defining' suggests that only a definition will do and (2) the definition of rationality is represented as just one among other definitions which it is the business of philosophy to provide. As to (1) see below. As to (2) a consideration of the principle that the meaning of a statement is the method of its verification will lead us to grasp that epistemology – puzzles of the form 'Do we really know?' 'How do we really know?' – and ontology – puzzles of the form 'What is it that we claim to know?' – are one. Consequently the problem 'What is rationality?' like the problems 'What is a statement?' 'What is a universal or predicate?' 'What is meaning?' 'What is understanding?' is involved in every philosophical problem and is consequently involved twice over in itself. Thus we ask 'What is the meaning of "meaning"?' 'What reasons are there for saying that a procedure is rational?'

2. The problem of induction is, surely, the problem 'Are inductive reasons really reasons?' It isn't 'the problem of finding a way to prove that certain empirical generalizations which are derived from past experience will hold good also in the future' (p. 49). That is a matter for the scientists. The problem of induction is a typical metaphysical problem. Mr. Ayer is out to

show that such problems are as ordinarily conceived not genuine, and as transfigured logical.

What is it to have reason for a scientific conclusion? Mr. Ayer's words in answer are a little confusing. One might for a moment suppose that he is saying (p. 50) that 'the only test to which a form of scientific procedure which satisfies the necessary condition of self-consistency is subject, is the test of its success in practice'. This might be said in metaphysics and be an illuminating paradox. But as a tautological account of what a rational, good, scientific procedure is it is as false as saying that the goodness of a pointer – the dog I mean – is a matter of his success in practice. The future, in a metaphysically extended sense of 'the future', is the only test of the truth of a scientific conclusion. But not even in this extended sense is it the test of the *propriety* of a procedure although, as with the dog's success, and his excellence, it is not so entirely disconnected with this as one pre-occupied with 'points' might pretend. And Ayer is aware that success is not enough. For he writes (p. 50) 'being rational entails being guided in a particular fashion by past experience'. If we ask 'In what fashion?' the only correct and complete answer in general terms is 'A scientific fashion'. As a platitude in metaphysics introducing or summarizing an explanation by samples and paradoxes this could be valuable. But by itself it's worth little.

3. On page 52 Ayer makes the important historical claim that Locke, Berkeley and Hume were not metaphysicians but were really analysts. They were not fully aware of this and half conceived themselves to be examining our fundamental assumptions about what is in the world. But really they were analysts. That, I venture to insist, is what Ayer wants to say really though of course he doesn't use the adverb 'really'. Isn't his whole book written against that adverb? We were very nervous of it in 1935.

Part of what Ayer means by saying that Locke, Berkeley and Hume were not metaphysicians is that they did not talk in what one may call 'the transcendental way', that is, they, or at least Hume, did not talk of, for example, physical things or the self as if they were realities over and above the appearances which are our evidences for them, as if they were related to their manifestations as a thing to its shadows. Is this true of Berkeley about the self? Is it altogether true of Berkeley about material things? I am not going to argue these matters here. For my point is that there is a great deal in what Ayer says about Locke, Berkeley and Hume, and that nevertheless they and Kant too were concerned with 'the systematic study of the ultimate nature of reality' (McTaggart's definition of metaphysics), with what things really are and whether and how we really know them. What it has taken us a long time to grasp is that the metaphysical inquiries put in these words are so very different from ordinary inquiries which may be put in the same words. We ask, for example, what certain suspicious-looking objects really are, who is really responsible for the robberies, whether Jones who claims to know the answer really knows the answer and if so how? What it has taken us a long time to grasp is that metaphysical questions which sound so matter-of-fact aren't, but are more like questions of logical analysis and may be called questions of analysis if we don't insist that there can't be analysis without definition. Perhaps the better way is to say that there can be philosophy without analysis. When he wrote his book Ayer wasn't clear about how there can be philosophy without analysis or, if you like, analysis without definition. In the Introduction he is clearer but even there he isn't fully aware, it seems to me, of the implications of the change, and this unawareness is an instance of doing philosophy as if it were science, not natural science of course but logical, mathematical, science. At the time he wrote *Language, Truth and Logic* Ayer was like many of us over-fascinated by the definition model, exemplified in 'that paradigm of philosophy, Russell's theory of descriptions'. In this 'theory' metaphysical puzzles were cleared up by finding and creating definitions. As Ayer says in his Introduction (p. 24) there are philosophical puzzles that can be cleared up without seeking a definition. There are indeed. But the example he has chosen to drive home this point could hardly be worse. The example is that of those puzzles about the existence of what doesn't exist which Russell's theory of descriptions demolished. It is true that these puzzles *can* be cleared up without bothering about definitions but, as it happens, they are among the very few metaphysical puzzles which can be dealt with in a convenient and impressive way by definition. And the fact that they were thus cleared up by definition contributed to our assuming that metaphysical puzzles could not be cleared up without definition.

So it happens that Ayer represents Berkeley as saying, when purified of theism, that it is possible to define material things in terms of sense-contents (p. 53). And from Chapter III, 'The Nature of Philosophical Analysis', we gather more of what sort of definition is contemplated when we gather that Berkeley's or, if you like, Hume's phenomenalism could have been put 'Material things are logical constructions out of sense contents'.

4. The first explanation of what this means is in the second paragraph of page 63 and is very liable to muddle people. There are places in philosophy where a lot of fuss about whether one is saying 'The symbol S has such and such features' or is saying 'S has such and such features' is unnecessary. But, as Moore taught us, if there is a place where it is very necessary not to mix up these two things it is where one is explaining the peculiarities of logical constructions, and at this place Ayer writes 'When we speak of certain objects b, c, d . . . as being elements of an object e, and of e as being constituted by b, c, d . . . we are not saying that they form part of e, in the sense in which my arm is part of my body . . . What we are saying is that all the sentences in which the symbol e occurs can be translated into sentences which do not contain e itself, or any symbol which is synonymous with e, but do contain symbols b, c, d . . . In such a case we say that e is a logical construction out of b, c, d . . .' What follows shows that Ayer means not that in such a case the symbol e is a logical construction out of the symbols b, c, d but that the object e is a logical construction out of the objects b, c, d. Unfortunately what precedes the words I have quoted, because it is concerned with the fact that symbols are logical constructions, may easily confuse the reader.

Ayer's symbolism too encourages a common misunderstanding. The average plumber is a logical construction out of Bert, Alf and so on. But of course these names do not occur in the translation of a sentence of the form 'The average plumber . . .' What occurs in the translation is the general term 'plumbers'.

Another common misunderstanding which Ayer's exposition encourages is that of supposing that from the fact that expressions of the forms 'The S', 'Every S', 'Some S' can be 'defined in use' in the sense implied by the theory of descriptions it follows that S's are logical constructions. But it is not the fact that sentences about the average plumber can be translated into sentences about the description 'the average plumber' that makes the average plumber a logical construction. What does this is the fact that sentences of the form 'The average plumber has P' can be translated into sentences of the form 'Plumbers have P'' or, if you like, 'The description "is a plumber" has P''.

5. But enough of this. We can now put things in a much simpler and more familiar way. For one of the best ways of saying that a material thing is a logical construction out of its appearances, sense-contents, sense-data, sensations or what not, is to say that a material thing is to these as the average plumber to plumbers, as a nation to its nationals, as energy to its manifestations, as the representative firm to firms, and *not* as a political representative to those he represents, not as an original to its copies, not as a mechanism beneath a bonnet to its manifestations, not as a sheep to shadows on the grass. In a word – down Plato with his cave, up Hume with his faggot. Another paradigm or model for explaining the meaning of 'logical construction' is the following. If you and I now speak with each other about dragons, the Greek gods, or the persons to be met with in Lilliput or the pages of Dickens we decide which of us is right by looking up the manuscripts, indeed we are talking about what Dickens or the Greeks said. And the fact that we are using this convenient shorthand is expressed by saying that the beings we speak of are logical constructions out of the stories told seriously or fantastically by others. The problem of what *they* were talking about cannot be solved by translation whether exact or rough.

It is easy to see the connection between a thing's being a logical construction and the problem of how we know what we know of it. The engine of a car is not a logical construction from the car's performance – the car might perform wonderfully and have no engine. True, we can in a sense read the condition of the engine from the car's performance. But we cannot do this by deduction, by translation, only by experience, so that error is always imaginable. In contrast to this we can read off the features of the average plumber from those of plumbers by calculation, deduction, translation – come what may he can't frown while too many plumbers smile.

It is now to be understood then that in saying that X's are logical constructions out of Y's one does not claim that for every X-sentence an exact translation in terms of Y's can be found. The fact that one does not refer to so definite a relationship as has sometimes been supposed does not imply that whether one is right or not is not a definite question. Suppose we ask 'Is the average carpenter a logical construction out of carpenters?' This means 'Are sentences about the average carpenter related to sentences about carpenters as sentences about the average plumber to sentences about plumbers?' And the answer is definitely 'Yes'. Is 'England to Englishmen as France to Frenchmen?' 'Yes, of course'. 'Is England to Englishmen as the average plumber to plumbers?' 'Not quite. But definitely near enough for us definitely to say that England is a logical construction out of Englishmen.'

But I now submit that the question 'Is a material thing related to its sense-contents as the average plumber to plumbers, as a nation to individuals?' has not a definite answer. It is a 'difficult' question. And though this difficulty arises in part from the *complexity* of the relevant considerations it arises also from their balance, that is from the *unsettleableness* of the question. The question has no answer because it isn't a question but a noise calculated to encourage us to look carefully and afresh at the pattern of the logical connections between material things and sense-contents.

The question has no answer because profoundly valuable though it is to say that the relation between a material thing and its sense-contents is analogous to the relation between the average plumber and plumbers, there is also profound reason to protest against this analogy and, indeed, against any analogy to a relationship between things and an abstraction or logical construction out of things. For sense-contents aren't things. Plumbers are. Statements about plumbers are statements. Statements about sense-contents aren't statements, aren't premisses. Or rather, in so far as statements about sense-contents, such as 'I see a dagger', are insusceptible of error, there is nothing which would make them wrong and nothing which would make them right. In so far as there is nothing which would make them wrong or right they are not statements, not premises, not something from which anything can be deduced. In so far as statements about sense-contents are statements, are verifiable, can be right, so far they can be wrong, and so far the Sceptic asks about them again 'How do we know them?' Suppose a Sceptic asks 'How do we know that matter exists?' we answer 'Well, here are two hands'.[1] The Sceptic replies 'But how do you know you have two hands?' We may reduce his doubts about this by reducing the claims involved in 'Here are two hands'. But when the risk reaches zero the implications do so too and the gap between our ultimate premises and our final conclusion, the gap which has been widening, becomes indeed unbridgeable when the premises vanish.

6. At this point the reader may well ask 'What in heaven's name *are* sense-contents? I can't agree that the question whether material things are to sense-contents as the average plumber to plumbers has or hasn't an answer until I know what sense-contents are'.

Ayer offers explanations. But they are insufficient. The reason for this insufficiency is worth mentioning because it operates throughout his book and throughout a great many philosophical disputes. In the controversies about the Trinity (A.D. 318) and in the controversies about the Incarnation (A.D. 400) I am sure people defined terms very carefully. And in A.D. 1922-32 we of the logico-analytic school used to be meticulous about such definitions. What we ignored was the less exact and less elegant work of ensuring that the defining but undefined general terms upon which our explanations finally depended were themselves understood. The application of these indefinables we knew could be explained only by examples, but the work of providing and arranging those examples and surrounding them with comment bringing out their interconnections we could not bring ourselves to do. And yet here, in this matter of sense-contents for example, the knowledge of the connections between the expressions 'sense-content', 'observation-statement', 'basic statement' are no use to us until we know with regard to

---

[1] Compare G. E. Moore's 'Proof of an External World'. *Proceedings of the British Academy.*

one of these expressions when it is to be applied and when not.
So, tediously, let us now inquire when we would say of a creature
that it is making or understanding a statement about sense-
contents. Consider a dog which whimpers as it hunts alone, a
cat which growls at another cat, a man who says 'Ow!' by himself,
a man who says 'Ow!' to his dentist, a man who says 'That sick
feeling again', a man who says 'Snakes again' but means nothing
about real snakes nor even that he is in for 'the horrors'.

Between these 'speakers' whose utterances tell us what *seem*
to be in the air before them or what *seems* to be in their minds
and those speakers who tell us what is *really* in the air before them
or what is *really* in their minds there are differences of first rate
philosophical importance. These differences are continually
thought of in terms of the following fantasy. Certain prisoners
live in cells with windows opening on to a common quadrangle.
But though the cells have windows the prisoners never look
through them and so never observe directly what is going on in
the quadrangle. Each is so shackled that he is obliged to rely
entirely upon reflections in a mirror which only he can see.
Some of the reflections come not from things happening at the
time in the outside world but from pictures stored and even
constructed in a mechanism built into each cell. This mechanism
is not itself observable but from time to time it throws reflections
of the pictures it contains into the mirror on the wall. And
besides the mirrors there are sound-reflecting devices as well. If
one of these prisoners sees snakes in his mirror he very naturally
calls out 'Snakes'. From what he sees in the mirror he infers that
there are snakes in the quadrangle and if his visual and auditory
reflectors don't soon show his neighbours talking and acting as
if they see snakes he will be very much surprised. Of course,
sometimes there may be something which makes him suspect
that though his mirror shows snakes the mirrors of others will
not, and in these cases he will sometimes think that his mirror
reflects the external situation but often he will think that it does
not. If he thinks that it does not he may confine himself to
remarking that his mirror shows snakes or that there are snakes
in his mirror.

The connections between the statements the prisoners make
about the external things in the quadrangle and the statements

they make about what is to be seen in their mirrors resemble at least superficially the connections between the statements people make about material things and the peculiar 'statements' which have often been described as descriptions of what is immediately observed and which Ayer calls statements about sense-contents.

7. Now Berkeley, Hume, Mill, Russell and Ayer in *Language, Truth and Logic* are very much concerned to make us face this fantasy of the prisoners and the mirror images and to recognize fully its inappropriateness to ourselves and our sense-contents.

The prisoners might, especially after several years, begin to wonder whether their mirrors were accurate and even whether anything at all went on in the quadrangle, and this doubt would the more readily occur to them if it occasionally happened that one of them failed to distinguish between (1) an internally generated reflection which would have no echo in the mirrors of his fellows and (2) externally generated reflections. Their scepticism would be indeed a very unpractical speculation since the penalty for turning from the mirrors and looking out of the windows at 'reality' is death, or the prisoners' heads are so fixed that they cannot do this. But though their question is exceedingly unpractical in such circumstances, one would hardly say that it had no meaning for them. For they remember how the matter would have been settled in the days of their freedom, and were they released they would quickly learn the truth in the old way; we cannot say that there is nothing they would count as relevant to a statement 'Snakes in the quadrangle' which they would not count as relevant to 'Snakes in all mirrors'. For it is still true of them that *if* they were placed as they now cannot hope to be placed they *would* count as very relevant to 'Snakes in the quadrangle' things quite beside the point as far as 'Snakes in all mirrors' is concerned. In short, the things in the quadrangle are not even for these prisoners logical constructions out of mirror images. The power which has imprisoned their bodies has not imprisoned their minds and they can still dream of what they now can never see. What philosophers like Ayer wish to emphasize is that people who ask 'Are material things like what we think them to be? Are they yellow sometimes or not? Are they round or square? Are there any material things at all?

Have appearances any causes whatever?' are dominated by the idea that men who are, as we say, 'describing their sense-contents' are to men who are describing material things as prisoners describing their own mirror images are to prisoners describing the things in the quadrangle. Hume and still more Russell and Ayer remind us that our language for describing the connection between how things seem and how things are is constructed as if this model were appropriate. What they urge is that it is inappropriate and that guided by this model we ask metaphysical questions about matter and approach their solution in an inappropriate way. In the case of the prisoners, once they are confident about the pattern of mirror images they may expect, any question about what is going on in the quadrangle is unpractical. But in our case, once we are confident about how things will seem, any question about how things are is not merely unpractical, it is not a question. For there is nothing we would call finding out that what in all ways to all people at all times seems to be so is yet not so. So far the phenomenalists are right – the model of the prisoners in the cells is inappropriate and misleading. Unfortunately in their efforts to explain how our position is not like that of the prisoners, they have very naturally tried to say what our position is like, and have shown that even they have not realized how fundamentally unlike it is to that of the prisoners. For they say that our position is like that of the prisoners in what I am going to call their second, or phenomenalistic, condition. This is as follows:

8. We can imagine that after a long time the prisoners come to mean no more by 'Snakes in the quadrangle?' than they have meant by 'All mirrors now and always will show reflections suitable for there now being snakes in the quadrangle'. It is important to remember exactly what this comes to. It is this: It is no longer true that *were* the prisoners to look out of the windows they *would* count what they then saw. It must not be supposed that in consequence they will be unable to make a distinction between real and hallucinatory snakes. There will still be cases where a man's mirror misleads him. His mirror will show perhaps a green snake coming nearer and nearer, growing larger and larger. He says 'A snake'. But instead of going on as a snake image usually does, to his horror, as it grows

larger it comes more and more to resemble the face of someone he once knew. Or again, maybe though his mirror shows a snake the mirrors of others don't and this is reflected in his room by his sound reflectors saying 'No, no snakes to-day'. Indeed the actual procedure of the prisoners will be little different from what it was when snakes were snakes. They will still speak of real and imaginary, real and hallucinatory snakes and so on. And because there will be no time when further watching of the reflectors will be definitely no longer to the point there will be no sharp line between cases where the question 'Is it a real snake?' is no longer a question which can be answered by further waiting and watching for what happens and cases where it can be so answered. Consequently the prisoners may, without realizing what they are doing, ask the question 'Even if all mirrors were at a certain time to show snakes and *all* mirrors were *always* to show scenes appropriate to there having been snakes at that time, would that guarantee that there really were snakes at that time?' They might ask this question without realizing that by its own provisions the question had ceased to be a factual one and had become a logical one to which the answer is definitely 'Yes'.

It would then indeed be appropriate to say to them 'But a snake you know, a snake in the quadrangle, is a logical construction out of mirror-snakes. The existence and character of snakes in the quadrangle are deductions from mirror images just as the existence and character of the average mirror is a deduction from the existence and characters of mirrors. A question about a snake in the quadrangle just is a question about mirror images'.

The prisoners might protest against this. They might say, for example, 'But surely a question about real snakes in the quadrangle cannot be the same as a question about mirror images. For suppose some mirror images favoured the snake hypothesis while others were against it and we knew that this "ambiguity" in the evidence would persist for ever. In such a case we should know the answer to the question "Do mirror images favour the snake hypothesis?" and yet not know the answer to the question "Are there snakes or aren't there?" This shows that the questions are not identical'.

Then the wise among them would have to reply: 'Suppose

that Englishmen spoke ferociously against the people of another
nation and even sent against them weapons of destruction while
yet whenever they came upon people of this nation they did
their best for them. In such a case we should know the answer
to the question "Are the feelings and actions of Englishmen in
favour of the hypothesis that they hate members of that nation?"
The answer would be "Some are, some are not". But if one
were asked "Does the average Englishman hate these people
or doesn't he?" one might well reply "Well I don't know".
Here, however, when one is not at all uncertain as to what further
research would reveal and is certain that the evidence will continue to be ambiguous this "I don't know" does not express
ignorance of the facts but hesitation as to what to say. Consequently although this shows that statements of the sort "The
average Englishman is of such and such a character" are not so
simply related to statements about Englishmen as is suggested
by the sample "The average Englishman is 5ft. 10 in." it remains
true that facts about the average Englishman just are matters
of fact about Englishmen. Likewise, in spite of what you remind
us of, facts about snakes in the quadrangle just are matters of
fact about mirror images'.

I will not trace further the parallels between the prisoners'
all-pervading doubts about things in the quadrangle and our
all-pervading doubts about material things. We have seen
enough to understand why Hume, Russell, Ayer and others
have urged that the first condition of the prisoners is a misleading model for describing the relation between material
things and their appearances and have also spoken as if the second
condition of the prisoners provides a model which is valuable and
adequate.

9. It *is* profoundly valuable and largely adequate. *But* I now
again submit that it is *misleading too*. And I offer the same reason
as before: Mirror images are things, sense-contents are not.
Mirror images are 'public', sense-contents are 'private'. If you
are not sure whether what you see is a real snake or not you can
ask someone else, put out your hand, watch what happens when
a rabbit passes or take a photograph. True, some of these moves
are not to the purpose when you are not sure whether there
really is a reflection of a snake in a mirror in front of you. But

some of them are; moves of the same sort are; you can ask someone, you can take a photograph, you can shake yourself and
look again and so on. In short whether you say 'A snake (real)'
or 'A snake in the mirror' someone else can correct you and you
yourself, taking a second glance or some other step, may correct
yourself. Of course, if you are right you won't need to be
corrected, but you could be if you were wrong. Now with
regard to a snake in the mirror of your mind it's very different.
With regard to the snakes in your unconscious mind, or with
regard to what your real sentiments or wishes or beliefs are, it's
not so very different. Other people may argue with you about
what is in the depths of your mind, and upon investigation you
may find that they are right. But with regard to what lies on its
surface, with regard to whether at a given moment you feel
pain or have a sick feeling or see stars or snakes, in a sense which
doesn't imply real snakes nor even 'the horrors', with regard to
these things, it's very different. For (1) anyone who seeing no
snakes tries to correct you has misunderstood you, has taken you
to be making an 'objective' statement about a 'public' snake.
(2) If you say 'I think I am in pain' people will take this to mean
that you are having a queer sensation which isn't definitely
painful, or else they just won't understand you at all, or they will
think you are making a joke, because of course 'I think' is quite
inappropriate here, suggesting as it does that you may upon
further investigation correct first impressions *in the way in which
you may if you say* 'I think I have a cold' or 'I think I am in love again'
or 'I think I again have the horrors'.

Some have tried to describe the peculiarity of statements
about sense-contents by saying that they are susceptible only
of verbal error. They meant that though if a man says 'A dagger'
we can't, if he is speaking of his sense-contents, correct him by
investigating and finding that really there is no dagger anywhere
near, we can ask him to draw what he sees and then if he draws
a carving-knife say 'You mean a carving-knife'. But to say that
statements about sense-contents are susceptible only of verbal
error obscures the fact that they are also not susceptible of verbal
error in the ordinary way. For if a man is describing his sense-
contents and exclaims 'A dagger' we cannot take a look at what he
is describing, find it's a carving-knife and then say 'You mean a

carving-knife'. Yet this is what we do in an ordinary case of detecting verbal mistake. The peculiarity of statements about sense-contents is better summed up by saying that they are true when the speaker says the same thing in all the ways he has of saying it – he not only says 'I have a headache' but sweat stands on his brow.

This immunity to error whether of fact or of ordinary verbal error which characterizes statements about sense-contents could also be described by saying that they haven't the usual implications. They can't be wrong in the usual ways. *Ipso facto* they can't be right in the usual ways. And therefore they aren't statements in the usual ways. In other words the very features which make us call certain of a man's utterances statements about his own sense-contents and 'not-objective' make it inappropriate to call these utterances statements at all. *A fortiori* they make it inappropriate to call these utterances 'statements of the premisses upon which he relies for conclusions about material things and from which in sufficient number he could deduce such conclusions'. Therefore it is absurd to say that statements about objective things, including material things, are related to, can be reduced to, statements about sense-contents just as statements about logical constructions can be reduced to statements about what they are logical constructions out of.

10. This doesn't mean that there has been no good in saying that material things are known from sensations as the average man is known from individual men. On the contrary this model of the logic of statements about material things has freed us from the power of the Sceptic's depressing model just as that freed us from the Innocent's model which gives a vulnerable optimism. True we have found that the logical construction model is inadequate too. But in doing so we have seen something of how it is inadequate. And, after all, our ultimate object is not to find a complete simile for the logic of matter any more than the poet's object is to find a complete simile for what he describes. It is to see it for what it is. Philosophy is not only less like discovery of natural fact than people once supposed, it is also less like the discovery of logical fact than they next supposed, and more like literature – which makes it again more like the discovery of natural fact, only now it is the rediscovery

of familiar fact through the recall of familiar logic dressed in not merely unfamiliar but scandalous clothes.

11. Ayer, of course, is not all unaware of the peculiarities of propositions about sense-contents – only he doesn't do justice to his own awareness. On pages 90-3 and in Chapter VII he writes about the connection between propositions about sense-contents and propositions about material things and propositions about mental things. And on page 93 there is a most important passage about the connection between propositions which describe the qualities of a presented sense-content and sensations. He comes very near to saying that statements about material things are based on sensations. This surely is the truth. If I say 'Mice' and you say 'What makes you think so?' I reply 'The smell' or 'I smell them' or 'Can't you smell them?' If I reply 'I smell them' then *your* reason for thinking there are mice is the fact that I can smell them, but *my* reason – or rather what makes it reasonable for me to think that there are mice – is different, it is the smell I smell, it is a sensation of smell. And as Ayer points out, the sensation is not a proposition about it. Now our vocabulary for talking about logical relations is suitable when we are dealing with the relations between propositions and propositions, statements and statements. When we try to apply it unmodified in other contexts we muddle ourselves. Nothing more can be said about this here. And unfortunately Ayer in the Introduction slurs the good things he said in the body of the book. For on pages 10 and 11 he writes '. . . I maintained that there could not be such things as basic propositions . . . I seem not to have perceived that what I was really doing was to suggest a motive for refusing to apply the term "proposition" to statements that "directly recorded an immediate experience", and this is a terminological point which is not of any great importance'.

I believe that on the contrary it is of the first importance. To fully understand Ayer's motive for refusing to apply the term 'proposition' to statements that directly record immediate experience would be to understand why one should refuse to call these statements statements, and to understand this would be to understand why one should refuse to call sensation knowledge. And as Professor Pritchard urged at Oxford in 1938,[1] this

[1] *Proceedings of the Aristotelian Society*, Supplementary Volume XVI.

is of the first importance. Without understanding this one cannot
understand the puzzles about knowledge of matters of fact,
whether psychological or physical, or indeed puzzles about
matters of value or validity.

12. In Chapter IV, 'The A Priori', Ayer writes, page 75, 'The
contention of Mill's which we reject is that the propositions of
logic and mathematics have the same status as empirical hypotheses; that their validity is determined in the same way. We
maintain that they are independent of experience in the sense
that they do not owe their validity to empirical verification. We
may come to discover them by an inductive process, but once
we have apprehended them we *see* that they are necessarily true'.
(Italics mine.) We *see* the necessary connection between a
proposition and what follows from it.

This answer by itself suggests a like answer about how we know
that an act or picture is good, and it reads like what Ayer calls
rationalism.

But he does not leave this answer without further explanation
of what this *seeing* is. On page 77 he writes 'The principles of
logic and mathematics are true universally simply because we
never allow them to be anything else. And the reason for this
is that we cannot abandon them without contradicting ourselves,
without sinning against the rules which govern the use of language
and so making our utterances self-stultifying. In other words,
the truths of logic and mathematics are analytic propositions or
tautologies'.

These general statements are supplemented with examples
though these examples are not carefully studied. Ayer does
wonders in his fifteen pages on the *a priori* but he necessarily
leaves many questions unanswered and he does not sufficiently
warn us of the inadequacy of his treatment.

Even after it is allowed that all necessarily true statements are
analytic it remains to consider how analytic statements are known,
what they are, how they are related to laws and regularities of
Nature and how to rules and regularities of language, how they
may be true and yet have no factual content not only in the
sense that they state no fact of Nature but also in the sense that
it is metaphysically misleading to talk of them as facts about
universals, abstract entities.

About the connection between analytic statements and the facts of language Ayer says in the Introduction that a logical proposition 'elucidates' the use of an expression (p. 17) and in the text (p. 79) he says that an analytic proposition 'illustrates' the way we use symbols, 'calls attention to linguistic usages of which we might otherwise not be conscious'. What is required is an explanation of what these suggestive but cryptic phrases come to.

13. And when this is done it will turn out that metaphysical statements are saved from senselessness in the very way in which Ayer says (p. 79) that logical ones are. For metaphysical statements too bring out the way we use certain symbols. True the logician is nothing if not photographic while the metaphysician confuses us with caricature. But the logician tells us only what would be obvious but for complexity, while the metaphysician shows us what all the structure of our language conspires to conceal.

14. What happens when we seek to substitute logic for metaphysics is beautifully illustrated in Ayer's Introduction. With meticulous care he dresses the verification principle so that it may gain access to those circles where he hopes it will exert a useful influence. '. . . a statement is . . . literally meaningful if and only if it is either analytic or empirically verifiable' (p. 9). This becomes (p. 16) ' . . . unless it [a non-analytic statement] satisfied the principle of verification it would not be capable of being understood in the sense in which scientific hypotheses or common-sense statements are habitually understood.' But even this, if it is to be unexceptionable, must mean no more than 'Unless a statement has the sort of verification a scientific or common-sense statement has it won't be a common-sense or scientific statement'. This draws attention to how we actually do classify statements by the way they are verified so that even now the principle is still not useless. But undoubtedly the poor thing is not what it was, and quite incapable of eliminating metaphysics or anything else.

15. Ayer is too acute not to realize that something has gone wrong and too honest not to own it (p. 16). And fortunately in the text he is not so concerned with the proprieties as he is in the Introduction. The fact is, the verification principle is a metaphysical proposition – a 'smashing' one if I may be permitted

the expression. After study of it we come to its complementary platitude 'Every sort of statement has its own sort of meaning' which by the verification principle itself becomes 'Every sort of statement has its own sort of logic'. This last is what Ayer is near to recognizing in the case of *a priori* statements.

By deduction we may pass from statements of one type to statements of the same type but not from statements of one type to statements of another type. We can pass from logical statements to logical, from ethical to ethical, from matter-of-fact to matter-of-fact, from psychological matter-of-fact to psychological matter-of-fact, from material matter-of-fact to material matter-of-fact. But we cannot pass from statements about sense-contents to statements about material things. And we cannot pass, neither by deduction nor by induction, from statements of fact, whether about things or about words, to logical statements. Nevertheless the basis of logical statements is experience and not a peculiar apprehension of a peculiar subject-matter. It is not the stuff of their foundation which is peculiar, it is the way it supports them. It is not their subject-matter which is peculiar, it is their purpose.

It is the same with ethical statements. And though light is thrown on their peculiar logic or verification by representing them as a mixture of empirical statement, exclamation and exhortation, this account of them still misleads. For it suggests that such statements as 'Tolstoy ought not to have refused the royalties on his books' or 'It's lovely' could be proved by establishing the relevant points of fact and then giving our opponent a 'shot' of some drug which would make him feel like us about what we are talking of. Yet this, it is certain, would not be altering his attitude in the way we also call 'showing him the beauty of the picture, the wrongness of the act'. For to do this his attitude must be altered by *rational* persuasion. And this is done by drawing attention rhetorically to the features of what we are talking about, insisting upon how different it is from this, how like to that, passing insensibly from the purely factual through the semi-factual, semi-critical, to the critical predicate at issue. Only this mixture is critical proof and the name of it is rhetoric.

'Induction' is the name for the process of justifying conclusions about the future from premisses about the present and the past. And of course if we mean by the proper justification of a probability claim only the transformation of a statement of alternatives, as when we talk of the probability of a head, given that there will be either a head or a tail, then induction isn't proper. But then it not only *isn't* but *can't be* proper: since a probability claim about the future cannot be a transformation of premises about the present and the past. The idea's absurd.

No doubt a study of the features of induction, an explicit recognition of how it differs from other rational procedures, alters our attitude to it. Reconsideration of the familiar features of anything, any procedure, any situation, any person is apt to alter our attitude to it. We see it better for what it is.

Sometimes our change of attitude may be described by saying that what once seemed good now seems bad or vice versa. But more often in these cases in which we are studying the familiar, even when we start our study with a view to deciding whether something is good or bad, valid or invalid, true or false, P or not P, in the end that question becomes of no importance. Sometimes it's 'unsettleable'. But it needn't be. It just becomes of no importance.

That is how it is with the questions (Chapter VIII and pp. 18-20) 'Do we really have reason for the claims we make about the minds of others?' 'Do statements about the mind of another amount to more than predictions about what he'll do and how he'll look?' It's easy to say that that's how it is with these questions but it's hard to show it.

PHILOSOPHY, METAPHYSICS AND
PSYCHO-ANALYSIS
I

I SHOULD like to say at once what I aim to do in these lectures and then do it. But there are difficulties about this. You already know more or less what philosophers do and more or less what psycho-analysts do, so that I feel like one does when someone asks 'What's the news?' and there isn't any news. How does anyone ever say to another anything worth hearing when he doesn't know anything the other doesn't know?

Well, of course, there are those who manage this. They say 'You look lovely in that hat' to people who know this already. But under these circumstances the words reveal nothing to the hearer except, possibly, something about the speaker. However, suppose now that someone is trying on a hat. She is studying it in a mirror. There's a pause and then a friend says 'My dear, the Taj Mahal'. Instantly the look of indecision leaves the face in the mirror. All along she has known there was something wrong with the hat, now she sees what it is. And all this happens in spite of the fact that the hat could be seen perfectly clearly and completely before the words 'Taj Mahal' were uttered. And the words were not effective because they referred to something still hidden like a rabbit in a hat. To one about to buy false diamonds the expert friend murmurs 'Glass', to one terrified by what he takes to be a snake the good host whispers 'Stuffed'. But that's different, that's news. But to call a hat the Taj Mahal is not to inform someone that it has mice in it or will cost a fortune. It is hardly to say that it's like the Taj Mahal; plainly it's very unlike and no less unlike now that this far-fetched analogy has been mentioned. And yet nothing will undo the work of that far-fetched allusion. The hat has become a monument and too magnificent by half.

Imagine that one of her friends says to a woman concerning the husband she has tried to love 'It might have been different if it had been just him you married but you had to marry his mother too. She's dead now but isn't it sometimes she who speaks when he speaks? Doesn't she still live in him and in spite of his struggles insist on an old ascendancy?' When this is said the woman's face may change. The horror of realization, the relief of understanding, may for an instant flicker there — but probably only for an instant. A proper expression is recovered, the absurd suggestion is dismissed. It is dismissed but not destroyed — for now secretly or openly so many familiar gestures, turns of phrase, modes of reaction, will assemble in the proof of the truth of this monstrous falsehood.

Socrates once asked a boy who had not been taught geometry about the properties of squares. And he begged Meno to remark particularly that although he, Socrates, told the boy nothing the boy was soon able to answer questions about squares which he at first answered wrongly or was unable to answer or, if you like, thought he was unable to answer. 'The boy said at first that a square twice the size of another would have sides twice as long. But after reflection the boy said that this first answer was wrong and he did this although Socrates told him nothing, but only asked him questions. Socrates at the end says 'Well what think you Meno? Has this boy in his answers, given any other opinion than his own?' Meno: 'None other: he has given his own opinion only'. Socrates: 'And yet but a little before, as we both observed, he had no knowledge of the matter proposed and knew not how to give a right answer.' Meno: 'True.' Socrates: 'But those very opinions, which you acknowledge to be his own were in him all the time: were they not?' Meno: 'They were.' Socrates: 'In a man therefore who is ignorant, there are true opinions concerning those very things of which he is ignorant.'

In courts of law there often arise questions which it is difficult to settle although the 'material' facts are known and agreed upon. For example, counsel for the plaintiff argues that there has been negligence, counsel for the defendant that there has not. Before the argument begins it is already agreed, perhaps, that the plaintiff found a snail in the bottle from which he drank ginger-beer and that this beer was bottled by the defendant though not sold by him and so on.

Mr. Glanville Williams in the *Law Quarterly*, 1945 in four articles called 'Language and the Law' insists that such questions are not questions of fact but questions of words. This is a bit of a shock. Is it questions of words we pay lawyers to settle? Why does Mr. Glanville Williams say so paradoxical a thing? It is in order to contrast such questions as 'All this being so was there negligence?' or 'All this being so was there consent to risk?' with such questions as 'Did Mrs. Barney shoot Stephens?' 'Did the nurse guide the hand that signed the will?' In these cases if only there had been a witness he could have settled the matter for us.

In the cases where 'the facts' are known and agreed upon it is not want of a witness that makes the question hard – it is not that nobody knows what happened but that though everybody knows what happened we don't know whether there was negligence or not, we don't know whether what happened constituted negligence or not. Even when we know whence a certain body derives its funds the question whether it is a public authority may be a hard one. When Mr. Glanville Williams calls these hard, 'chronic', questions questions of words he draws attention to the fact that in arguing them what we come to in the end are questions about parallel cases, questions which we may express like this. Wouldn't you call *this* negligence? Wouldn't you call *that* negligence? Wouldn't you say that *here* there was a duty to take care?

Nevertheless to call these hard questions questions of words is to distort and denigrate legal discussion. For such a description suggests that in such discussion what one is concerned with is either a question of linguistic fact 'Would most people apply such and such a word to this case?' or a question for linguistic decision 'Shall we apply such and such a word to this case?' And neither of these suggestions will do. Both of them obscure the fact that in the course of legal discussion certain features of what has happened are made to stand out and are assembled and ordered and the whole case set in a context of like and different cases in such a way that at the end we have a grasp, an understanding, an apprehension of the case before us which we lacked when we started. This can be clearly seen, for example, in Mr. D. M. Gordon's remarks on the case of Smith v. Baker in an article called 'Wrong Turns in the Volens Cases' in the *Law Quarterly*, April, 1945.

How seriously and widely misleading it is to call such thinking 'settling a matter of words' comes out if we ask Mr. Glanville

Williams 'Is the discussion as to whether legal discussion is verbal itself verbal or not?' For why does Mr. Glanville Williams argue that legal discussion is really verbal? Not because he wishes to persuade us that most people would call it verbal. On the contrary he is so insistent only because he is sure they would not. Is his argument designed to alter people's verbal habits and to persuade them to call legal discussion verbal in future? Not at all. He doesn't care whether they call it verbal or not as long as they are delivered from an inadequate apprehension of the character of legal discussion. The question 'Was there negligence?' asked *after* we have investigated, found witnesses, examined beer and so on is very different from what it is when asked *before* we have done all this. Nevertheless we call both questions questions of fact. Mr. Glanville Williams fears that in calling both these questions questions of fact we have not recognized how utterly different is the mode of inquiry suited to them. He fears that we may misconduct such inquiry because we have not recognized this difference. And his fear is not without justification. For example, when the most careful consideration of circumstances does not enable us to say that there was negligence or to say that there was not, we may feel our inquiry to be a failure in the way an inquiry as to what is happening behind a curtain is a failure when the evidences this side of the curtain do not enable us to decide what is happening behind it. And it is a muddle to feel like this. For, in the first place, when we have been able to fully investigate a matter, we know what happened. And, in the second place, the fact that in certain cases reflection does not yield a verdict, for example 'Negligence' or 'Not negligence', does not mean that in those cases reflection has not increased our comprehension of the case before us. It has, whether or no it has yielded an answer. When it yields an answer we have come to realize how close is the case before us to others where we would speak of negligence and how far it is from cases where we would refuse to speak of negligence, or we have come to realize the opposite. When it does not yield an answer we have come to realize how close and how far is the case before us from cases where we would and cases where we would not speak of negligence.

When we oppose Mr. Glanville Williams and insist that legal discussion is not a matter of words we do so because we fear that in freeing us from the misleading model or analogy suggested by the phrase 'question of fact' he is putting us in the power of another misleading analogy suggested by the phrase 'a question of words'.

It would therefore be utterly misleading to call the discussion as to whether legal discussion is a matter of words 'a matter of words'.

This opens our eyes to the *width* of the danger that lies in calling legal discussion verbal. That description not only distorts legal discussion, it also encourages us to distort discussion about the character of legal discussion — what we may call meta-legal discussion. And if we distort in this way discussion of the character of legal discussions we shall be tempted to distort in the same way discussion of the character of ethical discussion, of biological discussion, of physical discussion, of psychological discussion, in short we shall be tempted to distort all discussion of the character of kinds of discussion. We shall be tempted to call all meta-discussion a matter of words.

And, worse by far, we shall be tempted to describe all discussion in which no one gives anyone any news as discussion about words. We shall be tempted to call all reflective thought thought about matters of words. Indeed recently many metaphysicians have said that every question is either a matter for observation or a matter of words or nonsense. They said 'When one investigates like a policeman, watches like a bird watcher, experiments like a chemist, one discovers something. But what can one discover in an armchair?' The answer expected is 'Nothing'. For in an armchair one doesn't discover anything *in the way* a policeman or a chemist does — unless indeed one investigates the recesses of the armchair in which case one discovers lost property as frequently as policemen do. While one reflects, while one reviews only what one has viewed, one very naturally does not view a fox or find that this stuff makes all the difference in pneumonia. And yet, as we have just seen, one may come in reflection to see what one had not seen although it was before one's eyes — how near a hat is to the Taj Mahal, how far a square is from the double of another, how near is this to negligence and that to murder, how like is So and so to Hamlet, and a falling apple to a travelling star.

And these last two examples bring us to two points of importance. One is the close connection between discovery by reflection and discovery by investigation. The second is the difference between conventional reflection upon lines already laid down and unconventional reflection, in which it is necessary to introduce a new notation or remould an old one in order to express that new awareness of the known which this reflection brings.

We say that Newton discovered gravity. But now what was it he did? After all we didn't need Newton to tell us that apples fall. The well-taught child replies 'He explained why apples fall. He said they fall because of gravity.' But wasn't this explanation like the doctor's when we tell him how we feel and he tells us that we are run down. For what is gravity but the fall of apples and the like – in short, all these incidents we pretend to explain by gravity. 'Ah' the clever child replies 'gravity is much more than the fall of apples. It is the fall of apples and the like.' And this is true. With the word 'gravity', or the word 'attraction', used in a modified way, Newton connected apples in an orchard with stars in heaven, a mammoth in a pitfall with waves high on the beach. Till he spoke we had no word connecting every incident in nature by thin lines of likeness, thin as the lines of force but stronger than steel.

Unlike one who uses a pattern ready made for him Newton had to cut out a pattern in order to show the connections in a whole which no one had ever apprehended as a whole. We now are given the conceptions of gravity and of energy. Newton developed the conception of attraction and with it presented the power of the distant. Freud developed the conception of the unconscious and with it presented the power of the past.[1] Each introduced a word and from it bred a notation which encourages us towards new experience and also enables us to co-ordinate old experience.

The contrast between conventional reflection and unconventional reflection deserves attention. Socrates' boy when he found upon second thoughts that of course a square with sides twice as long as the sides of another will be much more than twice the size of the other did not attempt to bring things together in

[1] For the conception of the unconscious in pre-Freudian literature see for example, Anthony Trollope in *Framley Parsonage*, Chaps. XIII and XXI and in other places, and Dostoevsky, *The Eternal Husband*.

unheard-of ways or separate them from their usual associates. Consequently he did not need to introduce new words or stretch or narrow the use of old ones. Even a lawyer arguing a rather desperate case does not if he can possibly avoid it do any violence to ordinary or legal convention as to the use of the words at stake in his case.

But poets do mould the use of language to their needs. And so do philosophical scientists. Metaphysical philosophers do it too. Mr. Glanville Williams shocked us by saying that legal discussion is not really of the family of discussions of fact, as one might say 'George Forsyte wasn't really a Forsyte'. By doing this he induced us to recognize the contrast between 'Is there arsenic in the body?' asked before we have sent the organs for examination and 'Is there negligence in the case?' asked after we have found the snail. He induced us to recognize too the connections between legal discussion and the usage of words. It is true that he might instead have said quietly 'Between legal discussions and other discussions which we call discussions of questions of fact there are differences worth attention'. But if he had would he have got that attention to particular case after particular case necessary to the breaking of an old habit in grouping things? He might have. But after all why shouldn't he work with a paradox? Because he did we instantly followed, with annoyance or with pleasure, his proof. And more, we were stimulated to oppose him and even to defend the statement that legal questions are questions of fact in that, in considering them, we are endeavouring to apprehend properly what happened. By the time our metaphysical discussion was done we had apprehended the character of legal discussion in a way we never had before.

Those who say that discussions which are not to be settled by experiment and observation are discussions about words speak wildly — as wildly as one who calls a hat the Taj Mahal. So do those scientists, philosophers, or poets who say one cannot stir a flower without troubling of a star. What they say is mad but there's method in it.

II

Last time we reflected upon reflection. Sometimes this reflection does not at any point leave conventional lines and still is far from boring because of the complexity that is mastered in it. This happens in mathematical calculations. From a tangle of data about trains leaving Brighton and London a mathematician is able to tell us to our amazement at what point they passed each other. Sometimes the reflection has not this complexity and still is far from boring because it is not on conventional lines but presents familiar things as connected in ways in which we have not formerly connected them. Then new words and metaphors and paradoxes and counter-paradoxes are what we need. A philosopher since he has no news and also cannot amuse and amaze us in the way a mathematician can must be either paradoxical or boring. Metaphysical philosophers are no exception. Fortunately they are often paradoxical. They are indeed. For example, they say that discussions about right and wrong, good and bad are not discussions at all or, if they are, are nothing but discussions about how we feel to things. Or again, they say that discussions about the thoughts and feelings of others are just questions about the signs of those thoughts and feelings, that such a question as 'Outwardly he is friendly but is he inwardly?' is just the question 'This face smiles and smiles but will that hand stab me?'.

And these extraordinary doctrines which claim to reduce the mysterious to the obvious are reactions from other paradoxes still more paradoxical — declarations that we can never know what we all know we know. For example, the paradox that legal questions are merely questions about words comes in part from the fear that someone will say that they are questions the answers to which we can never know, that they are questions as to the presence or absence of the essence of negligence which is something so subtle that sometimes we can hardly detect its presence.

To say of cases where the facts however well known don't fix an answer, that we don't know the answer, that we don't know what is before us, is extremely misleading.

To say in cases where ordinarily we should say that we know the answer, that we don't really know the answer is still more misleading. And yet this is what is done by metaphysical sceptics. Their doubts are ridiculous and yet terrifying.

It's ridiculous to suggest that we never know what happens

behind our backs, never know to-day what happened yesterday, never really know from a face what happens in the soul. But what if it were true? It's ridiculous. And yet can we ever turn our heads quite quickly enough to make sure the trees behind us were not tittering and whispering? Can we ever know the past since 'we are obliged to rely on old stories, bones, stones, documents and fading photographs in family albums or our memories'? Isn't the whole material world perhaps a dream that we have always dreamed, a shadow show arranged by a super-illusionist whose powers guarantee that the performance goes without a hitch.

From the face of a clock we may guess at the mechanism behind, from the scenes in a mirror at what passes on the road or down the river. For, *in such cases* though for the moment we are obliged to guess from signs at what they signify, *on other occasions we have been better placed* and have seen beside the signs that which they signify. From what we see in the mirrors of our minds we guess at the reality beyond. But, *in these cases*, with what right? We have checked our memories by our records and our records by our memories, but when have we checked both by seeing beside a record and a memory the event they tell of in the past? What we suspect from a man's face we may confirm from his words, when we suspect his words we may await his actions. But we have never got behind all these still outward signs to the inward state. And, if we are asked to make sure in some other way that we are right about the thoughts and feelings that make a man do as he does, we are as helpless as an electrician if he is asked to make sure that a battery is charged, without connecting it to a tram, an electric light bulb, a clock or a bell.

But now Scepticism by its extremity begins to reveal its absurdity. This is the hard-headed metaphysician's opportunity. And he takes it. 'Exactly' he says 'exactly'. We *are* helpless in the face of these absurd questions. We are as helpless as the electrician *and in the same way*. The electrician is helpless in face of the extraordinary request made of him because the request is senseless. One who makes it pretends to ask the electrician to do something but he only *pretends* — like one who asks a statistician to ascertain the weight of the average child but without interrupting the studies of individual children by weighing them. We are helpless when someone asks us to ascertain the feelings of another without relying on what he says, how he looks, what he does now and later. We are helpless because this request is a self-contradictory one like that made of the electrician and the statistician. To see this, suppose that one of us tries to meet the demand made upon us. He is asked to find out whether Joan is angry but not from her words and behaviour. He is, of course, careful to avoid looking at Joan or listening to anything she says, or if he does he pays no attention to it. He consults the stars perhaps, gazes into a crystal, or answers according to how he himself feels. But then he will be told at once that this is nothing to the purpose since this is to misinterpret the question 'Is Joan angry?' and to turn it into a question about the stars or about how he himself feels. If, on the other hand, he *does* watch Joan and does listen to what she says he is again told that this is nothing to the purpose and will be nothing to the purpose however long he continues his investigation, since it will tell him only whether Joan's behaviour is at present, and from now on will be of the sort we expect upon being told that she is now angry.

The sceptic's doubts now seem again as absurd as ever. And yet — *is* consciousness quite like electricity? *do* we know of it in the same sort of way? *is* it in the same way no more than its effects? The sceptical metaphysician isn't done with. For amid the triumphant laughter of the hard-headed positivist he gravely replies 'It is indeed absurd to say that even when we know that a battery does all that can be expected of it we still don't know whether it is charged or not. But it is not in the same way absurd to say that even when we know that a thing does all that can be expected of an angry or intelligent being we still don't know whether it is angry or intelligent. It is senseless to talk of knowing that a thing has electricity in it without knowing this from what we misleadingly call the effects of the electricity. But it is not in the same way senseless to talk of knowing that a man has anger in his heart without knowing this from the effects of the anger. For the man himself does this. And if it makes sense to talk of one person doing a thing it also *makes sense* to talk of another doing it. If it is conceivable that Jack should follow the arguments of Einstein then it isn't meaningless to suggest that George could — even though in fact George lacks the training or ability required. Were it conceivable that Jack should learn the weight of the average child without weighing children then it would be conceivable that George should. It is absurd to talk of George's doing this because it is absurd to talk of *anyone's* doing this. But it is not absurd to talk of *anyone's* knowing how Joan feels without watching her face or listening to what she says. For Joan does this. And when it is said that no one but Joan really knows how Joan feels what is meant is that no one knows this like Joan does'.

In this reply truth and falsehood are subtly intermixed. It is undoubtedly true that the way we know of consciousness and the soul is different from the way we know of electricity and of such abstractions as the average child and the economic man. It is true that though one who is colour-blind can, in a sense, know from what others say and do that they see the sky as blue, the grass as green, he yet does not know this like one who is not colour-blind does. One who has never felt pain does not know like one who has how those in pain feel. He knows how they look, he knows what they say, he knows what they do. But that's different. Therefore it is false that to know people to be in pain is no more than to know how they look, what they say and what they do, and what they would do. To know people to be in pain is not like knowing that a thing carries a negative electric charge. It is also true that even one, A, who has felt pain and is sympathetically or telepathically feeling pain with another, B, does not know from his feelings that the other, B, is in pain in just the way that B knows that he, B, is in pain.

But it is quite false that it makes sense to talk of A's knowing B's feelings *as B does*. If the doctor asks A 'Well how d'you feel this morning?' A answers according to how he feels. But if B does just the same in order to answer the question the doctor puts to A then we say that B has misunderstood and takes the doctor's question to refer to himself. On the other hand if he does anything different he doesn't answer the question as A does.

It is therefore perfectly true that no one knows how a man feels as he does himself, because no one could, any more than one could have another person's child.

But this would be a good reason for saying that no one can ever know how another feels only if when we say 'A knows that B is pleased' we mean that he knows this *as B does*. And this we do not mean. It is what the sceptic means if the facts he refers us to are to justify what he says. But it is not what is ordinarily meant.

This doesn't show that we do know how others feel. But it does show that those features of our knowledge to which the sceptic draws attention by saying paradoxically that we don't know how others feel do not prove what he says in the literal, conventional and usual use of the words he uses.

What has happened in this discussion? We started from a ridiculous declaration of ignorance which then suddenly seemed serious. Then just as it seemed most serious it again seemed ridiculous. 'No one ever knows the feelings of another' at first sounded simply ridiculous. When the sceptic defended his paradox we realized that he had begun to penetrate a disguise which no one usually penetrates. For we always speak and think as if the mind of another were something behind his face which we learn about from the indications on this dial as one may learn about the course of currents in a very transparent stream from what floats on its surface or as one may try to guess from the outside of a house whether anyone is at home and what is going on within.

The sceptic pointed out that while in the case of the flotsam and in the case of the drawn blinds or shuttered windows we are justified in interpreting these signs as we do because on other occasions we have found these signs associated with other evidences which directly and completely confirm our interpretations, in the case of all the evidence one could have as to the feelings of another we have never had other evidences which are more direct and more complete.

The positivist then pointed out that we never have had such other more direct evidences because we never could have had evidences more direct, any more than we could have had evidences as to the weight of the average child more direct than those we have from weighing individual children. He substituted an utterly different model for consciousness. He said 'We talk of electricity and of energy as if they were something other than their effects, and we might by talking in this way make ourselves wonder whether we ever know whether there is electricity or energy in a thing. Such a "doubt" about electricity or energy would be engendered by the convenient but misleading way of speaking which prevents our realizing that to know that a thing is electrically charged or contains energy just is to know that it behaves in certain ways. In the same way our "doubt" about consciousness in others is engendered by a convenient but misleading way of speaking which prevents our realizing that to know that there is consciousness in a thing just is to know that it behaves in certain ways'.

In the next stage in the discussion we saw that the positivist's model for consciousness is also misleading. We saw that though it is true that to talk of everyone's having the same right to talk of the bugbear in B's mind as B has is self-contradictory, since the bugbears would then no longer be bugbears but bears, this is not because the logic of consciousness is the same as that of electricity. We set out, though somewhat sketchily, what makes people dissatisfied with the positivist's answer. And in doing this we came to notice just that peculiarity about knowledge of the mind which has made sceptics say what they do. This is the same peculiarity as that which has made people say that what is in the mind is 'private' as opposed to physical things which are open in the same way to the observation of everyone. That which makes people say that what is in the mind is private just is the fact that what is in the mind is 'not open in the same way to the observation of everyone', and this is the fact that if A answers a question as to how he feels according to how he feels this is answering a question about how A feels, while if B answers a question as to how A feels according to how he, B, feels this is misinterpreting a question about how A feels. In this discussion therefore we have come to see questions about the mind for what they are and not as unsuccessful or successful replicas of what they are not.

III

Last time we reflected upon how in metaphysical reflection one may come to see what has long been before one's eyes and we noticed what a wavering, oscillating process this may be. We saw how what had always seemed to be knowledge may suddenly seem to be not knowledge, and then to be knowledge but not quite what we had thought it, and then again to be not knowledge, and then to be knowledge different from what it had once seemed to be and yet neither more nor less. So what has seemed for years like sanity may in a moment look like madness, what has seemed to be love may suddenly seem to have been not really love, and then again to have been love.

Philosophers are notorious for reminding us of occasions on which what looked like gold was not, what seemed a man turned out to be a puppet. From these disappointments they pretend to demonstrate the impossibility of knowledge. Poets, dramatists, and novelists continually present the shocking continuities between love and hate, devotion and infatuation. Do they demonstrate the impossibility of love? Shall we be sensible and hard-headed and say that love, whether a lover's or a mother's, just *is* a sort of infatuation? Or shall we, rather than accept this denigration, say that love doesn't exist? Shall we accept the arguments of Proust and others and find ourselves in a world where dear despair is the somewhat sickly but only support of failing hope? Or shall we like Dostoevsky, Freud, and many other explorers of the spritual world, have the courage to refuse to deny the evil and also the further courage not then to deny the good.

The worst of it is Dostoevsky is extremely confusing. Behind the summer-houses a thunder storm is always coming up; in those enormous tenements where beside the remains of the last meal stands always another bottle of champagne, everything dissolves into what it was not. When someone remarked upon this lately I replied 'Well what about Freud? Doesn't he put some order into the chaos?' 'Yes,' he said 'yes, that's true but somehow . . .' 'Somehow what?' I said, 'Is it that under the chapter headings "The Psychology of Errors", "Fixation upon Traumas", "The Theory of the Libido" something is lost? The scientific terms give a wider but too distant view of reality — so distant that we no longer feel the sorrow and the joy. And as the detail of the concrete diminishes one loses grasp of what it is that is being talked about'. 'Yes, it's something like that,' he said. 'Well,' I said 'isn't the remedy for that to move to and fro from the concrete, presented by the artist, to the general, presented by the scientist'.

But this of course is easier said than done.

Besides the battle with illusion, disillusion and despair is something more personal than this. However able the artist, however great the insight he gives into someone else, this need not give insight into one's self. We have seen something of why people say that one knows oneself in a way no one else can. But it is notorious also that it is hard to see oneself as others see one, and this implies that it is hard to see oneself as one can see others, that the advice 'Know yourself' is not easy to follow. In psycho-analysis a determined attempt is made to do this with someone else's help. Concrete detail after concrete detail is assembled and slowly, very slowly, the bewildering chaos comes into order and the shifting shadows begin to have shape. But there are strong forces opposing this.

It is not only that the incidents one needs to recall are half forgotten. Added to this and bound up with it is the fact that there exists already a way of telling the story which selects, emphasizes and assembles things in certain constellations. For instance, the story is told in terms of loving certain people and hating others. You loved your kind mother and your good father and your little sister, who was weaker than yourself. You hated the people next door who poisoned the cat, and you despised Uncle Jack who disgraced the family name by selling on a prodigious scale, bogus shares. You despised him of course although he drove so magnificent a motor car. You loved your sister. Of course there were occasions when you lost your temper with her, but these were temporary aberrations when perhaps she broke your best soldiers or tore your best book. So far so good. It is only later, perhaps, that the adequacy of this picture begins to be suspected. You love your wife. You are of course sometimes angry with her. And here you are sorry to say that you are sometimes extraordinarily angry with her, unreasonably angry, much angrier than you would be with someone else who had done what she did. Perhaps of course she has done the same thing before. But sometimes she has not. And anyway why were you so angry from the first? You might be tempted to say sometimes that you detest your wife if it were not that you love her and love her very much. And now you come to think of it, though sometimes your sister was very provoking it is also true that you were sometimes angry with her about very little, and no less so when grown-ups in a certain tone of voice *again* said that she was smaller and weaker than you. Did you really detest her for the love she won so easily?

The suggestion is preposterous. But is it pointless? Isn't it in fact extremely pointed? The suggestion that a hat is a monument, that legal discussion is verbal, that knowledge of the minds of others isn't really knowledge are all preposterous. But they are not pointless. They force us to recognize things familiar but unrecognized. Psychological suggestions also, preposterous as they sometimes are, reveal to our dismay and our relief things we had felt creeping in the shadows and now must see in light.

Metaphysical paradoxes, such as 'Ethical discussion is propaganda', 'Reflective thought is thought about words', are dangerous and need to be balanced by the re-assertion of the old truths in their opposites. Psychological paradoxes are dangerous too and call for a dialectic process in which they are balanced. For example, the psychological paradox 'We are all mad' needs to be balanced by its opposite 'We are all sane' and by the re-assertion of 'Some of us are mad but some of us are not' — only now the old truth will no longer blind us to the continuities the paradoxes have revealed. The paradox that you hated your sister needs to be balanced by the re-assertion of the old truth that you loved her and the new truth that you loved her more than you knew when long ago you built houses in the trees or went pig-sticking in the orchard with her.

To gain a new apprehension of any part of reality we have to shake off old habits of apprehension crystallized probably in a well-known mode of presentation. In a recent book *Pleasure from Pictures* the author says in a note on the Impressionists 'They *found* (italics mine) that light can change colour completely, that a red dress may contain other colours than red'.[1] People were at first taken aback by the Impressionists' pictures. They had never seen trees like that. And yet they must have often had before their eyes what the Impressionists found. Oscar Wilde says 'There may have been fogs for centuries in London. I dare say there were. But no one saw them, and so we do not know anything about them. They did not exist till Art had invented them'.[2]

[1] Pamela Strain, *Pleasure from Pictures*, p. 100.   [2] *The Decay of Lying*, p. 37.

It is well recognized that poets may use words in unusual ways to present what they see when in a childlike and yet grown-up experience they look at things afresh.

But it is not so well recognized that people who are speaking or writing in prose may be doing the same. And yet they too may be trying to re-explore the manifold of particular things without seeing them always in the constellations imposed upon them by old names. They too may feel the need to free themselves from the power of a name. For example, the metaphilosopher struck by the peculiarity of a discussion does well to avoid calling it by its usual name – for example 'discussion of fact'. He may try a new name, for example 'verbal discussion'. This too will have its dangers unless he vigorously imagines, pictures, the faces, gestures, tones, words and circumstances of those taking part in the discussion and allows this to suggest to him the faces, gestures, tones, words of those taking part in other discussions. This way he may reach associations which might never have occurred to him, note features, note likenesses and contrasts, which he might never have noticed had he at once applied the usual name or too obstinately applied a new name to the discussion going on before him. For that name would have been powerful to lead him along familiar lines and thus to prevent his seeing new constellations. In trying to lead someone else to the unusual associations he has come upon the philosopher may apply not the usual name to what he was thinking about but an unusual one. So it comes about that in trying to express what they have seen metaphysical philosophers say surprising things. So do other philosophers. So do poets, novelists, and psycho-analysts, so, in general, do those who are philosophers, in the wide sense that they reflect on what has been observed in order to gain a new and greater apprehension of reality.

Imagine that till now all maps have been drawn on Mercator's projection. Mr. A has received as a wedding present what is in fact a map of the world on an extraordinary projection. Unfortunately he can make neither head nor tail of it, it is to him a meaningless pattern. However when his friend Mr. P, the philosopher takes a look at the thing he says 'Why can't you see, it's a map of the world'. These simple words may be enough. They may work on Mr. A like magic. But they may not. For he may say 'Whatever d'you mean?' because he has never dreamed of a map except on Mercator's projection. He has never seen Africa look like that. It will then be necessary to wean him from his unsophisticated conception of a map by putting before him first mild and then bolder and bolder departures from Mercator's projection. It may be only at the end of this procedure that he says 'Ha! Yes, yes I see it now' and as he says these words the pattern may look different to him as well as being no longer meaningless. Mr. A has made a discovery. The character of his discovery is worth careful consideration. When Mr. P said 'It's a map of the world' this came as a surprise to Mr. A. Just why it was a surprise to him is worth careful consideration. Mr. P justified his statement. The character of his justification is worth careful consideration.

Imagine that Mr. S, a scientist, points to a blank sheet of paper and says to Mr. A 'That's a map of the world'. Mr. A says 'What do you mean?' Mr. S then holds the sheet of paper before the fire and the invisible ink then shows up and there appears to the astonished eyes of Mr. A a map, a map in the ordinary conventional sense of a presentation on Mercator's projection of land and water. The discovery, the surprise, and the justification are very different in this case from what they were in the first case. Mr. S is able to astonish Mr. A because he knows something about the reactions of that about which he and Mr. A are speaking which Mr. A does not know. Mr. P did not in this way know anything that Mr. A didn't know and couldn't already see for himself.

Imagine now that Mr. M, a clear, acute and mathematically-minded man, points to a large-scale and extremely intricate map of the town through which he and Mr. B have been wandering all the afternoon and says 'That's a map of the place we were in this afternoon.' 'You don't say so,' says Mr. B. 'Why yes,' says Mr. M. 'Remember the cathedral? Here it is. From the cathedral ran that wide street with tram lines down to a canal didn't it? Here you are . . .' and so on. Mr. B is delighted. He hadn't realized that here was a map, a quite ordinary map of the place that had so bewildered him that very afternoon. Without producing any rabbits from a hat Mr. M is able to astonish Mr. B by showing him what he hadn't seen without showing him anything he hadn't seen. And unlike Mr. P Mr. M is able to do this by a proof on perfectly conventional lines. He doesn't have to stretch or narrow or press in any way the use of the word 'map' or any other word.

It is easy to see that there is a continuous connection between the two cases of discovery by reflection. For instead of imagining that the map before Mr. M and Mr. A is on perfectly conventional lines we may imagine that it is on slightly unconventional lines and then that it is on more and more unconventional lines. Mr. M's proof that it is a map of this or that will become correspondingly less and less on perfectly conventional lines and nearer and nearer to the proof of Mr. P.

In the many discoveries of our lives these sorts of surprise, proof and discovery are mixed in varying proportions. We are however inclined to proceed as if there were only two sorts of discovery, scientific discovery by observation and experiment and deductive discovery in strict accordance with well recognized customs of presentation. Indeed this habit of ours has found expression in the declaration that a statement has meaning only in so far as it can be verified either by observation or by calculation – otherwise it's an expression of our feelings, poetry, that sort of thing, not really a statement, not something which reveals the truth and about which reasons for and against can be given.

This habit of thought can have bad consequences. To begin with it has in fact led people to say that metaphysics is meaningless, that the paradoxes and counter-paradoxes of metaphysics are not really statements and that metaphysical reasoning is a muddled pretence at reasoning. And it has much wider and more serious consequences than this. For it leads not merely to the denigration of metaphysical reflective thought but to the denigration of all philosophical reflective thought, all reflective thought not within the bounds of ordinary convention. This comes about as follows. A person makes an unconventional statement, a paradoxical statement, only when however much reason there is *for* saying what he does there is also reason however superficial *against* saying what he does – otherwise his statement is not unconventional but conventional, not a paradox but a platitude.

But now if nothing is a paradox unless there remain reasons

against saying it *and* every statement that is really a statement is either one to be verified by observation or one to be verified by calculation then no paradoxical statement is really a statement and no reasons for it really reasons. For then the position is this: When a statement is not completely verified and still has in it an element of prophecy and thus lends itself to verification by observation then we may have at the same time reasons for it and reasons against it – for example, before we have operated or taken an X-ray picture there may be reasons for thinking that a patient has a duodenal ulcer and also for thinking that he has not. But if a statement can be verified by calculation from facts already known, then either the reasons for it or the reasons against it are complete, quite conclusive. For example, if the average age of the children in this form can be calculated from facts already known then it cannot be that there is at the same time reason for saying of a statement about that average age that it is true and also reason for saying that it is false. Hence statements which are not to be verified by observations and yet are not such that either there are only reasons for them or only reasons against them cannot really be statements, and reasons for and against them cannot really be reasons.

And this is not merely a piece of general and academic reasoning. It is the general and explicit formulation of a widespread habit of thought covertly at work in instance after instance. Imagine that a man and his wife are returning from an introductory lecture on psycho-analysis. They walk awhile in silence. Suddenly the husband says 'What stuff – and to call that science'. Wife 'I thought he rather proved his points.' 'Rather proved,' says the husband 'I have heard of mathematical demonstration and I have heard of scientific evidence. But I haven't heard of "*rather* proving" things.' The wife is silenced, we may imagine. But should she be? Not at all. For isn't what she means by 'rather proving' a thing exactly what proving a paradox is?

Usually when we make a statement it involves an element of prophecy. To give evidence for such a statement is to mention facts which give ground for expecting other facts which if they come along more and more completely prove the statement. For example, noticing certain symptoms the doctor says 'Duodenal ulcer', and the future course of the disease, perhaps also an examination of the body, confirms the diagnosis or does not. Occasionally however as we have noticed we make a statement which doesn't pretend to do more than sum up facts already known. For example when the disease has run its course the doctor may say 'There you are, it was duodenal ulcer'. In such a case the element of prophecy which was present in his diagnosis and is present in most statements has vanished, so the character of his statement has changed and the character of its proof. For the proof is now complete – it's a demonstration. We are apt to proceed as if these two types of statement and of proof are the only ones. But in doing so we distort those statements and their proofs which do not conform to these types. And there are such statements.

First, as we have noticed, there are cases in the courts in which all the relevant facts are known and yet the proof is not a demonstration and is in this way not complete. We tend to think of this incompleteness as like the incompleteness of the proof of a diagnosis which is still a prophecy. When we cannot arrive at an answer which is the right answer we tend to think that we are ignorant as to whether something hidden is or is not present. It was to combat this that Mr. Glanville Williams said 'There is nothing we are ignorant of in these cases. They are questions of words.'

It is like this also with paradoxical, unconventional, descriptions of what is known. Because they are unconventional convention does not link the words of the description fast to the facts. In this sense the proof of them must be incomplete. But this doesn't mean that the proof of them is incomplete like the proof of a prediction. In other words the way in which the proof of *these* statements is different from conventional demonstration does not make these statements precarious, dubious, uncertain.

The idea that the justification of a statement must be either of the *inductive* sort we have when we notice familiar symptoms and reckon, for example, that a patient is suffering from a certain disorder, or of the *deductive* sort we have when we have carried investigation so far that it would be senseless to deny that he is suffering from that disorder, has played a double part in metaphysics. It has encouraged and distorted its growth and also nearly brought about its premature death by hoisting it by its own inadequate petard. For in the first place metaphysicians have said that we have no real reasons for what we claim to know about right and wrong, the minds of others, and even the material world, because they have noticed that if we trace back the reasons a person has for the statements he makes about right and wrong, etc., until we reach what finally gives him a right to make these statements then the connection between these 'ultimate reasons' and the statements they are supposed to support is *never* deductive and therefore also never inductive. They have concluded that we haven't really any reasons at all for these statements.

At the same time it has always remained paradoxical to say that we never have any reason for saying one thing rather than another about what is right and wrong, what is going on in the mind of another and so on. These sceptical conclusions have never been deduced from familiar facts by a deduction as unquestionable, as impeccable, as a mathematical demonstration. They are clearly not conclusions which future investigation will verify or refute. And consequently meta-metaphysicians have concluded that we can never have reasons for metaphysical conclusions, that the paradoxes of metaphysics aren't really statements at all but merely manifestations of muddle.

They have pretended that their own meta-metaphysical conclusion is an exception and have pretended, like other metaphysicians, that their conclusion can be deduced in steps which no one who is really intelligent and really honest will question.

But the fact is that just as their second order paradox that there is no reason for saying one thing rather than another in metaphysics is not merely an expression of muddle but also an expression of a new grasp of the peculiarities of the justification of metaphysical statements, so also the first order paradoxes of other metaphysicians are not merely expressions of muddle, but also expressions of a new grasp of the peculiarities of the justification procedure proper to statements about right and wrong, the minds of others, etc. We have seen this in outline in the case of the paradox that no one really knows what is in the mind of another. And with time and care we could do the same for the others.

The evil effect of the cramping idea that every surprising,

revealing, statement must be justified either by giving information which the person surprised lacks or by taking him through a process of strict deduction which he has been incapable of carrying out is not so easily detected in our judgment of what psycho-analysts say. This is because *part* of the justification for the things psycho-analysts say which surprise us *does* lie in information which most of us have not possessed. A metaphysician never tells us anything we haven't heard before. But psycho-analysts do. As Freud says 'Errors and dreams are phenomena which were familiar to you ... The manifestations of neurosis, however, are an unknown region to you'. And though Freud works very much by recalling and connecting things familiar to us he also tells us astonishing stories. For example he tells us of an experiment carried out by Bernheim. 'A man was placed in a condition of somnambulism, and then made to go through all sorts of hallucinatory experiences. On being awakened he seemed at first to know nothing at all of what had taken place during his hypnotic sleep. Bernheim then asked him in so many words to tell him what had happened while he was under hypnosis. The man declared that he could not remember anything. Bernheim however insisted upon it, pressed him and assured him that he did know and that he must remember, and lo and behold! the man wavered, began to reflect, and remembered in a shadowy fashion first one of the occurrences which had been suggested to him, then something else, his recollection growing increasingly clear and complete until finally it was brought to light without a single gap'.[1]

Then there is Moreton Prince's story of the girl who while with her mouth she denied any memories connected with towers and the ringing of bells wrote with her hand an account of an experience which linked them with the grief and dread she had felt long ago when her mother was dangerously ill. In these cases it is new facts which make us say 'Really all that had happened was still in his mind though at first he couldn't find it'. 'Really she remembered although she seemed not to do so'. 'In the depths, in the unconscious was grief though on the surface there was only a ridiculous fear'. So does it come about that new facts give us a new apprehension of old ones and a new apprehen-

[1] *Introductory Lectures on Psycho-Analysis*, p. 85.

sion of old facts new freedom in looking for new ones. The metaphysician doesn't even remind us of things we had forgotten. The psycho-analyst may. All this is well known and well recognized. Indeed the idea that the psycho-analyst holds minds in a fire which makes stand out what is written there in invisible ink has only too powerful a hold upon us. What is not well recognized is how much the psycho-analyst reveals things to us in the way Mr. P, the philosopher, revealed to Mr. A what he had before his eyes without realizing it. Mr. P in order to reveal what he did to Mr. A modified and sophisticated Mr. A's conception of a map. Doctors narrow and widen the use of old names for disorders in order to present better their connections and disconnections, partly because of new discoveries but partly also because of an increased grasp of the welter of detail with which they are dealing. Psycho-analysts in order to reveal to us things about ourselves modify and sophisticate our conceptions of love, hate, jealousy, envy, sympathy, sense of responsibility. They use familiar words not with a disregard of established usage but not in bondage to it.

Such procedure is always open to misunderstanding. Because of the element of diagnosis, prognosis, prediction, in psychoanalytic interpretations and generalizations it is not inappropriate to look for support for them in the way of new facts from investigation. But in so far as there is an unconventional element in the use of the words in which these interpretations are expressed no investigation will provide a proof of them on utterly conventional lines. The consequence is that people half feel that astonishing as is the new material psycho-analysts bring forward and impressive as is their re-assembling of old material they still never 'quite prove' what they say.

They are right in a sense. The psycho-analysts' statements in so far as they are not expressed in strict accord with convention will never be proved in strict accord with convention. But this does not make them like statements which could be proved and are not. The psycho-analysts' statements will not be proved because they could not be. In so far as psycho-analysts' statements are conventionally expressed and precarious because they predict they may be in fact unproved but they are not incapable of proof. On the contrary in so far as they are conventionally expressed they are as capable of proof or disproof as any other prognosis, prophecy, prediction. It is only in so far as they are unconventionally expressed that they are incapable of conventional proof or disproof. But this doesn't leave them dubious, precarious, uncertain, or insusceptible of rational procedure. It means only that in so far as they are paradoxes they are paradoxical.

All this doesn't prove that psycho-analysts do prove what they say. Whether or no they do prove what they say in the manner appropriate to it is to be settled by considering with them what they draw attention to in justification of it — only this considering need not be a matter of coming upon something we have never come upon nor a matter of assembling what we have already come upon into a perfectly *conventional* proof.

IV

Last time we reflected upon the peculiar character of the proof of paradox and upon how an unconscious tendency to avoid recognizing this dangerous type of thought may make us miss what it can give us, and of how in particular this tendency can distort an understanding of the paradoxes of metaphysics and psycho-analysis.

And now someone may protest saying 'But surely no one does reject what psycho-analysts say merely because they do not always use words quite literally. Surely we all recognize an elasticity in the use of words or in your grand phrase "understand the logic of paradox", and surely we are prepared to apply this understanding'.

I answer 'Certainly we all recognize in some degree that language may be used paradoxically. And I do not claim that anyone rejects psycho-analytic claims merely because he does not recognize the power of paradox to reveal the truth or does not recognize it when considering what psycho-analysts say. But I do claim that in general we do not adequately recognize how often and how usefully people speak paradoxically, and I do claim that in particular our failure to recognize this adequately may contribute towards a person's rejecting psycho-analytic theories and psycho-analytic interpretations. I do claim that a person may use the paradoxical character of psycho-analytic statements in order to continue to reject them whatever evidence is assembled in support of them, and also in order to evade them by giving them a bogus acceptance'.

As to this bogus acceptance. It is not confined to psycho-analytic paradoxes. When someone says something astonishing, for example, 'St. Augustine wasn't a saint,' 'We're all mad really', 'Really we know nothing of the minds of others', 'Chairs and tables aren't really solid' we may at first expect him to produce in support of his statements facts unknown to the rest of us. When it turns out that he is not relying on facts not commonly known or only partly relying on these while it is also clear that no familiar facts could be conventionally described by his words, we may say, 'Ah I see you are using words in a special way of your own'; and when we say this we may no longer resist what is said and at the same time cease to pay much attention to it.

For example, when some metaphysical philosophers said 'Metaphysical questions are meaningless' some people took this paradox literally and opposed it vigorously. But others said 'Ah I see you are using the word "meaningful" in an extraordinary way of your own. If you mean by "a meaningful question" one that is either scientific or mathematical then of course metaphysical questions aren't meaningful.' And saying this they missed the point of the paradox. They aimed to castrate it, and did — as far as they were concerned. In the same way when Freud said of things which would not ordinarily have been called sexual that they are, some people opposed this but others cried 'Peace, peace' when there was no peace. For they said 'No doubt he is using "sexual" in a special sense of his own'.[1]

The consequence is that though it is true it is extremely dangerous to say that philosophers and psycho-analysts are not speaking literally. It is even dangerous to say that their paradoxes are paradoxes. For only in the shock of taking a paradox literally will people give that attention to concrete detail which will enable them to break old habits of grouping and recognize not merely *that* an old classification blinds and distorts but *how* it does.

[1] See Freud, *Introductory Lectures on Psycho-analysis*, Lecture XX 'The Sexual Life of Man'.

Even when the logical character of paradoxical statements is fairly recognized and it is realized that in dealing with them critical attention must not become unsympathetic *nor* sympathetic attention uncritical, the metaphysical philosopher and the psycho-analytic philosopher still have big difficulties to meet.

In the first place the material they have to deal with is subtle patterns in time which are hard to grasp. The characters of questions are a matter of the parts they play in discussions – not only in actual discussions but in discussions which might have been carried on. The characters of persons are a matter of the parts they play in life – not only the parts they actually play but the parts they might have played had things been different. Lives and discussions are patterns in time and cannot be covered by the eye at a glance. Consequently without recalling innumerable incidents, without selecting significant items and assembling them like a dramatist, one cannot grasp these patterns.

In order to grasp complex and unmanageable patterns we are always using models, other patterns which we have grasped. With every name we apply we compare one thing with another, with many others. For example, we do this when we speak of a *current* of electricity. But of course we don't always set out explicitly those things with which we compare the complex reality we now have to grasp. The comparisons we make are at once valuable and dangerous. Without them we cannot bring order into bewildering flux but with them we may in the interests of unity blind ourselves to the diversity of the individual.

The metaphysician brings into the light certain old-established and invaluable models which we use in order to grasp the characters of sorts of questions, statements, proofs. He does this not because he plans to discard these models as merely misleading but so that we may control them instead of their controlling us, so that we may see how they illuminate and how they distort. We saw how the model of a hidden stream has defects as a model for consciousness. It leaves us wondering when and where the stream pushes the bodily machinery and how we ever came to know of the presence of this stream. But we saw too how the model of electricity or energy also has defects. It obscures the fact that it makes sense to talk of a person answering questions about how he feels according to how he feels in a way in which it makes no sense to talk of another person, B, answering questions about how A feels according to how he, B, feels. The old model whatever its defects does not obscure this. It misrepresents the peculiar right a person has to make statements about what is in his mind, for it represents it as like that of a man who tells of the contents of a room to which he alone has the key. But at least it does not ignore this peculiar right. Nor does it ignore the fact that a person can know the sensations and feelings of another only in so far as he himself has had sensations and feelings of a like sort – a man, a god, who had never felt pain could not know that another was in pain, only that he groaned. No wonder we resist the attempt to substitute for a model which recognizes these things one which does not. The old one has served us well and will continue to do so; nor need we fear it once it no longer so fascinates us that we cannot recognize the differences between the model and that to which we apply it. But the fact remains that while this model has a monopoly in our minds it does on occasion lead us no end of a dance.

The psycho-analyst also tries to bring into the light models which dominate our thought, our talk, our feelings, our actions, in short our lives. And of course it is not the professional psycho-analyst only who does this – anyone who reflects upon people and tries to come at the truth does in some degree the same thing. Recently M. Blum broadcast some reflections on marriage and he then said again what we know has often been said, namely, that a woman in love tends to see her lover not as himself but as a prince charming. We might add, what also has often been said, that a man in love tends to see the woman with whom he is in love as a princess, a queen, an angel, a goddess. And we might add, what has less often been said, that a lover tends to see the person loved not only as a being with more than human, with divine, power, understanding, generosity, charm and unchanging love, but also as a being with demonic, Circe-like, wolf-like power, ruthlessness, and deceitfulness. We might say of someone 'He sees Eve – you remember Eve Brown? – well believe it or believe it not, he sees her as a mysterious, not to say curious, combination of the Madonna of the Rocks and the Venus of the Venusberg.' Or again we might say 'Deep down he sees every woman as a Cressida.'

When we try to bring out how someone sees something, say a goose, by saying that he sees it as something else, for example a swan, we may be concerned only to give an illuminating, co-ordinating, description of how he sees it but we may also be concerned to give at the same time an explanation of why he sees it as he does. For example it is sometimes said of someone 'He regards so and so as God Almighty', and this might be said even when the person in question had never heard of God. In that case however although what we say might be an illuminating description of him it would give no explanation of why he regarded so and so with such reverence. On the other hand if the person of whom we speak had heard of God and believed in Him and then perhaps lost that belief we might say 'He sees so and so as God Almighty' and with these words give not merely a description but part of the explanation of his attitude to so and so. The psycho-analyst tries to describe the present in terms which do not merely connect the present with the present but also connect the present with the past. For example, suppose we say 'Jack regards every woman as a Cressida'. This won't satisfy the psycho-analyst. What we have said is well enough as a description. But it explains nothing. *Why* does Jack regard every woman as a Cressida? He was never himself deceived by Cressida. Nor by anyone like her. But is this last true? For hasn't he known a woman who gave him all the love and all the good in all the world he knew and then too often suddenly withdrew it and gave that love and good to another? He has — in his mother's arms. No wonder that even when the lips of Venus are those of the Madonna they still smile like the Mona Lisa.

The psycho-analyst seeks to bring into the light those models from the past which for good and evil so powerfully influence our lives in the present, so powerfully distort reality and so powerfully illuminate it. For, of course, these models don't only distort. By no means. No doubt the lover sees what we see isn't there. But doesn't he also see what we can't see? Unquestionably Miss E. Brown is not Aphrodite nor Diana. But then may be she isn't the Miss Brown we think we know. Hate may blind, but hate, even neurotic hate, also reveals. The subtle evidence assembled to prove suspicions of Albertine may not prove precisely those suspicions but they don't prove nothing.[1]

The phantasies and models, illuminating but distorting, which metaphysical philosophers and psycho-analysts try to bring to light are unconscious. This makes the work of bringing them to light difficult in a way intimately bound up with a difficulty we have already looked at, the difficulty which lies in the proof of statements in which the ordinary usage of words is followed and yet left behind, in which words are used so that we cannot say that they are not being used in their old sense nor yet that they are. Asked of such statements as these whether they are true or false we are obliged to say 'Well they are and they aren't'.[2] And those situations in which we say of someone that he unconsciously thinks this, imagines that, unconsciously wishes this, feels that, are always ones in which when asked whether he thinks this, imagines that, wishes this, feels that, we are inclined to say 'Well he does and he doesn't'. No wonder the logic of paradox is important to the understanding of statements of the sort 'Unconsciously he. . . .'

Take now the statement 'Unconsciously we think of the soul as a hidden stream, as a little bird within'. Someone may protest 'What nonsense. Primitive people may have had this idea but we are aware that consciousness or the mind or the soul is not a material thing at all, however transparent or elusive'.

It is true that we do not watch for the soul leaving the body

[1] Consider also William Sansom's *The Body*.

[2] It is sometimes said that the unconscious knows nothing of logic and even that it is not bound by logic. But this is a mystery-making way of talking. The unconscious knows as much as any one else about logic. And the laws of logic can no more break down in the world of the unconscious than they can in any other world. What is true is that in any sphere whatever to connect our statements in accordance with the laws of logic serves us well only in so far as the language in which we make those statements is applicable to the phenomena with which we are dealing without distorting those phenomena in those respects with which we are concerned. There are no doubt some cows which are more like horses than others but upon the whole the animals which we actually come across fall very definitely under one or other of the animal names in our vocabulary and the law 'If it's a cow it can't be a horse' serves us well. But if Nature were to begin to produce beasts as much like cows as horses, as much like dogs as cats, our language would begin to break down again and again and the law 'If it's a cow it can't be a horse' though it would not become false would become as much a menace as a help.

Now in describing people, though our language serves us well enough up to a point, we are often concerned with likenesses and differences which it not only fails to reveal but in so far as we rely upon it conceals. Consequently for any minute understanding of people's spiritual states laws such as 'If he loves he doesn't hate', 'He can't think this and also not think it' become as much a menace as a help.

in sleep or at death or cut open skulls extremely quickly in order
to catch a glimpse of the soul. Further, for ascertaining the truth
about birds and clouds we count Jack as good as his neighbour
while for ascertaining the truth about a soul we count Jack better,
if the soul is his.

Nevertheless it is also true that we seldom consciously and in
so many words recognize the difference between souls and minds
on the one hand and on the other hand ghosts, winds, clouds
and streams. And even people who pay lip service to this difference may not recognize the difference between this difference
and the difference between stone, ice and water. We sometimes
ask 'How when and where does the soul act upon the body?'
We sometimes say 'The most careful physiologist cannot find
thoughts or feelings, the mind or the soul' and say it either with
ill-concealed satisfaction at there being still something which
eludes the scientist or with an equally inappropriate innuendo
that to believe in mind or the soul is unscientific. In these ways
we betray the feebleness of our grasp of the idiosyncrasy of the
logic of the soul, that is of the way questions about the soul are
settled. We betray this again when we are perplexed by a
sceptical person who suddenly, by reasoning which every feature
of our language seems to condone, forces us towards a formula
of doubt which seems to express the metaphysical confirmation of
our worst fears. We are at once dominated by the model of
the stream, the bird, the manikin, the ghost and yet unconscious
of it.

Someone may protest 'I see that while there are features of our
thought about the soul which are in favour of saying that we are
not dominated by the model of the bird and the stream, there are
also features of it which are in favour of saying that we are. But
why say that we are unconscious of this model? We talk openly
enough of the stream of consciousness.'

It is true that we talk openly of the stream of consciousness,
of the stream of thoughts and feelings, and even of the mysterious
inhabitant that in sleep may leave the body and visit again places
it used to know. But if a metaphysician says 'The soul you know
is not a bird nor a stream nor even a wind' then we are apt to
reply 'Well of course. We know the soul isn't a bird or a stream
or a wind. Primitive people may have thought so but we are

aware that the soul is not a material thing at all however elusive or transparent'. And with these words we may, while admitting that the myth of the bird lingers in our language and even in a sense in our thought, avoid recognizing its power, its power to lead us a purely metaphysical dance and even to bewilder us in factual inquiries by mixing with the difficulties of getting the facts a feeling of mystery which comes from metaphysical misunderstanding. For example when the question is asked 'Do animals, do dogs, think?' the inquiry is sometimes bedevilled by mixing with the difficulty of finding out what dogs are capable of, a difficulty which is expressed by saying 'We can only find out how dogs *behave*. We can't know anything about their minds or indeed whether they have any'. This last doubt is nothing but a special case of 'No one can know anything about the mind of another, only about how he behaves'. Again, Mr. Bernal in a discussion about science and ethics which was carried on in *Nature* accuses Mr. Waddington of believing in dubious and elusive entities such as the super-ego. And this accusation though it arises only in part from metaphysical misunderstanding of the logic of mental events does arise in part from this and in part from another metaphysical misunderstanding which comes from thinking of the mind, the soul, the super-ego, as something not only behind bodily events but also behind mental events. And people are suspicious of the unconscious and of unconscious mental events not only because they misunderstand the logic of paradox but also because they think of unconscious mental events as behind, below, deeper down than, the conscious ones as there are deeper and deeper depths in a stream. The two misunderstandings encourage each other. We are at once dominated by the model of the stream and the ghost, and yet unconscious of its power.

It is the same with the models the power of which the psychoanalyst tries to bring home to us. He says perhaps 'In your feelings your parents are inside you, watching every act you do, cognizant of every thought you think, and consequently hurt, pleased, angered not only by what you do but also by what you think of doing', or 'Unconsciously you think your parents are inside you'. We say perhaps 'What nonsense' or 'If you mean that I hear from time to time what used to be called the voice of conscience why don't you say so instead of talking in this ridiculous new way'.

Just as the metaphysician must assemble evidences in support of his claim that we not only speak as if the soul were a hidden manikin but from time to time think and feel as if this were so the psycho-analyst must wait until the person to whom he speaks provides the evidences which show how inadequate is the expression 'You hear from time to time the voice of conscience' to cover the facts he refers to by the words 'You have always the idea that your parents are within you'.

In thinking of the metaphysician and the psycho-analyst as trying to bring to light unconscious models we come again upon what I have called bogus acceptance but now of a rather different sort. For example, the metaphysician says perhaps 'You have the idea that language is an exact calculus'. Someone may reply 'I know, I know. Words are vague and we don't sufficiently recognize this'. What is one to say then? And yet the person who says this may have an utterly inadequate idea of how insufficiently we recognize the vagueness of language.[1] A moment later he may be found treating a question which because of the vagueness of language has no definite answer as if it had one, or insisting that it is a different question, one which has a definite answer, or insisting because it hasn't a definite answer that it isn't a question.

In a like way someone may say to a psycho-analyst 'Yes I know it has been discovered that many men secretly envy women their role in life' or even 'I know I secretly envy women their role in life' while having the feeblest apprehension of the concrete detail which backs these statements. The envy itself makes it the harder to accept the humiliation of recognizing it. A man may say 'All right, all right, I know that old stuff about seeing the woman I am in love with as my mother' and still not be alive to the ramifications of the power of that model from the past which illuminates and distorts the present.

Besides all these ways in which the procedure, the difficulties, and the aims, of psycho-analysis are reflected in metaphysics there is another connection, so I believe, which brings them closer

---

[1] Compare Karin Horney in *New Ways in Psycho-Analysis* on the meaning of the word 'unconscious'.

still. As I have said I believe that metaphysics arises from applying, in a peculiarly profound study of what gives us the right to make statements of this type or that, models which are inappropriate. In particular the deductive model is appropriate only in a non-profound study of what gives one a right to make this or that statement of a given type. While we are concerned only with what gives a person a right to make a *particular* statement of a certain type – ethical, mathematical, physical, psychological – and are prepared to admit as giving him a right to make that statement other statements of *the same type* the inductive-deductive models described in books on logic are adequate. But sometimes we are concerned to push further the inquiry as to what gives him a right to make the statement he does. Then when he submits premisses which consist of statements of the same type we ask him what right he has to accept those premisses. At once the inductive-deductive models are no longer adequate. For only statements of the same type are connected on the inductive-deductive models. Consequently if we are dissatisfied with premisses which are of the same type as a certain statement and yet insist that only what is connected with a statement inductively or deductively really gives a right to make that statement we are bound to conclude that in the end no one really has any right to make that statement or any other of the type in question. There is therefore logical confusion and logical penetration at the back of metaphysics.

But if we now ask 'What drives people to pursue to such lengths questions of the sort' 'Do we know this?' 'What right have we to make these statements?' and what preserves the power of those models which keep us for ever seeking but never finding the knowledge we seem to want, then it occurs to us to wonder whether the forces at work in this curiously unsatisfactory struggle which never ends in success nor in failure aren't in part the same as those at work in those other struggles in which something is for ever sought and never found, struggles which in their turn are connected with an earlier time when there was something, namely the world of the grown-ups, knowledge of which we desperately desired and equally desperately dreaded.

When we consider the obstinate doubts of the metaphysician 'Can one ever know what's right or wrong?' 'Can one ever know what others think or feel?' they readily remind us of the chronic doubts of the neurotic and the psychotic 'Have I committed the unpardonable sin?' 'Aren't they all against me really?' On the road to Solipsism — which is the doctrine not that I matter to nobody but that nobody exists but me — on the road to Solipsism there blows the same wind of loneliness which blows on the road to the house with walls of glass which none can break. In the labyrinth of metaphysics are the same whispers as one hears when climbing Kafka's staircases to the tribunal which is always one floor further up. Is it perhaps because of this that when in metaphysics we seem to have arranged by a new technique a new dawn then we find ourselves again on Chirico's sad terraces, where those whom we can never know still sit and it is neither night nor day?

We may hurry away and drown the cries that follow from those silent places — drown them in endless talk, drown them in the whine of the saxophone or the roar from the stands. Or, more effective, we may quiet those phantasmal voices by doing something for people real and alive. But if we can't we must return, force the accusers to speak up, and insist on recognizing the featureless faces. We can hardly do this by ourselves. But there are those who will go with us and, however terrifying the way, not desert us.